THE SOCIAL SCIENCES
IN THE ASIAN CENTURY

THE SOCIAL SCIENCES
IN THE ASIAN CENTURY

Edited by Carol Johnson,
Vera Mackie and Tessa Morris-Suzuki

Australian
National
University

PRESS

Published by ANU Press
The Australian National University
Acton ACT 2601, Australia
Email: anupress@anu.edu.au
This title is also available online at http://press.anu.edu.au

National Library of Australia Cataloguing-in-Publication entry

Title:	The social sciences in the Asian century / Carol Johnson, Vera Mackie, Tessa Morris-Suzuki.
ISBN:	9781925022582 (paperback) 9781925022599 (ebook)
Subjects:	Social sciences--Pacific Area.
	Social sciences--Study and teaching--History.
	Education and globalization--Pacific Area.
Other Creators/Contributors:	
	Johnson, Carol, 1955- editor.
	Mackie, Vera C., editor.
	Morris-Suzuki, Tessa, editor.
Dewey Number:	300.95

Cover image: Adapted from photograph of the First National Library of China by Xioabawang. Source: Wikimedia Commons.

Cover design and layout by ANU Press.

ACADEMY OF
THE SOCIAL SCIENCES
IN AUSTRALIA

Contents

PART III: AUSTRALIAN SOCIAL SCIENCES IN THE ASIAN CENTURY AND BEYOND

Contributors

Chua Beng Huat is Professor of Sociology at the National University of Singapore (NUS) and is affiliated with the Asia Research Institute at NUS. He is a co-founder of the journal *Inter-Asia Cultural Studies*, and has published widely on urban planning and public housing, comparative politics in Southeast Asia and the emerging consumerism across Asia. He has held visiting professorships at universities in Malaysia, Hong Kong, Taiwan, Germany, Australia and the United States.

Raewyn Connell, FASSA, is Professor Emerita at the University of Sydney and has received awards from the American Sociological Association and the Australian Sociological Association. Her books are listed among the most influential in Australian sociology and her work has been translated into 18 languages. Her book *Southern theory* (Allen & Unwin 2007) discusses theorists unfamiliar in the European canon of social science, and explores the possibility of a genuinely global social science.

Sylvia Estrada-Claudio is Professor of Women and Development Studies in the College of Social Work and Community Development at the University of the Philippines. She is a qualified medical doctor and psychologist. She formed the Medical Action Group to organise health missions to treat psychological trauma and injuries, and co-founded Likhaan, an organisation working with grassroots women on issues of reproductive health and rights. She has worked with various international networks and regional networks, including Women's Global Network for Reproductive Rights, the Isis International feminist advocacy organisation (Manila) and ARROW.

Ken Henry AC, FASSA, was special adviser to the prime minister in 2011 and 2012. In that role, he led the development of the White Paper on *Australia in the Asian Century*. Today, he is a member of the boards of National Australia Bank Limited, the Australian Securities Exchange (ASX) and Reconciliation Australia. He was secretary to the Treasury from 2001 to 2011.

Ariel Heryanto is Professor at the School of Culture, History and Language, The Australian National University. He is the author of *Identity and pleasure: The politics of Indonesian screen culture* (NUS Press 2014) and *State terrorism and political identity in Indonesia: Fatally belonging* (Routledge 2007), editor of *Popular culture in Indonesia: Fluid identities in post-authoritarian politics* (Routledge 2008), and co-editor of *Pop culture formations across East Asia* (Jimoondang 2010). His current research investigates Indonesia's postcoloniality.

Kanishka Jayasuriya is Professor of International Politics and a Director of the Indo-Pacific Governance Research Centre at the University of Adelaide. His books include *Statecraft, welfare and the politics of inclusion* (Palgrave 2006), *Reconstituting the global liberal order: Legitimacy and regulation* (Routledge 2005) and *Asian regional governance: Crisis and change* (Routledge 2004).

Carol Johnson, FASSA, is Professor of Politics in the Department of Politics and International Studies at the University of Adelaide, and a member of the University of Adelaide's Indo-Pacific Governance Research Centre. She has written extensively on Australian politics and political culture, including issues of Australian national identity, and has a particular interest in how governments manage social and economic change. Her books include *Governing change: From Keating to Howard* (UQP 2000; second edn, Network Books 2007). She also co-edited and contributed to a special issue of the *Australian Journal of Political Science* on 'Re-engaging Asia' in 2010, and has written on the comparative politics of social issues, information technology and e-governance in the Asia-Pacific region.

Leong Liew is Professor in the Griffith Business School. His research interests focus on China's political economy, the political economy of Sino–US relations, development economics and the political economy of international business, trade and finance. He co-authored *The making of China's exchange rate policy: From plan to WTO entry* (with Harry X. Wu; Edward Elgar 2007).

Vera Mackie, FASSA, is Senior Professor of Asian Studies in the Faculty of Law, Humanities and the Arts at the University of Wollongong. Her publications include *The Routledge handbook of sexuality studies in East Asia* (co-edited with Mark McLelland; Routledge 2015); *Ways of knowing about human rights in Asia* (Routledge 2015); *Gender, nation and state in modern Japan* (co-edited with Andrea Germer and Ulrike Wöhr; Routledge 2014); *Gurōbaruka to Jendā Hyōshō* [Globalisation and representations of gender] (Ochanomizu Shobō 2003); *Feminism in modern Japan: Citizenship, embodiment and sexuality* (Cambridge 2003); and *Human rights and gender politics: Asia-Pacific perspectives* (co-edited with Anne-Marie Hilsdon, Martha Macintyre and Maila Stivens; Routledge 2000).

Simon Marginson, FASSA, MAE, works as Professor of International Higher Education in the Institute of Education, University College London. He was previously a professor at Monash University (2000–06) and the University of Melbourne (2006–13). He is Joint Editor-in-Chief of the journal *Higher Education*, and joint author of *International student security* (Cambridge 2010) and *Imagination: Three models of imagination in the age of the knowledge economy* (Peter Lang 2011). He focuses primarily on globalisation and comparative and international higher education, including higher education systems in East and Southeast Asia. In 2014 he was the University of California's Clark Kerr Lecturer in Higher Education and the recipient of the US Association for the Study in Higher Education's Research Achievement Award. From October 2015 he will be director of the ESRC/HEFCE Centre for Global Higher Education, a five-year Economic and Social Research Council centre based at the UCL Institute of Education.

Tessa Morris-Suzuki, FAHA, is Professor of Japanese History and holds an Australian Research Council Laureate Fellowship at The Australian National University. Her research focuses on aspects of modern Japanese and East Asian regional history, particularly cross-border movement between Japan and its Asian neighbours; issues of history, memory and reconciliation in Northeast Asia; and grassroots social movements in Japan. Her most recent books include *East Asia beyond the history wars: Confronting the ghosts of war* (with Morris Low, Leonid Petrov and Timothy Y. Tsu; Routledge 2013), *Borderline Japan: Foreigners and frontier controls in the postwar era* (Cambridge University Press 2010) and *Exodus to North Korea: Shadows from Japan's Cold War* (Rowman & Littlefield Publishers 2007). In 2013 she was awarded the Fukuoka Prize (academic award) for contributions to the study of East Asian history.

Sujata Patel is Professor of Sociology at the University of Hyderabad. She edited the *ISA handbook on diverse sociological traditions* (Sage 2010) and is editor of a number of book series, including Studies in Contemporary Society, Cities and the Urban Imperative, and Sage Studies in International Sociology.

Preface and acknowledgments

This collection focuses on the challenges of practising the social sciences in the Asia-Pacific region in the twenty-first century. Most of the chapters draw on papers presented at the 2012 Annual Symposium of the Academy of the Social Sciences, Australia, on 'Australian Social Sciences in the Asian Century' (see www.assa.edu.au/events/symposium/2012). The symposium developed from discussions between several fellows of the academy—Carol Johnson, Vera Mackie, Pal Ahluwalia, Dennis Altman, Raewyn Connell and Michael Dutton (with Tessa Morris-Suzuki also a strong supporter)—and was co-convened by Carol Johnson and Vera Mackie. We also worked closely with Tim Rowse, chair of the academy's Public Programs Committee. We were keen to open up a dialogue between social scientists in the Asia-Pacific region. The symposium took shape over several years of planning. During this period, the Australian government released the White Paper on *Australia in the Asian Century*, in 2012. The White Paper became one focus of our discussions, although our concerns were more wide-ranging. We would like to express our thanks to the current and former president, executive and secretariat of the Academy of the Social Sciences in Australia, for their support of the symposium and this publication. We would also like to thank Professor Marian Sawer and Professor Renee Jeffery of the ANU Press Social Sciences Editorial Board, and the anonymous reviewers for constructive comments.

—Carol Johnson, Vera Mackie and Tessa Morris-Suzuki

Australia, the Asia-Pacific and the social sciences

Vera Mackie, Carol Johnson and Tessa Morris-Suzuki

In 2013, Australia's Abbott Liberal government announced a 'New Colombo Plan', which supports Australian undergraduates to visit selected Asian countries to study, research or undertake internships, mentorships and practicums. One year earlier, the Gillard Labor government had released a White Paper, *Australia in the Asian Century*, which emphasised the importance of developing an education system that encourages Australians to be 'Asia-literate' and 'Asia-capable'. The White Paper stressed the importance of strengthening 'research and teaching links between Australian institutions and those in the region' (Commonwealth of Australia 2012: 16–17; Department of Foreign Affairs and Trade n.d.).

In this volume, we argue that in the twenty-first century not only will the study of Asian societies and languages be important but also the study of the diverse forms of knowledge produced outside the Euro-American centres. These diverse forms of social science knowledge, coming from differing intellectual traditions, can make important methodological and theoretical contributions as well as filling empirical gaps. They will be relevant not just for those who study Asian societies but also for those who study a range of societies grappling with similar problems, including Australia. To understand why such a fundamental intellectual engagement is so important, it is necessary to understand both the historical background to the development of the social sciences in Australia and the changing geopolitics of knowledge in which the contemporary social sciences are situated.

We therefore begin by outlining the historical origins of, and intellectual influences that helped to shape, the social sciences in Australia. We will outline the impact of those origins and influences on Australian social scientists' study of the region and argue for the need to develop more contemporary approaches, especially a deeper and more reciprocal intellectual engagement, in the conditions of the twenty-first century.

Modes of engagement

By juxtaposing the New Colombo Plan of the twenty-first century with the original Colombo Plan of the 1950s, we can gain insight into the changing relationships between Australia and its neighbours since the mid-twentieth century and the changing conceptions of intellectual engagement that have resulted.

The original Colombo Plan was established in 1950, at a Commonwealth Conference of Foreign Ministers, and provided infrastructure and skills development to scholars from developing countries. The original members were Australia, Britain, Canada, Ceylon, India, New Zealand and Pakistan. There are currently 26 member nations, no longer restricted to the British Commonwealth. In Australia, the Colombo Plan is firmly lodged in national cultural memory, as it brought international students from a range of developing nations to study at Australian universities over several decades (Indelicato 2015: 1–16; Kartomi 2013: 240–57; Oakman 2004), and helped forge relationships with individuals who would often go on to be leaders in their own countries. Tens of thousands of students studied in Australia under this scheme, and many more Australians came into contact with these students in classrooms, dormitories, student union activities and the homes of host families (Downer 2005; Lowe 2014).

In the 1950s, when the original Colombo Plan was established, Australia was firmly aligned with the Anglophone powers: the United States and the United Kingdom. Australia had been founded on the basis of a series of British colonies from the mid-eighteenth century, but by the mid-twentieth century it had taken on a similar colonial role in the Asia-Pacific region as the administrator of territories such as Papua New Guinea. As a relatively wealthy nation, Australia also provided scholarships and other forms of development aid to the countries of the region. Between the 1950s and the 1970s, Australia gradually dismantled the White Australia Policy, repealing the *Immigration Restriction*

Act and moving to an official policy of multiculturalism. By the 1990s, hosting international students was no longer a matter of benevolence, but rather a major 'export' industry, with international students' tuition fees and their purchases of other goods and services providing a major boost to the Australian economy. Although Australia still provides a small number of international student scholarships through AusAID and individual university scholarship schemes, the majority of our international students are fee-paying. The Rudd–Gillard Labor governments introduced the Endeavour Fellowships, a two-way scheme that allowed Australians to travel overseas, and brought scholars from neighbouring countries to Australia (Australian Education International n.d.). This was in the spirit of the government's White Paper, *Australia in the Asian Century*, which had a vision of a reciprocal relationship between Australia and other countries in the region, and demonstrated a recognition that learning could be a multidimensional and multidirectional process (Commonwealth of Australia 2012). By contrast, the New Colombo Plan funds only Australians to travel overseas, 'complementing the thousands of students from the region coming to Australia to study each year' (DFAT n.d.).

This snapshot of different forms of engagement through the participation of young people in higher education provides an introduction to the concerns of this book. While there are diverse elements to the relationship between Australia and the Asia-Pacific region—economic, political, diplomatic, military, strategic, cultural and interpersonal—we are particularly interested in exploring the role of academic social scientists. This volume grew out of an annual symposium of the Academy of Social Sciences in Australia, which focused on 'Australian Social Sciences in the Asian Century'.[1] As with the example of international education described above, we argue that there can be several different models of social scientific engagement with the region.

In the past, we can identify a colonialist view that saw Anglophone societies as producers and dispensers of knowledge, primarily engaged in describing 'other' societies and engaging with 'other' societies in a pedagogical manner. Australia's own Indigenous peoples were also the objects of academic knowledge. In this sense, Australia can be seen as inheriting Euro-American social scientific traditions. Australia's first universities were established in the mid-nineteenth century, in the separate colonies that would come together under Federation in 1901. They were modelled on the British universities of the time, and there was a period of expansion of the university sector in the early post–World War II period, which closely paralleled developments in the United Kingdom (Connell 2007; Connell in this volume; Patel in this volume).

---

1   For information about the 2012 Annual Symposium of the Academy of the Social Sciences in Australia (convened by Carol Johnson and Vera Mackie), see www.assa.edu.au/events/symposium/2012. Consulted 7 October 2013.

With respect to the study of societies in the Asia-Pacific region, from the mid to late twentieth century, we can identify an instrumentalist model in which knowledge of 'other' societies is primarily for the purposes of advancing Australian economic interests. Much of the late twentieth-century interest in Asian languages and studies focused on economic and strategic reasons for studying the societies and cultures of Indonesia, Japan, China and (South) Korea (COAG 1994; NALSAS 1998).[2] In this volume, however, we will propose a dialogical model whereby societies in the region are engaged in the common pursuit of solutions to regional problems, and the flows of knowledge necessarily move in multiple directions.

To consider the role of the social sciences in Australia's engagement with the Asia-Pacific region, we need some historical background and context. We need to survey Australia's engagement with the Asia-Pacific region, describe Australia's inheritance of a particular Euro-American view of the social sciences, acknowledge recent paradigms that challenge Eurocentric models, situate the social sciences in the age of globalisation, and consider what this means for practising the social sciences in the twenty-first century.

Engaging with the Asia-Pacific region

David Walker and Agnieska Sobocinska point out that every Australian generation seems to rediscover Asia, all the time imagining that theirs is the first to be conscious of the changing economics and geopolitics of the region. They quote Australian prime minister Andrew Fisher, who commented in 1915 that the 'rise' of Japan had 'no parallel in our history', and journalist George Johnston, who at mid-century thought we stood 'at the very beginning of another great cycle of civilisation', which, one day, would 'push the centre of gravity of civilisation back to the Orient' (Walker and Sobocinska 2012: 3).

As several commentators have noted, Australia's relationship with the region has often been associated with ambivalence and anxiety (d'Cruz and Steele 2003; Walker 1999; Walker and Sobocinska 2012: 1–23). The first Japanese language program in Australia was established at the University of Sydney in 1917, perhaps in response to anxiety about Japan's increased role in the region. Just two years later, in 1919, the Australian government succeeded in opposing Japan's proposal for a 'racial equality' clause in the founding charter of the League of Nations after World War I (Shimazu 1998). Although there was some development of trading relationships with Japan in particular in the early twentieth century, this was cut short in the 1930s as Japan withdrew from

2   Some plans also included Thailand, Vietnam and India.

the League of Nations in the wake of criticism of its invasion of Manchuria, culminating in trade embargoes against Japan in the mid-1930s (Jones 2001: 133–62).

After the bombing of Pearl Harbor in 1941 and the fall of Singapore in 1942, the Asia-Pacific region was the site of warfare between the Allies and Japan. As Prue Torney-Parlicki points out, for many in mid-century Australia, the dispatches of war correspondents were a major source of their knowledge about the region (Torney-Parlicki 2000). For a generation of Australian men, their contact with the Asia-Pacific region was as combatants in World War II, as occupiers of the defeated Japan from 1945 to 1952, or as combatants in the Korean and Vietnam wars. Women, too, supported these military actions: as nurses, as members of the women's services or in other ways. Meanwhile, on the home front, opposition to the Vietnam War was the focus of civil society activity from the 1960s. In 1965, MP Jim Cairns argued that Australians needed to know more about Asia, proposing a relationship based on pacifism rather than militarism:

> The most significant recent change in the outlook of Australians is their growing awareness of Asia. We are all aware of Asia. Many of us are afraid of it. Few of us understand it (Cairns 1965: 1).

Asia has been constructed in Australian political discourse as a source of both fear and hope (Johnson et al. 2010: 59–79). There is also a long history of Australian governments pursuing policies that emphasise the importance of trading with Asia (McFadyen 1949; on the 1930s, see Jones 2001: 133–62). By the late twentieth century, Australian governments were becoming more aware that the international economy would be transformed by the economic development of countries in the Asian region. One consequence was that intellectual aspects of the engagement with Asia began to be taken more seriously, even if the impetus for such engagement was largely economic. In 1988, then prime minister Bob Hawke made a speech at the conference of the Asian Studies Association of Australia on the importance of studying Asian languages. This speech was widely credited with contributing to that year's massive rise in Asian-language enrolments at universities. This was congruent with the Hawke–Keating governments' embrace of the Asia-Pacific Economic Cooperation (APEC) concept, starting with Hawke's speech in Seoul in 1989 (APEC n.d.). Former prime minister Paul Keating (1992) argued that Australians needed to improve their cultural and language skills to engage with Asia, and that we needed to draw on the skills of Australia's multicultural population.

By the twenty-first century, prime minister Kevin Rudd (2008) went even further, arguing that China and India were 'looming to dominate the 21st Century, just as the United States and the United Kingdom had dominated the 20th'. Drawing on knowledge gained as a student of Asian studies at The Australian National

University, Rudd (2009) emphasised the important intellectual contributions of countries such as India and China, both historically and in the contemporary period. Foreign minister Stephen Smith argued that '[w]e have to make Australia's understanding of Asian literacy and Asian culture almost second nature to us' (*The Advertiser* 21 April 2008).

We have had several iterations of government interest in policies on teaching Asian languages and studies. There has also been a long history of lobbying on behalf of Asian languages and studies.[3] The Commonwealth government's (2012) White Paper on *Australia in the Asian Century*, however, provided fresh context for questions about practising the social sciences in the twenty-first century.

The *Australia in the Asian Century* White Paper was different from earlier such reports in taking a 'whole of government' approach, with the Gillard government appointing a minister to have explicit responsibility for policies related to the 'Asian Century'. There is some continuity, however, in its focus on instrumentalist reasons for engaging with the region: economic relationships; the fact that our major trading partners come from the Asia-Pacific region; and the fact that there is a growing middle-class market for consumer goods, tourism and educational services in the region. Several contributors to this volume comment on the *Asian Century* White Paper from diverse points of view, as we shall see below.

The Abbott government did not always give the concept of the Asian Century the kind of emphasis given by the Rudd and Gillard governments. Indeed, when she was shadow minister for foreign affairs, Julie Bishop (2013a) suggested that while the term 'Asian Century' had currency, the 'Global Century' might be an even better term, given 'the rise of different powers challenging the established powers'. Nonetheless, then Prime Minister Tony Abbott (2014) acknowledged that 'with a combined population of 1.5 billion and a GDP of $15 trillion, China, Japan, and Korea collectively have decisively shifted the world's centre of economic gravity'. He argued that we are no longer 'at the wrong end of the world but the right one', and expressed his confidence that 'the Asian Century will be Australia's moment too' (Abbott 2014). Significantly, Abbott's successor as Prime Minister, Malcolm Turnbull (2015), has stressed the importance of 'the great geopolitical transformation of our time—the economic rise of emerging Asia'. Bishop (2013c) has focused on the importance of 'economic diplomacy' in engaging with Australia's region, given the increasing economic importance of the Indian Ocean and Asia-Pacific regions. Bishop (2013b) has also emphasised the importance of engaging intellectually with Asia, noting the importance of

---

3   See Auchmuty (1971); Asian Studies Association of Australia (2002); Asian Studies Council (1988, 1989); COAG (1994); FitzGerald (1980); Kersten et al. (1996); NALSAS (1998).

top-ranked universities in the region.[4] Under the New Colombo Plan, young Australians are encouraged not only to learn Asian languages but also to engage in study exchanges as a significant form of regional engagement (Bishop 2013b; 2013c: 4). Indeed, the new scheme is described as being 'designed to be a rite of passage for young Australians' and intended to ensure that it is 'the norm for young Australians to spend time living in the region' (Bishop 2013c: 12).

Recent statements on the New Colombo Plan focus on the 'Indo-Pacific', covering an area from the Indian Ocean to the Pacific (DFAT n.d.). In other words, this refers to a region that encompasses South Asia, Southeast Asia, East Asia and the Pacific. Indeed, the revival of the place name 'Colombo' might also suggest a (re)orientation towards South Asia. These changes in the terminology to describe Australia's neighbourhood underline the fact that 'the Orient', 'Asia', the 'Asia-Pacific' and the 'Indo-Pacific' are all constructed categories. The different nuances and connotations of each term reflect shifting geopolitics, different ways of imagining Australia's place in the world, and changing views of which countries are important to Australia.[5] In this introductory essay, we sometimes refer in different places to 'Asia', the 'Asia-Pacific' or the 'Indo-Pacific', depending on the particular period we are writing about. Chapters variously focus on particular countries, ranging from Pakistan, India, China and Japan down to the Philippines and Indonesia, with Australia included as part of the broader Asia-Pacific region. We are also, however, keenly interested in the interconnections between these places, and recognise that the Australian population includes a significant proportion of nationals and residents of Asian heritage (Martin et al. 2015). Now let us turn to a brief consideration of the historical role of the social sciences in contributing to Australia's engagement with the region.

Social sciences, area studies and beyond

Australia's first universities were established in the mid-nineteenth century, in the capitals of the separate colonies. The late nineteenth-century universities in Australia provided a combination of liberal arts and fields of study with some vocational or practical application—law, medicine, engineering, economics. These universities were established with a professoriate drawn from British

4   One of the most influential university ranking systems, the Academic Ranking of World Universities (ARWU)/'Shanghai Jioatong', is based in China.
5   On the instability of the category 'Asia', see, *inter alia*, Spivak (2008); on the 'Asia-Pacific', see Wilson and Dirlik (1995). Many thinkers in diverse countries in the region commonly described as Asia have also, of course, resisted this homogenising label (Wang 2007; Hall 2009). It should also be noted that while the term 'Asian Century' has gained currency in Australia, elsewhere the twenty-first century has been referred to as the 'Pacific Century' (Nguyen and Hoskins 2014).

universities, with some appointments from the United States and a few home-grown academics who were likely to have completed higher degrees overseas (Dale 2012). At the end of World War II, there were six universities in Australia (the Universities of Sydney, Melbourne, Adelaide, Tasmania, Queensland and Western Australia), with 16,000 students. The Australian National University was established in 1946. The tertiary education system expanded in the 1950s and the 1960s. There were nine universities with a total of 31,000 university students in 1955, and 14 universities with 81,000 students in 1965. The university system underwent further expansion in the late 1980s when the older universities were amalgamated with former teachers' colleges, technical colleges and colleges of advanced education, bringing total enrolments to 420,000. By 1996 there was a total of 630,000 university students in Australia (Macintyre 2010: 22–5). In 2014 there were about one million university students in the country (Universities Australia 2014). Each period of growth also saw changing configurations of the international student population. About 20,000 students came from mainly Asian countries in the period of the Colombo Plan, with a similar number of private overseas students. There was growth in the full-fee-paying international student population from the 1980s. By 2011, one in five students at Australian universities were international students (Martin et al. 2015).

The social sciences originally grew out of Enlightenment rationalism in Europe in the eighteenth century. They are 'a product of modernity, their point of departure the emergence of society as a separate and autonomous realm of human activity' (Macintyre 2010: 4). They were established as separate disciplinary areas of study in universities in the United States in the late nineteenth century. Australia was slower to establish similar programs. Sociology had a difficult beginning in Australia, with short-lived attempts to establish sociology programs in the 1920s, although training in social work was established by the mid-1930s (Miller and Nicholls 2014: 21–33). The first chair in anthropology was established in 1926, and anthropology programs were seen to be highly relevant to Australia's involvement in the policing and administration of the territory of Papua New Guinea (Macintyre 2010: 18).

Australia was thus in an ambivalent position. In the late nineteenth and early twentieth centuries, Australia was seen as a 'social laboratory', with its universal suffrage, pioneering Labor governments, wage arbitration systems, non-contributory old-age pensions and strong union movements. At the same time, it was a former colony of the United Kingdom, nominally independent after 1901, but still beholden to the British Privy Council and the British monarchy (through the Governor-General and state governors). Australia was a colonial-settler society that asserted its difference from other British colonies like India and Malaya through the White Australia Policy. Australia's Indigenous peoples were the focus of Euro-American anthropological research, as were the peoples of Papua New Guinea and the Pacific (Wolfe 1999).

The social sciences were important in both wartime Australia and the early post–World War II reconstruction period. As far as Asian studies is concerned, Japanese-language training was vital for military intelligence during World War II, for the conduct of war crimes trials at the end of the war and in the Allied occupation of Japan from 1945 to 1952. Some of these military specialists went on to teach in universities. The Australian Defence Force continues to teach Asian languages at the Australian Defence Force Language School near Melbourne, and Asian studies is part of the curriculum at the Australian Defence Force Academy in Canberra (Department of Defence 2000).

In the United States, the study of societies outside the Euro-American centres in the post–World War II period was brought together under the rubric of 'area studies'. That is, these fields of study were defined by a geographical focus rather than a disciplinary focus. Area studies had its roots in World War II and the subsequent establishment of the Cold War world view. Area studies teaching and research were closely aligned with US defence and foreign policies.

There have been spirited debates around area studies, modernisation theory and the social sciences in North America. The *Bulletin of Concerned Asian Scholars* (now known as *Critical Asian Studies*) was established in 1968 by academics concerned about the direction of US foreign policy in Asia, particularly the military conflict in Vietnam (Committee of Concerned Asian Scholars 1968), in which Australia was also involved. As early as 1975, John Dower, in his essay on modernisation theory, pointed out that area studies in the United States had been implicated in US government foreign policy objectives (1975: 3–108).

A generation of scholars of Asia has been influenced by Edward Said's book *Orientalism*, in which he argued that Orientalism is a Western style for 'dominating, restructuring, and having authority over the Orient' (1978: 3). While Said's book largely focused on European representations of the Middle East, conceptions of the 'Orient' also included Asian countries, as has been pointed out before and after Said's book (Breckenridge and van de Veer 1993: 3–4). In any case, the term Orientalism has been adapted to a range of situations where scholars and their objects of study are embedded in structured relationships of inequality. What is important about Said's intervention is not so much whether he was writing about the Middle East, South Asia or East Asia, but rather his recognition of the relationship between power and knowledge. In addition to the perspectives provided by Said's rethinking of the concept of Orientalism, the field of postcolonial theory considers the relationship between academic knowledge and the history of colonialism, whether this concerns former colonies, former colonising powers or places that do not neatly fit this schema (Young 2001).

Miyoshi and Harootunian's (2002) collection, *Learning places*, considered the place of area studies in the early twenty-first century, with a focus on North America. While acknowledging the critiques of the power relations inherent in the 'area studies' model, Gayatri Chakravorty Spivak (2003) has also argued for the importance of the rigorous language training and the deep familiarity with the society and culture that were nurtured in area studies and comparative literature programs.

Australia has a strong tradition of 'area studies', particularly in such places as the former Research School of Pacific and Asian Studies at The Australian National University (Lal and Ley 2006; Macintyre 2010: 58–59). Indeed, the establishment of this school (originally the School of Pacific Studies) was intimately connected with Australia's position as colonial administrator of Papua New Guinea, as noted above (Macintyre 2010: 66). In this sense, Australian social sciences from the beginning had much in common with the colonialist focus of Euro-American social sciences.

Some of the other newer universities included a focus on Asian studies after World War II. Monash University, established in 1961, appointed a historian of Indonesia, John Legge, as its foundation Professor of History. Legge went on to chair the world-renowned Centre for Southeast Asian Studies and also became Dean of Arts. In 1966, Prague School linguist Jiří V. Neustupný established a Japanese-language program at Monash based on a communicative model—different to existing 'Oriental studies' programs, which tended to focus on classical literatures rather than the real-world usage of language and the study of contemporary societies. Several other universities established programs in Asian languages and studies in the 1960s, including the University of Queensland, the University of Melbourne, Swinburne, and the West Australian Institute of Technology (now Curtin University). In the 1970s, secondary schools also started to teach some Asian languages.

There has been less reflection on the meaning of this history in the Australian context compared with the above-mentioned debates in the United States, though some contributors to this volume have undertaken critical reflection on the construction and role of area studies in Australia.[6] Australia was also the site for much of the early work by the subaltern studies group, which interrogated the colonial basis of European knowledge about South Asia. Ranajit Guha was based at The Australian National University, and Dipesh Chakrabarty completed his doctoral dissertation there.[7]

One of the purposes of this volume is to engage in a discussion about the intellectual basis of our pursuits, in a dialogue between social scientists from Australia and the region. Ideally, this will encourage a more contemporary model of the social sciences, which is based on a recognition of international connectedness, and also of the diversity of social science traditions from which we can learn. In other words, the Australian social sciences need to continue to move beyond their origins in Euro-American traditions, and beyond the purely pragmatic focus of some forms of area studies, to embrace other sources and forms of knowledge, while still retaining all that is beneficial and useful about those traditions. A further impetus for developing this broader intellectual dialogue comes from the conditions of globalisation and the changing geopolitics of knowledge.

Social sciences and globalisation

The contemporary world is characterised by changing economic relationships accompanied by the increasingly rapid and intensified circulation of finance, commodities, people, signs and symbols—often called globalisation. Many forms of corporate activity are carried out on a global scale; production and consumption transcend the scale of the nation-state; and institutions of global governance are gradually developing to deal with issues that go beyond the boundaries of one nation-state.[8] New forms of transnational activism have also developed to deal with these changing relationships. Globalisation has been

---

6   See Jayasuriya (2012); Mackie (2007: 103–20; 2013: 293–301); Morris-Suzuki (2000, 2011); and chapters by Jayasuriya and Morris-Suzuki in this volume; see also Jackson (2015). In the late 1990s, the Australian Research Council, the Academy of the Humanities and the Academy of the Social Sciences surveyed academic disciplines in Australia. There are no specific chapters on Asia or the Pacific in the social science volumes, but there are several chapters on area studies in the humanities volumes (Academy of the Social Sciences in Australia 1998; Aveling 1998: 29–39; Brasted 1998: 239–49; Coaldrake and Wells 1998: 151–63; Denoon and Ward 1998: 209–14; Hooper 1998: 57–66; Ingleson 1998: 251–60; Milner and Morris-Suzuki 1998: 113–27; Saikal 1998: 199–207). For a more recent survey of humanities, arts and social science disciplines, see Turner and Brass (2014; on 'Asia-related' research, see pp. 66–67). In November 2013, the Australian Council of Learned Academies (ACOLA) brought together a group of Australia-based academics to consider 'Science and Research Collaboration with Asia and the Pacific'. For a report on this meeting, see Ang et al. (2015).
7   See Amin and Chakrabarty (1996); Arnold and Hardiman (1994); Bhadra et al. (1999); Chakrabarty (1992: 101–8; 2014: 194–206); Chatterjee and Pandey (1992); and Guha (1982–89).
8   See, *inter alia*, Grewal and Kaplan (1994); Hannerz (1987: 546–49; 1989: 66–75); Mattelart (1983); Tambiah (2000: 163–94); and Tolentino (1996: 49–76).

described as 'a process of intensifying global social inter-relatedness, whereby space and time are compressed and previously separated locations [are] brought into a new proximity' (Eschle 2002: 316). One of the challenges faced by social scientists is to shift from addressing issues in a largely national frame to addressing issues that necessarily cross national borders. Our focus is on the challenges faced in the Asia-Pacific region, and how social scientists can contribute to the solution of pressing regional problems.

The world is currently undergoing major shifts in economic and social power. These shifts have been explored by writers as diverse as Kishore Mahbubani in *The new Asian hemisphere* (2008) and Michael Spence in *The next convergence* (2011). These shifts have particular implications for Australia in its location in the Asia-Pacific region. As we have seen, the former Australian Labor Party government referred to the 'Asian Century' (Commonwealth of Australia 2012), a term that was also used at times by then Prime Minister Abbott (2014). The United States recognised the shifting geopolitics, particularly the rise of China, in 2011 when President Obama stated the policy of a 'pivot to Asia' (Foreign Policy Initiative 2011).[9]

In this volume, we argue that dealing with these shifts involves not just a reorientation of economic and political power but also a changing geopolitics of knowledge. Consequently, in the twenty-first century, it is necessary not just to make the languages and societies of the region objects of study but also to engage with the diverse forms of knowledge produced outside the Euro-American centres. It is particularly important to recognise the methodological and theoretical as well as empirical contributions that the diverse forms of knowledge and diverse intellectual traditions in the region can generate. There has been a long history of university academics in Asian countries being encouraged to engage with 'Western' thought (Huang 2007: 422). The original Colombo Plan itself reflected these pressures, as a range of professionals in the region, including academics, was encouraged to study abroad. This pressure has intensified with the internationalisation of university education, and academics are increasingly being encouraged to publish in English in high-ranking international journals—a development that has led to critiques that more 'local' issues are being neglected in favour of issues that will attract an international readership (Mok 2007: 446).[10] The exchange has been excessively one-sided: there has not been sufficient reciprocal pressure on academics in Western countries to engage with the knowledge being produced in the

9   There was also criticism that the US government failed to back up its policy on Asia with adequate budget initiatives (Stewart 2013: 1–3).
10   See also the chapters by Patel, Chua and Jayasuriya in this volume. Peter Jackson (2015: 24) has recently argued that the current conditions of transnational academic publishing and research quality auditing regimes entrench Euro-American dominance.

Asia-Pacific region (even when this knowledge is being produced in English). Here, we argue that a new approach is needed and that we need to develop a far more ambitious idea of what intellectual engagement with the region involves, one that goes beyond the approaches embedded in the early years of the development of the social sciences in Australia. To begin with, we need to go beyond the area studies model of taking 'other countries' as an object of study in order to determine their difference from some abstract Euro-American ideal. Rather, we need to take time to reflect on the intellectual rather than simply instrumental underpinnings of our engagement with the region (Morris-Suzuki 2000: 9–23; 2011: 123–42; and in this volume).

Furthermore, if Australian students are to understand the specificities of Australian society, and of other societies in the region, they need to understand that, for example, the concepts of state and civil society, modernity, and gender and sexuality that are prevalent in Australia are not universal.[11] They need to be aware of other concepts, of other ways of seeing the world, as well as their implications for other forms of governance and for analysing the policy challenges that Australia faces in the twenty-first century.

This will involve an openness to engaging with the knowledge being produced in many diverse parts of our region, and it will require a consciousness of the political, economic and social issues arising from the increasing integration of Australia's society and economy into the Asia-Pacific region. As Kanishka Jayasuriya (among other contributors to this book) points out, we face many shared problems and issues that are regional in nature, including the political and social challenges of inequality in the region, urbanisation, access to public space and infrastructure, the funding, governance and provision of regional public goods, and transnational environmental challenges.

Furthermore, as the twenty-first century progresses, it will be increasingly difficult for even those Australian academics who focus primarily on domestic economic, social and political analyses to divorce their work from broader regional considerations. Australia is increasingly integrated into the Asia-Pacific region in ways that affect many aspects of Australian domestic policy. For example, the former Labor government noted the impact of the Asian Century-driven resources boom on Australia's 'patchwork economy' (Gillard and Swan 2011) and justified the National Broadband Network proposal partly on the grounds that Australia was falling behind key Asian competitors in internet speeds (Conroy 2007; Singh and Johnson 2013: 129–51).

---

11   On differing concepts of state and civil society, see, for example, Lyons and Gomez (2005); and Wang (2011: xxv–xxviii). On differing concepts of modernity, see, for example, Hobson (2004); and Wang (2011). On differing concepts of gender and sexuality, see Jackson (2001); Mackie (2000; 2007: 103–20); and Mackie and McLelland (2015: 1–17).

Meanwhile, Abbott government Treasurer Joe Hockey (2012) suggested while in Opposition that the Asian Century would require a reduction in Australian government benefits and entitlements, given that Australia would be competing with countries in the region that spend a much smaller percentage of gross domestic product (GDP) on 'public welfare and health care and pension costs'. Engagement with Asia also has implications for Australia's institutional structures, as our state and federal governments try to engage in trade and industry development with Asian competitors and markets where the units of decision-making may be very different. Consider, for example, the key role of city and regional governments in Chinese industry policy, including in areas such as biotechnology and information technology. Engaging with the region will therefore have multiple implications for public policy analyses.

The scope of this book

The authors of this volume draw on insights from economics, education, gender studies, history, political science, psychology, sociology and urban planning. Issues covered range from the internationalisation of Australian tertiary education to the contributions to be made to understanding shared regional problems such as climate change, reproductive control, trade liberalisation and financial governance by engaging with diverse social science traditions.

As discussed above, this process of reflection impels us to re-examine the history of the social sciences and to consider how Australian academics are positioned as inheritors of Euro-American and Anglophone ways of thinking about the social sciences (Connell 2007). This also means recognising Australia's position as an Anglophone colonial-settler society with a significant Indigenous population, located geographically in the Asia-Pacific region. Indigenous Australians were in communication with the places now known as Indonesia, Timor-Leste and Papua New Guinea well before white settlement. Furthermore, a significant component of our population consists of international students from the Asia-Pacific region (some of whom will become immigrants), other immigrants from the region and the descendants of Asian Australians who immigrated in earlier generations (Jupp 2007; Martin et al. 2015).

A further context for our discussions, as noted above, is the question of how to practise the social sciences in an age of global connectedness in which people, products and images are engaged in constant mobility across national borders.[12] Many of the issues that engage the social sciences are problems that, by their

12   Donald and Mackie (2009: 1–14); Mackie (2013: 293–301); Mackie and Pendleton (2010); Mackie and Stevens (2009: 257–73).

very nature, cross national boundaries. These include questions of climate change, environmental disasters like earthquakes and tsunamis, labour mobility and the political economy of inequality, asylum-seeking, and pandemics that spread rapidly across the globe.

The chapters in this volume present the diversity of the social sciences in the region. Our aim is to bring diverse ways of doing social sciences into dialogue with each other; to consider the role of Australia-based social scientists in mediating between different ways of doing social sciences in the region; to provide an intellectual, social scientific framework for calls to engage with the Asia-Pacific region and to develop Asia literacy; and to consider the role of the social sciences in addressing pressing transnational social concerns in the region. A key aim of the volume is to draw the attention of Australian social scientists to some of the exciting insights that can be gained from engaging with the rich and diverse social science traditions in our region.

The book begins with chapters that address broad issues of how contemporary social science was and is constructed and the implications for developing a twenty-first-century social science. Raewyn Connell draws on her previous work in her path-breaking book *Southern theory* (2007). She acknowledges that the social sciences in Australia were originally influenced by the impact of colonialism on the development of European social sciences with a corresponding neglect of other social science traditions from Africa, South America and Asia. Connell gives examples of major social science work that has been neglected as a result. She draws out some of the implications of this changing geopolitics of knowledge for Australian higher education policy, including the need to develop a research evaluation policy that values broader intellectual traditions.

Sujata Patel argues that the social sciences in the twentieth century inherited a colonial form of knowledge from the nineteenth century that divided them into separate disciplines having distinct national traditions. Some of these national traditions were then privileged over others. Some, particularly those associated with the West, were considered universally applicable forms of knowledge, while others were considered more localised and particular. Patel analyses some of the problems associated with this world view, and argues for a more global social science that incorporates useful insights from a range of national traditions. Such a global social science, she suggests, would be better able to address issues and problems in an increasingly globalised and interconnected world.

Chua Beng-Huat emphasises that it is important for scholars in Asia to accept the West as one particular point of reference among others and to multiply the points of reference to include Asian instances that can also be compared with each other. In the process, the West is no longer privileged as the point of comparison, and Asia and the West can be treated as relative equals. He argues that such comparisons of political and economic practices can generate concepts that explain developments in Asia more adequately than the mere application of presumed 'universal' concepts generated outside Asia. For example, one can better understand the differing economic models and strategies pursued in South Korea and Singapore if one contrasts and compares these countries with each other, rather than merely making comparisons with a supposedly universal model. Chua gives additional examples from urban planning, cultural production and democratic institutions.

Kanishka Jayasuriya explores how the concept of the Asian Century problematises key assumptions of both area studies and social sciences. He argues that area studies is based on a view of Asia as 'out there' rather than 'within' the mainstream of academic disciplinary inquiry. Rather than regarding the study of Asia as a special case, such study should be incorporated into all levels of analysis, including the social, political and institutional. Jayasuriya proposes that we also need to draw on the methodological and analytical insights of important work being produced in Asian universities, which provides new insights into common social science problems. Examples he gives include Cui Zhiyuan's (2005) work advocating new forms of economic decentralisation and property rights in China; Neera Chandhoke's (1995) innovative work on Indian civil society and new forms and patterns of representation; and Pasuk Phongpaichit et al.'s (1998) work on Thai society and economy. Through mainstreaming such research and issues, we can develop an interdisciplinary, problem-oriented approach that enables us to build research around key issues, problems and puzzles of social, economic and political transformations pertaining to the region as a whole. Such regional issues range from those of inequality and urbanisation to those of public goods and environmental issues.

Having analysed the ways in which the contemporary social sciences were constructed and arguing for the development of a more flexible, inclusive and global social science that draws on diverse traditions as required, subsequent chapters in the book undertake more specific analyses of case studies in the region, while others engage with the *Australia in the Asian Century* White Paper.

Sylvia Estrada-Claudio shows how reproductive health issues in the Philippines have involved a process of mediating the claims and perspectives of the national government, the church, medical professionals, non-governmental organisation (NGO) activists, multilateral aid agencies and individuals. Her chapter focuses on the local and international alliances forged between politicians, activists, medical professionals and academics, and the implications for our understanding of citizenship, political activism and social science scholarship in a regional frame.

Tessa Morris-Suzuki's chapter brings important social science analyses to bear on common ways in which the issue of Asian engagement is imagined, in the process illustrating some of the contributions that such analyses can make to our understanding of key issues in the region. Morris-Suzuki argues that placing the rise of Asia so squarely in an economic framework obscures some important dimensions of regional change and regional interaction. For social scientists and other researchers, it is also important to consider the region through a different prism: that of the end of the Cold War and the creation of a post–Cold War order. Such a prism provides additional insights into the economic rise of Japan, South Korea, Taiwan and other economies, with implications for both foreign and economic policy and for our understanding of key issues in the region.

Leong Liew analyses economic thought in China, noting both similarities and differences in approaches and methods compared with conventional Western economics, including differing views on the nature and role of the state in regard to markets. This has major policy impacts. He argues that such differences need to be grasped if we are to have a thorough understanding of the Chinese economy. The role of the state in the Chinese economy highlights the need to rethink some key aspects of contemporary Western economic thought.

The final group of articles addresses and moves beyond the concept of the Asian Century. Ken Henry—who oversaw the process leading to the White Paper on *Australia in the Asian Century*—analyses the background of the White Paper. Henry outlines the social, political and economic challenges facing Australia in the twenty-first century, emphasising the need for a compelling narrative and vision of Australia's future. In particular, he argues that we need Australians with the knowledge and skills to develop strong relationships in the region. In order to build partnerships, we need the capacity to understand and operate in cultures, languages and mindsets other than our own. Within Australia we need to ensure that we have the advisory, decision-making and representational structures in place to make informed decisions in an increasingly complex environment. Social scientists in Australia have important contributions to make in developing these skills and capacities and contributing to developing the knowledge necessary for making well-informed policy decisions.

Ariel Heryanto points out that the White Paper on *Australia in the Asian Century* is the latest in a string of government documents and statements to emphasise 'Asia literacy'. Heryanto explores what is meant by the concept of literacy and the ways in which it can lead to biases when examining and interpreting social practices in modern but oral-oriented societies. Heryanto points out that in Indonesia some of the most valued information and messages are usually shared through face-to-face communication, in which body language is as important as words. He therefore draws attention to the need for Asia literacy knowledge, analyses and policies in Australia to engage with such differences.

Simon Marginson analyses the changing geopolitics of higher education in the light of the rise of Asian and Southeast Asian universities in the Asian Century. Marginson compares the higher education systems in the United States, Asia and 'Westminster' (the United Kingdom, Australia and New Zealand) in terms of differences in the role and nature of the state, educational cultures, financing of higher education and politico-economic dynamics of research. He then draws out the implications for the Australian social sciences and for Australian education policy.

Just as we wish to introduce readers to the diversity of 'doing' social sciences in the region, so too have we incorporated a diverse range of views and approaches in this book. While all of our contributors welcome the increased attention to Australia's interactions with the Asia-Pacific region, many wish to challenge the instrumentalist focus of much of the existing discussion. As we have seen, Connell, Patel and Chua all recognise the colonial background to Anglophone social sciences (as it has been practised in Australia, too) and argue for a decolonisation of social science methodologies. Several authors are critical of the focus on economics in the discussion of 'engagement with the Asia-Pacific region'. Morris-Suzuki argues for a more historically informed approach, which recognises that much of our earlier engagement with the region was informed by a Cold War world view and that we need to come to terms with the post–Cold War order. Heryanto points out the limitations of the Asia literacy model that informs the discussion of Asian studies education. We believe that encouraging such diversity of views and approaches not only contributes to a better understanding of the nature and range of social science knowledge, it also encourages academic discussion and debate on the important issues that this book addresses. Indeed, pursuing differing approaches can help to provide a more complete picture of the complex events and processes that are occurring in the Asia-Pacific region, producing forms of knowledge that can complement rather than contradict each other. In this introduction, we have drawn attention to complex interactions between cultural, political and economic factors that have helped to shape Australian understandings of, and responses to, our region.

Conclusion

In a radio interview, Kishore Mahbubani, Dean of the Lee Kuan Yew School of Public Policy at the National University of Singapore, has claimed that '[b]oth the Australian population and, what is even more frightening, the Australian intelligentsia at large, is out of touch with the new realities of Asia' (Mahbubani 2012). He argues that Australians have lived in a comfortable Western bubble and that the intelligentsia has 'become complacent'. Consequently, Mahbubani (2012) argued that the Australian education system had failed and that there was a need for a 'mental revolution' in Australia and a substantial 'mindset' change. This book is an indicator that Mahbubani has underestimated the determination of Australian academics to engage intellectually with the diverse social science knowledge produced in the Asia-Pacific region. Indeed, we see such an engagement as being part of our role in an intellectual 'intersection' society and that such mediation is an important part of the contribution that Australia-based academics can make to international social science.

This book demonstrates that there are diverse social science traditions from various parts of the world that can usefully be drawn upon. Australian universities are particularly well placed to seize the teaching and research opportunities arising from Australia's geographical location and intellectual history. We can become an intersection university system, drawing on all that is best of the knowledge produced in European and North American universities and all that is best of the diverse forms of knowledge being produced in the great universities of the Asia-Pacific region. In doing so, we will position ourselves well to operate successfully in the international higher education system of the twenty-first century. These shifts in the geopolitics of knowledge make this an exciting time to be a social scientist, facilitating an intellectual engagement between diverse traditions. Indeed, Australian social scientists are arguably already at the forefront of such engagement. This book is intended to be a contribution to an international discussion about how to best practise the social sciences under conditions of globalisation when there is a shifting geopolitics of knowledge.

References

Abbott, Tony. 2014. Address to the Asia Society. 25 March, Canberra. URL: www.pm.gov.au/media/2014-03-25/address-asia-society-canberra. Consulted 20 October 2014.

Academy of the Social Sciences in Australia. 1998. *Challenges for the social sciences and Australia*. 3 vols. Canberra: Commonwealth of Australia.

Amin, Shahid and Chakrabarty, Dipesh. eds. 1996. *Subaltern studies: Writings on South Asian history*. Vol. 9. Delhi: Oxford University Press.

Ang, Ien, Tambiah, Yasmin and Mar, Phillip. 2015. *Smart engagement with Asia: Leveraging language, research and culture*. Report for the Australian Council of Learned Academies (ACOLA). Canberra: ACOLA.

APEC [Asia-Pacific Economic Cooperation]. n.d. History. URL: www.apec.org/About-Us/About-APEC/History.aspx. Consulted 15 September 2014.

Arnold, David and Hardiman, David. eds. 1994. *Subaltern studies: Essays in honour of Ranajit Guha*. Vol. 8. Delhi: Oxford University Press.

Asian Studies Association of Australia. 2002. *Maximising Australia's Asia knowledge: Repositioning and renewal of a national asset*. Melbourne: Asian Studies Association of Australia. URL: asaa.asn.au/publications/Reports/ asia-knowledge-book-v70.pdf. Consulted 7 October 2013.

Asian Studies Council. 1988. *A national strategy for the study of Asia in Australia*. Canberra: Australian Government Publishing Service.

Asian Studies Council. 1989. *Asia in Australian higher education: Report of the inquiry into the teaching of Asian studies and languages in higher education*. Canberra: Asian Studies Council.

Auchmuty, James J. 1971. *The teaching of Asian languages and cultures: Report of the Commonwealth Advisory Committee*. Canberra: Commonwealth Government Printing Office.

Australian Education International. n.d. Endeavour Scholarships and Fellowships. URL: aei.gov.au/scholarships-and-fellowships/Pages/default. aspx. Consulted 24 August 2014.

Aveling, Harry. 1998. Asian languages and literatures. In Reference Group for the Australian Academy of the Humanities, ed. *Knowing ourselves and others: The humanities in Australia into the 21st century*. Vol. 2. Canberra: Commonwealth of Australia.

Bhadra, Gautam, Prakash, Gyan and Tharu, Susie. eds. 1999. *Subaltern studies: Writings on South Asian history and society*. Vol. 10. Delhi: Oxford University Press.

Bishop, Julie. 2013a. Address to Liberal Friends of India launch. *Speeches*. URL: www.juliebishop.com.au/speeches/1269-address-to-liberal-friends-of-india-launch.html. Consulted 6 October 2013.

Bishop, Julie. 2013b. A new vision for engaging in the region. Address to the Australasian Council of Deans of Arts, Social Sciences and Humanities 2012 Conference, The Australian National University, Canberra. *Speeches*. URL: www.juliebishop.com.au/speeches/1178-a-new-vision-for-engaging-in-the-region.html. Consulted 11 September 2013.

Bishop, Julie. 2013c. Australian foreign policy debate. 7 August 2013, Lowy Institute for International Policy, Sydney. URL: www.lowyinstitute.org/files/ documents/events/australianforeignpolicydebate_transcript_7august2013. pdf. Consulted 6 October 2013.

Brasted, Howard. 1998. South Asian studies. In Reference Group for the Australian Academy of the Humanities, ed. *Knowing ourselves and others: The humanities in Australia into the 21st century*. Vol. 2. Canberra: Commonwealth of Australia.

Breckenridge, Carol A. and van de Veer, Peter. 1993. Orientalism and the postcolonial predicament. In Carol A. Breckenridge and Peter van de Veer, eds. *Orientalism and the postcolonial predicament: Perspectives on South Asia*. Philadelphia: University of Pennsylvania Press.

Chakrabarty, Dipesh. 1992. Trafficking in history and theory: Subaltern studies. In Ken K. Ruthven, ed. *Beyond the disciplines: The new humanities*. Canberra: Australian Academy of the Humanities.

Chakrabarty, Dipesh. 2014. Communing with magpies. *History Australia* 11(3): 194–206.

Chandhoke, Neera. 1995. *State and civil society: Exploration in political theory*. New Delhi: Sage.

Chatterjee, Partha and Pandey, Gyan. eds. 1992. *Subaltern studies: Writings on South Asian history and society*. Vol. 9. Delhi: Oxford University Press.

Chen, Kuan-Hsing and Huat, Chua Beng. 2002. An introduction. *Inter-Asia Cultural Studies* 1(1): 9–12.

COAG [Council of Australian Governments]. 1994. *Asian languages and Australia's economic future: A report prepared for COAG on a proposed national Asian languages/studies strategy for Australian schools*. Canberra: Australian Government Publishing Service.

Coaldrake, William and Wells, Ken. 1998. Japanese and Korean studies. In Reference Group for the Australian Academy of the Humanities, ed. *Knowing ourselves and others: The humanities in Australia into the 21st century*. Vol. 2. Canberra: Commonwealth of Australia.

Committee of Concerned Asian Scholars. 1968. *CCAS Newsletter* (1)(May). URL: criticalasianstudies.org/assets/files/bcas/v01n01.pdf. Consulted 23 September 2014.

Commonwealth of Australia. 2012. *Australia in the Asian Century*. White Paper. Canberra: Commonwealth of Australia. URL: pandora.nla.gov.au/pan/133850/20130914-0122/asiancentury.dpmc.gov.au/white-paper.html. Consulted 17 July 2014.

Connell, Raewyn. 2007. *Southern theory: The global dynamics of knowledge in social science*. Oxford: Polity.

Conroy, Stephen. 2007. ALP media statement. 25 March. URL: www.alp.org.au/media/0307/mscom250.php. Consulted 27 March 2007.

Cui, Zhiyuan. 2005. Liberal socialism and the future of China: A petty bourgeoisie manifesto. In Cao Tianyu, ed. *China's model for modern development*. London: Routledge.

Dale, Leigh. 2012. *The enchantment of English: Professing English literatures in Australian universities*. Sydney: Sydney University Press.

d'Cruz, J. V. and Steele, William. 2003. *Australia's ambivalence towards Asia*. Melbourne: Monash Asia Institute/Monash University Press.

Denoon, Donald and Ward, Gerard. 1998. Pacific Islands studies. In Reference Group for the Australian Academy of the Humanities, ed. *Knowing ourselves and others: The humanities in Australia into the 21st century*. Vol. 2. Canberra: Commonwealth of Australia.

Department of Defence. 2000. Defence gets new state-of-the-art language school. URL: www.defence.gov.au/minister/2tpl.cfm?CurrentId=269. Consulted 23 September 2014.

DFAT [Department of Foreign Affairs and Trade]. n.d. *New Colombo Plan*. URL: www.dfat.gov.au/new-colombo-plan/about.html. Consulted 24 August 2014.

Donald, Stephanie Hemelyrk and Mackie, Vera. 2009. Working in the space between. *Journal of Multidisciplinary International Studies* 6(1)(January): 1–14. URL: epress.lib.uts.edu.au/journals/index.php/portal/article/view/1220/1236. Consulted: 7 October 2013.

Dower, John. 1975. E. H. Norman, Japan and the uses of history. In John Dower, ed. *Origins of the modern Japanese state: Selected writings of E. H. Norman*. New York: Pantheon.

Downer, Alexander. 2005. Speech on the launch of 'Australia and the Colombo Plan, 1949–1957'. URL: www.foreignminister.gov.au/speeches/2005/050523_colombo_plan.html. Consulted 8 March 2015.

Eschle, Catherine. 2002. Engendering global democracy. *International Feminist Journal of Politics* 4(3): 315–41.

FitzGerald, Stephen. 1980. *Asia in Australian education: Report of the Committee on Asian Studies to the Asian Studies Association of Australia*. Canberra: Asian Studies Association of Australia.

Foreign Policy Initiative. 2011. The Obama administration's pivot to Asia: A conversation with Assistant Secretary Kurt Campbell, moderated by Robert Kagan. 13 December. URL: www.foreignpolicyi.org/files/uploads/images/Asia%20Pivot.pdf. Consulted October 2013.

Gillard, Julia and Swan, Wayne. 2011. Transcript of joint press conference. 22 August, Canberra. Press Office. Canberra: Department of Prime Minister and Cabinet. URL: www.pm.gov.au/press-office/transcript-joint-press-conference-canberra-14. Consulted 20 September 2012.

Grewal, Inderpal and Kaplan, Caren. eds. 1994. *Scattered hegemonies: Postmodernity and transnational feminist practices.* Minneapolis: University of Minnesota Press.

Guha, Ranajit. ed. 1982–89. *Subaltern studies: Writings on South Asian history.* Vols 1–6. Delhi: Oxford University Press.

Hall, C. Michael. 2009. 'A long and still-unfinished story?': Constructing and defining Asian regionalisms. In Tim Winter, P. Teo and T. C. Chang, eds. *Asia on tour: Exploring the rise of Asian tourism.* London: Routledge.

Hannerz, Ulf. 1987. The world in creolization. *Africa* 57(4): 546–59.

Hannerz, Ulf. 1989. Notes on the global ecumene. *Public Culture* 1(2)(Spring 1989): 66–75.

Hobson, John M. 2004. *The Eastern origins of Western civilisation.* Cambridge: Cambridge University Press.

Hockey, Joe. 2012. Interview. *Lateline.* 18 April. Sydney: Australian Broadcasting Corporation. URL: www.abc.net.au/lateline/content/2012/s3480665.htm. Consulted 9 May 2012.

Hooper, Beverley. 1998. Chinese studies. In Reference Group for the Australian Academy of the Humanities, ed. *Knowing ourselves and others: The humanities in Australia into the 21st century.* Vol. 2. Canberra: Commonwealth of Australia.

Huang, Futao. 2007. Internationalization of higher education in the developing and emerging countries: A focus on transnational higher education in Asia. *Journal of Studies in International Education* (3–4): 421–32.

Indelicato, Maria Elena. 2015. Australia's 'Colombo Plan': The beacon of Western knowledge in the Asia-Pacific region. *Critical Race and Whiteness Studies* 11(1): 1–16.

Ingleson, John. 1998. Southeast Asian studies. In Reference Group for the Australian Academy of the Humanities, ed. *Knowing ourselves and others: The humanities in Australia into the 21st century*. Vol. 2. Canberra: Commonwealth of Australia.

Jackson, Peter A. 2001. Pre-gay, post-queer: Thai perspectives on proliferating gender/sex diversity in Asia. In Gerard Sullivan and Peter A. Jackson, eds. *Gay and lesbian Asia: Culture, identity, community*. New York: Harrington Park Press.

Jackson, Peter A. 2015. *Spatialities of knowledge in the neoliberal world academy: Theory, practice and 21st century legacies of area studies*. Bonn: Crossroads Asia Working Series.

Jayasuriya, Kanishka. 2012. A teachable moment. *Global Asia* 7(2): 88–91.

Johnson, Carol, Ahluwalia, Pal and McCarthy, Greg. 2010. Australia's ambivalent re-imagining of Asia. *Australian Journal of Political Science* 45(1): 59–79.

Jones, Paul. 2001. Trading in a 'fool's paradise'? White Australia and the trade diversion dispute of 1936. In Paul Jones and Vera Mackie, eds. *Relationships: Japan and Australia, 1870s–1950s*. Melbourne: History Monographs and RMIT Publishing.

Jupp, James. 2007. *From White Australia to Woomera: The story of Australian immigration*. 2nd edn. Cambridge: Cambridge University Press.

Kartomi, Margaret. 2013. Growing up in a musical Quaker family. In Susan Blackburn, ed. *Growing up in Adelaide in the 1950s*. Sydney: GHR Press.

Keating, Paul. 1992. Asia-Australia Institute address. 7 April. In M. Ryan, ed. *Advancing Australia: The speeches of Paul Keating, Prime Minister*. Sydney: Big Picture Publications.

Kersten, Rikki, Sebastian, Eugene and Williams, Leslie. 1996. *Asian Studies in Australia's higher education sector*. Sydney: Research Institute for Asia and the Pacific.

Lal, Brij V. and Ley, Allison. 2006. *The Coombs book: A house of memories*. Canberra: Research School of Pacific and Asian Studies.

Lowe, David. 2014. New Colombo Plan can change how we see Asia: If done right. *The Conversation* 25 June. URL: theconversation.com/new-colombo-plan-can-change-how-we-see-asia-if-done-right-28301. Consulted 24 August 2014.

Lyons, Lenore T. and Gomez, James. 2005. Moving beyond the OB markers: Rethinking the space of civil society in Singapore. *Sojourn: Journal of Social Issues in Southeast Asia* 20(2): 119–31.

McFadyen, C. H. 1949. Acting Director of the Division of Industrial Development, column. *Exports of Australia* February: 27–28.

Macintyre, Stuart. 2010. *The poor relation: A history of social sciences in Australia.* Melbourne: Melbourne University Press.

Mackie, Vera. 2000. The metropolitan gaze: Travellers, bodies, spaces. *Intersections: Gender and Sexuality in Asia and the Pacific* 4(September): unpaginated. URL: intersections.anu.edu.au/issue4/vera.html. Consulted 9 October 2013.

Mackie, Vera. 2007. Sexuality in a transnational frame: Australian stories, Japanese stories. In Leigh Dale and Masayo Tada, eds. *On the Western edge: Australia and Japan.* Perth: Network Books.

Mackie, Vera. 2013. Ways of knowing about human rights in Asia. *Asian Studies Review* 37(3): 293–301.

Mackie, Vera and McLelland, Mark. 2015. Framing sexuality studies in East Asia. In Mark McLelland and Vera Mackie, eds. *Routledge handbook of sexuality studies in East Asia.* London: Routledge.

Mackie, Vera and Pendleton, Mark. 2010. On the move: Globalisation and culture in the Asia-Pacific region. *Intersections: Gender and Sexuality in Asia and the Pacific* 23(January): unpaginated. URL: intersections.anu.edu.au/issue23/mackie_pendleton.htm. Consulted 7 October 2013.

Mackie, Vera and Stevens, Carolyn S. 2009. Globalisation and body politics. *Asian Studies Review* 33(3): 257–73.

Mahbubani, Kishore. 2008. *The new Asian hemisphere: The irresistible shift of global power to the east.* New York: Public Affairs.

Mahbubani, Kishore. 2012. Interview. *Radio Australia.* 2 November. URL: www.radioaustralia.net.au/international/2012-11-02/asian-century-white-paper-timely-and-overdue-mahbubani/1038068. Consulted 4 November 2012.

Martin, Fran, Healy, Chris, Iwabuchi, Koichi, Khoo, Olivia, Maree, Claire, Yi, Keren and Yue, Audrey. 2015. Australia's 'Asian Century': Time, space and public culture. *The Asia-Pacific Journal* 13(6)(February). URL: www.japanfocus.org/-Audrey-Yue/4268. Consulted 9 March 2015.

Mattelart, Armand. 1983. *Transnationals and the Third World: The struggle for culture*. Trans. D. Buxton. South Hadley, Mass.: Bergin & Garvey Publishers.

Miller, Jane and Nicholls, David. 2014. Jocelyn Hyslop, the little-known story of the founding director of social work at the University of Melbourne. *Lilith: A Feminist History Journal* 20: 21–33.

Milner, Tony and Morris-Suzuki, Tessa. 1998. The challenge of Asia. In Reference Group for the Australian Academy of the Humanities, ed. *Knowing ourselves and others: The humanities in Australia into the 21st century*. Vol. 3. Canberra: Commonwealth of Australia.

Miyoshi, Masao and Harootunian, Harry. eds. 2002. *Learning places: The afterlives of area studies*. Durham, NC: Duke University Press.

Mok, Ka Ho. 2007. Questing for internationalization of universities in Asia: Critical reflections Asia. *Journal of Studies in International Education* 11(3–4): 433–54.

Morris-Suzuki, Tessa. 2000. Anti-area studies. *Communal/Plural* 8(1): 9–23.

Morris-Suzuki, Tessa. 2011. Japan and its region: Changing historical perceptions. *Sungkyun Journal of East Asian Studies* 11(2): 123–42.

NALSAS [National Asian Languages and Studies in Australian Schools]. 1998. *Partnership for change: The NALSAS strategy*. Canberra: NALSAS.

Nguyen, Viet Thanh and Hoskins, Janet. 2014. Introduction: Transpacific studies—interventions and intersections. In Janet Hoskins and Nguyen Viet Tanh, eds. *Transpacific studies: Framing an emerging field*. Honolulu: University of Hawai'i Press.

Oakman, Daniel. 2004. *Facing Asia: A history of the Colombo Plan*. Canberra: Pandanus Books.

Phongpaichit, Pasuk, Piriyarangsan, Sungsidh and Treerat, Nualnol. 1998. *Gangs, gambling, gaming: Thailand's illegal economy and public policy*. Bangkok: Silkworm.

Rudd, Kevin. 2008. Address at the launch of *Inside Kevin 07* by Christine Jackman. 22 July, Sydney. Prime Minister of Australia Media Hub 2008. URL: www.pm.gov.au/media/Speech/2008/speech_0373.cfm. Consulted 15 April 2009.

Rudd, Kevin. 2009. India–Australia joint declaration on security cooperation. 12 November, New Delhi. URL: www.pm.gov.au/node/6324. Consulted 19 November 2009.

Said, Edward. 1978. *Orientalism*. Harmondsworth: Penguin.

Saikal, Amin. 1998. Middle Eastern studies. In Reference Group for the Australian Academy of the Humanities, ed. *Knowing ourselves and others: The humanities in Australia into the 21st century*. Vol. 2. Canberra: Commonwealth of Australia.

Shimazu, Naoko. 1998. *Japan, race and equality: The racial equality proposal of 1919*. London: Routledge.

Singh, Amita (with a special Australian contribution by Carol Johnson). 2013. *A critical impulse to e-governance in the Asia Pacific*. New Delhi: Springer.

Spence, Michael. 2011. *The next convergence: The future of economic growth in a multispeed world*. New York: Farrar Straus & Giroux.

Spivak, Gayatri Chakravorty. 2003. *Death of a discipline: The Wellek Library lectures on critical theory*. New York: Columbia University Press.

Spivak, Gayatri Chakravorty. 2008. *Other Asias*. Oxford: Blackwell.

Tambiah, Stanley J. 2000. Transnational movements, diaspora and multiple modernities. *Daedalus* 129(Winter): 163–94.

Tolentino, Rolando B. 1996. Bodies, letters, catalogues: Filipinas in transnational space. *Social Text* 14(3): 49–76.

Torney-Parlicki, Prue. 2000. *Somewhere in Asia: War, journalism and Australia's neighbours*. Sydney: UNSW Press.

Turnbull, Malcolm. 2015. Assessing the future of the Asia-Pacific–US/Australia dialogue. 31 January. URL: www.malcolmturnbull.com.au/media/future-of-the-asia-pacific. Consulted 27 February 2015.

Turner, Graeme and Brass, Kylie. 2014. *Mapping the humanities, arts and social sciences in Australia*. Canberra: Australian Academy of the Humanities.

Universities Australia. 2014. Key facts and data. 7 July. URL: www.universitiesaustralia.edu.au/australias-universities/key-facts-and-data#.VCD531aOWlI. Consulted 23 September 2014.

Walker, David. 1999. *Anxious nation: Australia and the rise of Asia, 1850–1949*. Brisbane: University of Queensland Press.

Walker, David and Sobocinska, Agnieszka. 2012. Introduction: Australia's Asia. In David Walker and Agnieszca Sobocinska, eds. *Australia's Asia: From yellow peril to Asian century*. Perth: UWA Publishing.

Wang, Hui. 2007. The politics of imagining Asia: A genealogical analysis. *Inter-Asia Cultural Studies* 8(1): 1–33.

Wilson, Rob and Dirlik, Arif. eds. 1995. *Asia-Pacific as space of cultural production*. Durham, NC: Duke University Press.

Wolfe, Patrick. 1999. *Settler colonialism and the transformation of anthropology: The politics and poetics of an ethnographic event*. London: Cassell.

Young, Robert. 2001. *Postcolonialism: An historical introduction*. Oxford: Wiley-Blackwell.

PART I: ENGAGING DIVERSITY IN THE SOCIAL SCIENCES

2

Australia in the global dynamics of social science: De-centring Europe and de-mythologising the 'Asian Century'

Raewyn Connell

Introduction

This chapter addresses two major challenges facing the social sciences in Australia. The first is the situation of Australian social science in a world context, which must be considered in the light of the postcolonial thinking that is now developing in all the social sciences worldwide. The challenge is all the greater because, in Australia, that reconsideration is taking place in institutions situated on the dispossessed land of Australia's Indigenous peoples. The second challenge is that this reconsideration is occurring in the context of the promotion of government plans for Australian capitalists to exploit what are seen as the vast growing markets of Asia, under the rubric of the 'Asian Century'. In this chapter, I will discuss both agendas, and the contradiction between them.[1] I will also argue that the engagement with social science in the

---

1   Indeed, the Academy of the Social Sciences in Australia's Annual Symposium on 'The Social Sciences in the Asian Century', from which this book arose, reflected these two strikingly different agendas.

Asia-Pacific region needs to be seen in the broader context of a global economy of knowledge, including the history of colonialism and the development of neoliberal economics.

The global economy of knowledge

In the social sciences, we usually work with the convenient fiction that the disciplines we work in, and the concepts we work with, do not come from anywhere in particular. They are just 'in the air', so to speak. When we cite a particular author or study—'Smith, Jones and Robinson 2009'—we rarely stop to think what ethnic group Smith comes from, to whom Jones is married or what untenured job Robinson is currently holding. Indeed, the most influential epistemological viewpoint in the social sciences tells us that these details do not matter, that the more abstract and decontextualised the knowledge, the better it is, and the more scientific. Even highly context-focused social sciences, like history and anthropology, tend to see their methodology in this way.

There is, however, a counter-current of thought in social science that has never been persuaded that decontextual is good; arguing, indeed, that social determinations shape all intellectual work—and not superficially but at the most profound level. This thinking has nineteenth-century roots but was stated with great brilliance by Gyorgy Lukács in *History and class consciousness* (1971), originally published in 1923 and rapidly suppressed by authoritarian regimes on both the right and the left. His ideas were taken up by Karl Mannheim in his 1929 masterpiece *Ideology and utopia* (1985), and turned into the sociology of knowledge. In a later generation, Michel Foucault's immensely influential work on cultural history showed how systems of knowledge were not only embedded in social power but themselves functioned as techniques of power and social control (Foucault 1977). At much the same time, studies of the impact of gender relations on knowledge formation were developed by scholars such as Dorothy Smith (1990) and became known as standpoint epistemology. The more recent development of critical whiteness studies has begun to do the same kind of job for race relations.

These developments, important as they have been, were nevertheless focused on the societies of the global North, the imperial powers of Europe and North America that in a postcolonial era remained the centre of the global capitalist economy. In the past generation, the relation of global power structures to the making of knowledge systems has finally come under close scrutiny. A decisive step occurred with the publication of Edward Said's *Orientalism* (1978), which examined the construction of European knowledge about the Arab world and the 'East' in the context of European world power. Said's work, together with other contributions—of which perhaps the most important was the work of the Subaltern Studies group leading up to Dipesh Chakrabarty's *Provincializing Europe* (2000)—opened up a broad set of issues that have come to be called 'postcolonial studies' in the humanities.

This is the territory now being explored by social scientists in a vigorous literature on the global dynamics of knowledge. The strands of this literature include research on alternative traditions in social science (Alatas 2006; Patel 2010), southern theory (Connell 2007; Meekosha 2011), postcolonial sociology (Bhambra 2007; Reuter and Villa 2010), indigenous knowledge (Odora Hoppers 2002), the psychology of liberation (Montero 2007), decolonial thought (Mignolo 2005; Quijano 2000), the decolonisation of methodology (Smith 2012) and more.

For our present discussion, the most important resource is the global sociology of knowledge developed by the Beninese philosopher Paulin Hountondji in *Endogenous knowledge* (1997; see also Connell 2011). Hountondji identifies the problem not as the simple imposition of Western perspectives, but as a global division of labour in the realm of knowledge, with its roots in imperialism. The colonial world served as a rich source of data for science; figures as famous as Charles Darwin and Alexander von Humboldt shared in the collecting. The data were shipped back to the metropole—that is, the imperial centre—which became the site of the *theoretical* moment in knowledge production. Data were classified and intellectual structures built and debated in the universities, museums, botanic gardens, scientific associations and research institutes of the imperial powers. Here, specialised workforces were created, and practical fields were transformed into applied sciences such as engineering, agronomy and medicine. In this form, science was returned to the periphery, and applied by colonial powers in the mines, in agriculture and in government.

In the contemporary world, the periphery continues to be a rich source of raw materials for the new biology, pharmaceuticals, astronomy, social science, linguistics, archaeology and more. The metropole continues to be the main site of theoretical processing, now including corporate research institutes and giant databanks. Intellectual workers in the periphery are pushed towards a stance Hountondji calls 'extraversion'—a key concept.

To function successfully as a scientist in the periphery—whether in Africa, China or Australia—one *must* read the leading journals published in the metropole, learn the research techniques taught there and gain recognition there. Career paths include advanced training in the metropole, attending conferences in the metropole and, for the more successful, getting a job in the metropole. The theoretical frameworks developed in the metropole become embedded in the intellectual work of the periphery, not by the exercise of direct control, but by the way the whole economy of knowledge is organised, and the extraversion this economy requires.

It is not hard to see this economy of knowledge at work in social science. The foundation stories of our disciplines are told with heroic figures from Europe at the centre: Adam Smith, Leopold von Ranke, Karl Marx, Max Weber, and so on. With very few exceptions, the theorists of Europe and North America are the ones who still provide our paradigms: Michel Foucault, Howard Becker, Jürgen Habermas, Gilles Deleuze, Pierre Bourdieu, Judith Butler, and so on. Most journals in the social sciences are published in the global North, and all of the most prestigious ones. Output in the global South is marked by extraversion: in Brazil, South Africa, Colombia, New Zealand, Australia or China, the usual structure of papers in a local journal is hybrid, consisting of a theoretical discussion derived from Europe and North America, plus data derived locally. There is a steady traffic of social scientists going to the North to study for doctorates, to work on sabbatical or to seek jobs.

To acknowledge the global economy of knowledge is surprisingly difficult, though the data are very clear. Many social scientists do not like to be told this; many careers are deeply invested in the current Northern paradigms. Within the dominant conventions of our disciplines, the works of Foucault, Habermas, Deleuze, Bourdieu, and so on are simply 'theory'; they are not read as specifically European ideas arising from the social experience of the global North. Social scientists, like natural scientists, often think they are part of a search for universal knowledge that is untainted by place or local interest. They can even become angry when asked to think about the global structures of power in which their knowledge work occurs.

Australian social science in the global context

Australian universities were created as a branch of the British university system, importing professors, curricula and ceremonials alike. Creating the first ones was a remarkable and even heroic thing to do in these rough and remote settler colonies, but the founders were determined to bring European culture to leaven the local lump. The relationship was beautifully expressed by the founders of the University of Sydney when they chose the motto for the university's coat of arms, *Sidere Mens Eadem Mutato* ('Under changed skies, the same mind'). Familiar disciplinary structures of knowledge were adopted without question.

A century and a half later, despite a great change in scale and sophistication, the position of Australian social science in the global economy of knowledge is only slightly changed. We do now generate data locally. Apart from that, our disciplinary structure—as shown by the organisation of the Academy of the Social Sciences in Australia itself—faithfully reflects European and North American customs. Our curricula and reading lists closely resemble those of the metropole and we often use, or modestly adapt, textbooks from the metropole as the basis of our courses.

We send our promising students to the metropole for advanced training, and if they come back to Australia, having a doctorate from Cambridge, Harvard or the Sorbonne is a great career asset. We try to publish in metropolitan journals—indeed, that has become essential for serious career advancement in all the social sciences (except possibly history, and even there it is highly desirable). When we publish in local journals, our Australian data are typically framed by ideas from North American and European theorists. When we organise social science conferences in Australia, we typically bring keynote speakers from Britain and North America—rarely from Asia and almost never from Latin America or Africa. The pattern of extraversion can be traced empirically among Australian intellectual workers from a variety of institutions (Connell et al. 2005).

The condition of academic dependence on the metropole is so *normal* that most social scientists hardly notice it at all; it is just the way things are, like gravity. It really requires a conscious effort—of the kind made by sociologists of knowledge, standpoint epistemologists and postcolonial theorists—to see Australian social science as being in a historically produced situation that could be otherwise. Yet there have already been other possibilities.

One is given by the fact that some intellectuals in the settler population began to think in ways outside the existing metropolitan disciplinary framework—began, in fact, to produce theoretical perspectives of their own. The most illustrious of these—probably the most influential social scientist ever to emerge from Australia—was Vere Gordon Childe. He was a radical democrat who became an unorthodox Marxist. His sharp, disillusioned account of Australian working-class politics, *How labour governs*, long stood as the classic text on Australian party politics (Beilharz 1995).

But it was prehistory that made Childe famous, and it is there that his power as a social theorist is best seen. Childe did some digging in sites in Scotland and Ireland; however, synthesis and interpretation on a continental, and then world, scale were his forte. I see him fundamentally as a historical sociologist who poured an immense knowledge of archaeological detail into the reconstruction of ancient social structures and dynamics of change.

Childe's masterwork, *The dawn of European civilization* (1925), was a tremendous compilation of Mesolithic, Neolithic and Bronze Age data from eastern, western, southern and northern Europe, carefully sorted by region and time, out of which Childe mapped the succession and overlap of cultures, and debated the issues of dating, diffusion and autonomy from the urban civilisations of Egypt and Mesopotamia. Characteristics of his work were a massive empirical base, a vigorous classification, a concern with the cultural meanings of material remains and an attempt both to reconstruct the functioning societies that gave rise to these remains and to construct an intelligible narrative of large-scale social change.

Is there anything Australian about this? Technically, it could have been written by someone brought up in Europe, and Childe never described it as a perspective from the colonies. Yet there is something about Childe's powerful sense of space and distance, and his concern with the complexities of centre–periphery relations in the ancient world, that seems to reflect colonial experience. There is a memory of structure here that is different from the concerns with racial ancestry, with national distinctiveness or with schemes drawn from Engels, which preoccupied many of his contemporaries in European archaeology.

In his later writing, Childe produced syntheses of prehistory on a canvas broader than *The dawn*—an influential account of urbanism, a historically based social ontology and a sophisticated sociology of knowledge that differs markedly from the Mannheim tradition (see, for example, Childe 1949). It is thought-provoking that the university system in Britain did find a place for him, while the university system in Australia did not. Yet he kept an emotional connection with Australia to the end.

The other significant possibility was eliminated at the start of the university story by the adoption of a European, not just a Eurocentric, curriculum. There was already on the Australian continent an ancient civilisation with highly developed knowledge systems. Indigenous knowledge was categorically excluded from the new higher education institutions in the 1850s, and has only to a small degree, a century and a half later, been brought in.

Indigenous societies and cultures have of course provided *data* for a well-established social science in Australia, anthropology and, in the past generation, the relations between Indigenous and settler societies have also concerned history and to a lesser extent sociology. But *Indigenous knowledge* as a whole—involving conceptualisation, representation, observation, data, symbolic recording and practical know-how—has not yet been regarded as institutionally significant for the higher education system or for the social sciences in general (for the beginnings of recognition in one discipline, see Walter et al. 2006.)

This has been different in other areas of the postcolonial world. One response to the disruption imposed by colonialism has been to reassert indigenous knowledge, though presenting it in new genres. This has been a particularly powerful response in Africa, where a whole literature of 'African philosophy' emerged after 1945—a project renewed under the banner of the 'African Renaissance' promoted by the then South African president Thabo Mbeki. Folktales, songs and poems, language forms and other elements of indigenous culture were brought together as evidence of an implicit African ontology or epistemology, which could stand as an alternative to Western knowledge (Kagamé 1956). This procedure has also been applied to generate an indigenous sociology, based on concepts drawn from the traditional poetry of Yoruba society (Akiwowo 1986).

Akiwowo's project provoked a vigorous debate (Lawuyi and Taiwo 1990) and remains controversial. I am not persuaded that it does yield a generalisable sociology, but it does produce an interesting *diagnosis* of the critical problems of contemporary Nigerian society, and of other countries in the region by extension—specifically, a reading of the process of change from a kinship-based society under the impact of colonialism and the postcolonial economy. The broad question of the relationships between knowledge systems, and the alternatives to Western framings of knowledge, has been widely debated across Africa (Odora Hoppers 2002).

The African debate is dramatic, but it is not alone. There have been debates about the project of an Islamic framing for science (Ghamari 1996), and about decolonial thought in South America (Mignolo 2007). Nandy (1987) argues that Gandhi's struggle against British rule in India not only created a particularist opposition, but also confronted British power with an alternative universalism. Vinay Lal's *Empire of knowledge* (2002) attempts to build on this idea a broad critique of mainstream social science. There is no reason to be shy about the reach or relevance of ideas coming from subordinated or marginalised knowledge systems.

In suggesting that Akiwowo's work commands attention for the diagnosis of social change in West Africa contained in it, I wish to make a wider argument. The *knowledge of social situations* embedded in non-metropolitan discourses about society is knowledge of the same order—and is likely to be as detailed, subtle, grounded in experience and contestable—as metropolitan discourses about metropolitan society. But as Hountondji shows, the *practical conditions* under which knowledge production occurs in the periphery are very different, creating severe difficulties in circulating social knowledge that goes beyond metropolitan paradigms.

Hountondji (1983) mounted a famous critique of the genre of 'African philosophy' as not actually indigenous knowledge. Ironically, it is a construction that reflects the coloniser's gaze. It presents African culture as static and local, in defiance of what we now know about the dynamism of African history, and it is based on a model of 'primitive unanimity'—that is, cultural consensus that is supposed (wrongly) to exist in traditional societies. We see the same patterns in traditional Australian anthropology—now fortunately changing, as shown in research like Gillian Cowlishaw's (2004) study of the hidden injuries of race.

Hountondji does not deny that indigenous knowledges survive, though he is aware that their forms and contexts change. In the volume *Endogenous knowledge: Research trails* (1997), he and a number of West African colleagues explore indigenous mathematics, agronomy, metallurgy and other forms of knowledge. Hountondji argues that these knowledge systems now exist as marginalised forms of knowledge within a context of extraversion. Hountondji argues, to avoid being swallowed in the global economy of knowledge, there is a need for a 'critical validation' of endogenous knowledge. This implies a search for, and affirmation of, the *truth* in indigenous knowledge systems. It also implies a *critique* of the elements of ideology that they carry—that is, a study of their limits and distortions, arising from their origins in unequal societies.

This is, doubtless, the most uncomfortable part of Hountondji's analysis. It is important, however, and necessary. If indigenous knowledge is to function in a world dominated by the knowledge systems of the colonising society, if it is to be validated and made effective, it must be capable of development and growth—and that means it must be open to critique and evaluation.

As I have argued in *Southern theory* (Connell 2007), and as Colin McFarlane argues in 'Crossing borders' (2006), there has to be a mutual learning process. This is not just a matter of individual learning (though that is certainly part of the process). Crucially, it is collective learning that happens at the level of whole knowledge systems.

A *condition* for this learning process is a certain external relationship—one of recognition. Noel Pearson (1997) has observed that 'native title' is not a concept in Aboriginal law. Nor is it a concept in European law. It is, rather, a recognition concept, which arises in the space between the two systems and allows them to interact. Specifically, this concept allows settler society's law to recognise a certain kind of rights. In his recent *Rethinking social justice*, Tim Rowse (2012) has given us a fascinating history of the changing forms of recognition, at least concerning the intellectuals of white settler society in Australia.

Australian neoliberalism, social science and the Asian Century story

The policy agenda in Australian higher education since the 'Dawkins revolution' of the late 1980s has definitely been to reinforce the pattern of extraversion, not to encourage alternatives.

Policy now emphasises competition and ratings within certain measures of excellence: university league tables, citation indexes, journal rankings. These measures are centred on the global North. (Although one of the well-known global rankings of universities is produced in China, paradoxically this confirms the point: it was invented as part of an effort to find out which institutions should be used as models while the Chinese university system was built up.)

These measures of performance, and the material benefits they are increasingly linked with, produce formidable pressure to copy the elite institutions of the global North. In late 2012, then prime minister Julia Gillard announced a national policy goal to promote 10 Australian universities into the 'top 100' globally. (In mid-2013, the same government announced a funding cut for the university sector; neoliberalism has its contradictions.) Meanwhile, the commodification of higher education and the pressure to reduce costs—salaries are the largest item in university budgets—are producing online resources that allow Northern curricula to be accessed more directly. Massive open online courses (MOOCs) are the most discussed but are not the only form of this.

This policy regime for higher education is part of a much broader shift in Australian politics since the 1980s that has reshaped the public sphere on market models. First called 'economic rationalism' in Australia (Pusey 1991), and now (as is more usual internationally) 'neoliberalism', this regime is most familiar as a set of economic policies. The 'free market' is the central image, and deregulation measures that were supposed to free the markets, especially capital markets, were among the earliest and most important neoliberal policies.

Neoliberalism seeks to make existing markets wider, and to create new markets where they did not exist before. This is central to the interests of the businesspeople who fund and sustain neoliberal politics; an expanding terrain of profit-making *is* their definition of development. Neoliberalism pushes towards the wider, and potentially universal, commodification of services, including the realm of social reproduction. The most dramatic form is the privatisation of public assets and services, such as land and electricity. Neoliberals have, however, been quite inventive in finding other ways to commodify services, including higher education. The impact of these policies reaches far beyond economic policymaking, into the realms of everyday life and culture (Braedley and Luxton 2010).

Neoliberal policies have not rolled back the state—indeed, the state's repressive capacity has grown—but they have gone far to halt the growth of public sector expenditure on social reproduction, translating into a real squeeze on many public services. This gradual process in the economies of the global North was packaged in a more drastic form in the structural adjustment programs of the 1980s and 1990s for countries of the global South—a logic still active, as we see in the recent devastation of Greece. In the remaining public sector, a new ethos of managerialism appears. Managers' salaries and bonuses rise, in both the private and the public sectors, to unprecedented levels. Management practice in government increasingly resembles that in corporations. An overlap of elite personnel and policymaking between the public sector and corporate capitalism develops, illustrated by the careers of top managers such as Ken Henry—not long ago secretary to the Treasury, more recently appointed director of the National Australia Bank (NAB) and the Australian Securities Exchange (ASX), and at an earlier stage of his career a representative at the rich countries' neoliberal think tank, the Organisation for Economic Cooperation and Development (OECD).

In the metropole, neoliberalism has dismantled the Keynesian welfare state, the system of regulated capitalism and state-supplied services that was dominant in the generation from 1945 to 1980. In the global periphery, neoliberalism has dismantled the social-democratic developmentalist state and broken up the social alliances around it—most successfully in Latin America, Africa, Australia and New Zealand. Both major parties in Australia now are substantively neoliberal, and the former Gillard and current Liberal leaderships strongly so.

The forces driving neoliberalism are generally understood through a systems model of capitalism, focused on the global metropole, which is curiously reminiscent of neoclassical economics itself (Duménil and Lévy 2004; Harvey 2005). But the first country to adopt a strongly neoliberal economic regime, in the 1970s, was Chile under the Pinochet dictatorship. It was in New Zealand and Australia that labour governments in the 1980s pioneered the shift from social democracy to neoliberalism. In the 1990s, the great triumph of neoliberalism was in the former Soviet bloc. In the 2000s, neoliberalism has been working its way through the Arab world and consolidating in South Asia. Since 2000, Latin America is where the most powerful contestation of neoliberalism has emerged. Along with Samir Amin (1997), I consider that neoliberalism has as much to do with the restructuring of metropole–periphery relations as with crisis tendencies internal to the metropole.

In Australian politics, as in most parts of the global periphery, neoliberalism appears as a development agenda, a strategy for growth and prosperity. An early dramatisation of this was Paul Keating's 'banana republic' statement. A more recent version is the White Paper *Australia in the Asian Century* (Commonwealth of Australia 2012). In this remarkable document, neoliberal educational mechanisms are presented as essential preparation for 'Australia' (more exactly, Australian business elites) to tap the rivers of gold about to flow from the rising middle class of rising Asia.

Since the White Paper has been promoted as a serious contribution to thinking about Australia's future, I strongly encourage readers of this volume to read it. Chapter 6 is particularly interesting for those in the education sector. Some of the White Paper's views on inequality within Australia will also intrigue sociologists.

Commentators at the time of the White Paper's release correctly identified it as an attempt to develop a re-election narrative for the troubled Gillard government, which was long gone by the time the current book was published. As the Liberal government is even more militantly neoliberal, however, and the general approach is widespread in the Australian ruling class, the White Paper has continuing evidential value.[2] John Lenarcic's (2012) tart comment about the document—'A melange of bland rhetoric and generic management-speak, leavened with policy points as mantra'—accurately indicates its representativeness.

Here are some brief reasons why it is interesting. There is little social science in the White Paper. This is not really surprising; apart from a simplified market-friendly economics, neoliberalism generally does not have much use for social science. Disciplines such as history are put in their place by culture wars, while disciplines such as sociology are increasingly residualised, given contracts to research the lives of groups considered market failures.

Australia does in fact have highly knowledgeable social scientists who have done rich and detailed research in Southeast, South and East Asian societies. Practically none of their research appears in the references of the *Asian Century* White Paper, and the text shows little sign of this knowledge base. Its account of 'Asia' is a breathless story of benevolent governments and economic booms caused by deregulation and free trade. To the extent that the White Paper has any ideas about the nature of societies in the region, they are schematic and overgeneralised, especially the idea that their most important feature will be an ever-expanding 'middle class' with ever-expanding consumption demands.

What was considered important—indeed, what provided the framing ideas for the White Paper—was the output of corporate ideologues, especially management consultants. A number of management consultancies and corporate research units are specifically cited as sources in the White Paper—among them Boston Consulting, Deloitte Access Economics, HSBC, McKinsey, ANZ,

---

2 The Liberal government's continued commitment to an engagement with Asia, and the government's emphasis on economic imperatives, is discussed in Chapter 1 of this volume.

PricewaterhouseCoopers and Goldman Sachs. More generally, the document is framed in their style and within their characteristic approach to the world. Management consulting is an industry whose elite has now acquired the role of organic intellectuals to corporate business, increasingly providing the formulaic common sense of the public realm—the language in which politics and journalism, as well as business, speak. Collectively, management consultants understand 'Asia' as a gigantic, swelling market for the products and services of transnational corporations.

The main concern of the White Paper is that Australian corporations should put their foot on as large a share of this market as possible, and that Australian governments should organise their policies to facilitate this. I am putting it bluntly, but truly, the White Paper's main line is as blunt as this. It ends with these inspiring words:

> Right across our nation—in governments, businesses, unions, educational and cultural institutions and broad community groups—we need to become even more innovative, efficient and adaptable. All of us will need to work smarter to maximise prosperity. (Commonwealth of Australia 2012: 272)

As a blueprint for a rich country's future relations with poorer countries in the neighbourhood, the White Paper is breathtakingly cynical. But it is strictly in line with the main tendency of neoliberalism in the global periphery: to see the path of development in complete integration into global markets, via a search for comparative advantage. In recent decades, Australia's comparative advantage is mainly found in the minerals extracted by transnational mining corporations. In pursuit of that advantage, manufacturing and public infrastructure have been run down.

To do it justice, the White Paper is trying to think beyond coal and iron ore. In his role as an economic advisor to government, its principal author, Ken Henry, was a proponent of a serious tax on mining profits. In his role as a director of the NAB, he has a fiduciary duty to foster banking profits, and as a director of the ASX his responsibility is to expand the corporate economy from which come stock exchange transactions. Framed with ideas from that corporate world, the White Paper cannot think beyond the neoliberal logic of commodification and the restless search for advantage in global markets.

As a guide to the future of Australian social science, this is bleak indeed. Basically, it suggests social science is irrelevant. It encourages neither serious thought about Australian society nor engagement with the multiple intellectual worlds beyond the withered neoliberal imagination.

Global social science and Australian society

To rethink Australian society in a world context, an essential starting point is to recognise the wealth of social thought in the global South, existing in many genres and going through its own development. In this chapter, I can only gesture towards this wealth.

Around the colonial encounter itself, intellectuals of colonised societies developed the analysis and critique of colonialism and the study of its impact. Pioneering figures here included al-Afghani, whose famous *Refutation of the materialists* (1968 [1881]), along with his journalism, contains a cultural critique of imperialism from an Islamic standpoint, and elaborates an alternative strategy of modernisation. At the other end of the Islamic world, in the Dutch East Indies, in the early years of the twentieth century, Kartini wove together a critique of the colonial regime with a critique of local patriarchy into a strategy for the educational advancement of Javanese women (2014). José Rizal, the central intellectual figure in the Philippine struggle for independence, wrote wide-ranging critiques of colonial society in the form of two famous novels, *Noli Me Tangere* and *El Filibusterismo*. Sun Yat-sen, known as the first president of the Republic of China, produced sharp social analysis in his late essays *San Min Chu I* (1975), with incisive observations about cultural hybridisation as well as economic and technological development. Perhaps the most striking example was Solomon Plaatje's *Native life in South Africa* (1982). Plaatje, the secretary of the organisation that was forerunner to the African National Congress (ANC), studied the impact of the *Natives Land Act* of 1913. He travelled the country doing fieldwork, and on this basis told the story of indigenous families displaced from their land by this racial enclosure Act. He wove this together with analysis of the colonial state, the attitudes of settler society and the relevant political history.

Following on from this, intellectuals of the South have made analyses of the societies produced by colonialism and the changing forms of their relationship with the metropole. Pride of place goes to the rich Latin American literature on dependence and development. Raúl Prebisch's *The economic development of Latin America and its principal problems* (1950) and Octavio Paz's *The labyrinth of solitude* (1990), first published in the same year as Prebisch's remarkable work, represent this moment on the economic and cultural sides respectively. They were followed by a growing literature of political economy and sociology, in which Cardoso and Faletto's *Dependency and development in Latin America* (1979), a vast synthesis of historical sociology, is a high point.

Ashis Nandy (2003) centres his critique of contemporary Indian society on the modernising state—which was split, but not dismantled, at independence in 1947—and the secularised middle classes whose interests it mainly represents.

Such analyses are not easily confined within one academic discipline. Nandy weaves together sociological, psychological, historical, literary and media analysis (see *An ambiguous journey to the city*, 2001). Veena Das's *Critical events* (1995) moves far beyond her discipline of anthropology, and Bina Agarwal's tremendous *A field of one's own* (1994) goes far beyond her discipline of economics. Ali Shariati (1986) in Iran worked on the basis of an intimate connection between theology and the social sciences. So does Abdolkarim Sorush in political theories developed in the period since the Islamic revolution of 1979 (Ghamari-Tabrizi 2004).

These forms of knowledge are not utterly separated from knowledge systems in the metropole. Indeed, most of the intellectuals just mentioned have made a critical appropriation of metropolitan knowledge systems, combining them in new ways with the experience and knowledges of the periphery. Thus, Linda Tuhiwai Smith has adapted social research procedures, especially those of qualitative social science, and combined them with Maori culture and political experience in her influential *Decolonizing methodologies* (2012). The point is not an absolute separation of Southern knowledge systems from Northern; it is, rather, to achieve the recognition and mutual learning described earlier.

For that, our current main task is to recognise and engage with the wealth of social thought around the global South, despite the pressure of the global economy of knowledge to focus on the thought of the North. Aids to this task exist. There are conceptual statements and reviews of non-metropolitan social thought, such as Farid Alatas's *Alternative discourses in Asian social science* (2006), and Chilla Bulbeck's *Re-orienting Western feminisms* (1998). There are case studies such as Wiebke Keim's *Vermessene Disziplin* (2008) and, in a different register, Lydia Liu et al.'s *The birth of Chinese feminism* (2013). Attempts are being made to decolonise social sciences and even philosophy in the global North (Go 2013; Gutiérrez Rodríguez et al. 2010; Harding 2008). There are compilations and surveys such as Sujata Patel's *International handbook of diverse sociological traditions* (2010). This is just a beginning with the resources available; many more can be found via institutions such as the Council for the Development of Social Science Research in Africa (CODESRIA) and the Latin American Council of Social Sciences (CLACSO). All of these texts concern a shift of intellectual authority, actual or potential, to the global periphery—and that provides a new context for understanding Australian society.

Since most of the work remains to be done, I cannot summarise conclusions here, but I will conclude by suggesting some of the dimensions of the rethinking possible.

First is the task of rethinking the nature of Australian society. Much of our work in social science presumes that it is continuous with European or North American society, so we can apply Bourdieu or Butler or Foucault without hesitation. Learning social perspectives from the global South will encourage us to think about the specificities of a settler-colonial society, a dependent primary-exporting economy, a dependent or satellite polity, and a Southeast Asian, Oceanic and Antarctic environment—with tensions and complexities in all the relationships implied by those categories. Our own neighbourhood provides interesting models of thought about, for instance, society in the context of the Pacific Ocean (Hau'ofa 2008).

Second is to grapple with the issue that Aboriginal intellectuals and Aboriginal politics persistently point out: the land. As the work of Bina Agarwal (1994) in India and João Maia (2011) in Brazil shows, the significance of land in social relations is not a uniquely Australian concern; indeed, it is a central issue in colonisation generally. A society formed in and through the violent taking of land from indigenous communities embeds a structural violence. This continues to surface in Australian society in important ways—most troublingly, at present, in the persistence of racism and the toxic politics of the 'intervention' and 'border protection'. The land is also reasserting itself in the form of environmental issues, which will certainly become more important to Australian social science.

A third dimension concerns the practice of social science in Australia: curriculum and teaching, research agendas and methods, and career structures. Paying attention to the conditions of intellectual work in other parts of the periphery (such as those described by Mkandawire 2005) will be illuminating. The postcolonial world offers many alternatives, good and bad, to the patterns engraved in the Northern-centred global economy of knowledge. Under the pressures of neoliberal management, however, it involves effort and cost to explore these alternatives. Here, social science organisations, including the Academy of Social Sciences in Australia, could do much to support new directions of practice and to legitimate Australian participation in the de-centring of world social science.

A fourth dimension concerns the global division of labour in the mainstream economy of knowledge that locates the formation of theory (including methodology) basically in the metropole. In fact, there is a lively theoretical dimension in intellectual production in the periphery, though it is greatly under-recognised except in the 'indigenous knowledge' debates. Australian social science can, in principle, be greatly enriched by opening up to new resources of concepts and methods.

Finally, a deeper connection with social thought around the global periphery has strategic potential for the social sciences in Australia. I have mentioned the tendency under neoliberalism for the social sciences to become residualised. It is already clear that social science has a declining role in Australian public policymaking; the *Asian Century* White Paper is only one among many examples of this. A collective learning process that encounters the social experience and intellectual practice of the rest of the periphery will, among other things, offer multiple new models for the engagement of social science in the practical world.

In his book *The redress of poetry*, the great poet of postcolonial Ireland Seamus Heaney remarks that '[t]he poet must in some sense set the world free to have a new go at its business'. I think that is one of the roles of social science, too. In Australia, the real encounter with the social world of the South around us, and not just the social world of the global North, is critical to making it happen.

References

Agarwal, Bina. 1994. *A field of one's own: Gender and land rights in South Asia.* Cambridge: Cambridge University Press.

Akiwowo, Akinsola A. 1986. Contributions to the sociology of knowledge from an African oral poetry. *International Sociology* 1(4): 343–58.

Al-Afghani, Sayyid Jamal ad-Din. 1968 [1881]. *An Islamic response to imperialism: Political and religious writings of Sayyid Jamal ad-Din 'al-Afghani'.* Trans Nikki R. Keddie and Hamid Algar. Berkeley: University of California Press.

Alatas, Syed Farid. 2006. *Alternative discourses in Asian social science: Responses to Eurocentrism.* New Delhi: Sage.

Amin, Samir. 1997. *Capitalism in the age of globalization: The management of contemporary society.* London: Zed Books.

Beilharz, Peter. 1995. Vere Gordon Childe and social theory. In Peter Gathercole, T.H. Irving and Gregory Melleuish, eds. *Childe and Australia: Archaeology, politics and ideas.* Brisbane: University of Queensland Press.

Bhambra, Gurminder K. 2007. Sociology and postcolonialism: Another 'missing' revolution? *Sociology* 41(5): 871–84.

Braedley, Susan and Luxton, Meg. eds. 2010. *Neoliberalism and everyday life.* Montreal & Kingston: McGill-Queen's University Press.

Bulbeck, Chilla. 1998. *Re-orienting Western feminisms: Women's diversity in a postcolonial world.* Cambridge: Cambridge University Press.

Cardoso, Fernando Henrique and Faletto, Enzo. 1979 [1971]. *Dependency and development in Latin America.* Berkeley: University of California Press.

Chakrabarty, Dipesh. 2000. *Provincializing Europe: Postcolonial thought and historical difference.* Princeton, NJ: Princeton University Press.

Childe, Vere Gordon. 1925. *The dawn of European civilization.* London: Kegan Paul, Trench, Trubner & Co.

Childe, Vere Gordon. 1949. *Social worlds of knowledge.* L.T. Hobhouse Memorial Trust Lecture No. 19. London: Oxford University Press.

Commonwealth of Australia. 2012. *Australia in the Asian Century.* White Paper. Canberra: Commonwealth of Australia. URL: pandora.nla.gov.au/pan/133850/20130914-0122/asiancentury.dpmc.gov.au/index.html. Consulted 15 March 2015.

Connell, Raewyn. 2007. *Southern theory: The global dynamics of knowledge in social science.* Sydney: Allen & Unwin.

Connell, Raewyn. 2011. *Confronting equality: Gender, knowledge and global change.* Sydney: Allen & Unwin.

Connell, Raewyn, Wood, Julian and Crawford, June. 2005. The global connections of intellectual workers: An Australian study. *International Sociology* 20(1): 5–26.

Cowlishaw, Gillian. 2004. *Blackfellas, whitefellas and the hidden injuries of race.* Oxford: Blackwell.

Das, Veena. 1995. *Critical events: An anthropological perspective on contemporary India.* New Delhi: Oxford University Press.

Domingues, José Maurício. 2008. *Latin America and contemporary modernity: A sociological interpretation.* New York: Routledge.

Duménil, Gérard and Lévy, Dominique. 2004. *Capital resurgent: Roots of the neoliberal revolution.* Cambridge, MA: Harvard University Press.

Foucault, Michel. 1977. *Discipline and punish: The birth of the prison.* New York: Pantheon.

Ghamari-Tabrizi, Behrooz. 1996. Is Islamic science possible? *Social Epistemology* 10(3–4): 317–30.

Ghamari-Tabrizi, Behrooz. 2004. Contentious public religion: Two conceptions of Islam in revolutionary Iran. *International Sociology* 19(4): 504–23.

Go, Julian. 2013. For a postcolonial sociology. *Theory and Society* 42(1): 25–55.

Gutiérrez Rodríguez, Encarnación, Boatcă, Manuela and Costa, Sérgio. eds. 2010. *Decolonizing European sociology: Transdisciplinary approaches*. Farnham, UK, and Burlington, VT: Ashgate.

Harding, Sandra. 2008. *Sciences from below: Feminisms, postcolonialities, and modernities*. Durham, NC: Duke University Press.

Harvey, David. 2005. *A brief history of neoliberalism*. Oxford: Oxford University Press.

Hau'ofa, Epeli. 2008. *We are the ocean*. Honolulu: University of Hawai'i Press.

Heaney, Seamus. 1995. *The redress of poetry*. New York: Farrar, Straus & Giroux.

Hountondji, Paulin J. 1983 [1976]. *African philosophy: Myth and reality*. Trans Henri Evans and Jonathan Rée. London: Hutchinson.

Hountondji, Paulin. ed. 1997. *Endogenous knowledge: Research trails*. Dakar: CODESRIA.

Kagamé, Alexis. 1956. *La philosophie bantu-rwandaise de l'être*. Brussels: Académie royale des sciences coloniales.

Kartini. 2014. *Kartini: The complete writings 1898–1904*. Edited and translated by Joost Coté. Melbourne: Monash University Publishing.

Keim, Wiebke. 2008. *Vermessene disziplin: Zum konterhegemonialen potential afrikanischer und lateinamerikanischer soziologien*. Bielefeld: Transcript Verlag.

Lal, Vinay. 2002. *Empire of knowledge: Culture and plurality in the global economy*. London: Pluto.

Lawuyi, O.B. and Taiwo, Olufemi. 1990. Towards an African sociological tradition: A rejoinder to Akiwowo and Makinde. *International Sociology* 5(1): 57–73.

Lenarcic, John. 2012. Asian Century White Paper. *The Conversation* 28 October. URL: theconversation.edu.au/asian-century-white-paper-experts-respond-10370. Consulted 20 March 2015.

Liu, Lydia H., Karl, Rebecca E. and Ko, Dorothy. eds. 2013. *The birth of Chinese feminism: Essential texts in transnational theory*. New York: Columbia University Press.

Lukács, Gyorgy. 1971 [1923]. *History and class consciousness: Studies in Marxist dialectics*. London: Merlin Press.

McFarlane, Colin. 2006. Crossing borders: Development, learning and the North–South divide. *Third World Quarterly* 27(8): 1413–37.

Maia, João Marcelo Ehlert. 2011. Space, social theory and peripheral imagination: Brazilian intellectual history and de-colonial debates. *International Sociology* 26(3): 392–407.

Mannheim, Karl. 1985 [1929]. *Ideology and utopia: An introduction to the sociology of knowledge*. San Diego: Harcourt Brace Jovanovich.

Meekosha, Helen. 2011. Decolonizing disability: Thinking and acting globally. *Disability and Society* 26(6): 667–81.

Mignolo, Walter D. 2005. *The idea of Latin America*. Malden, Mass.: Blackwell.

Mignolo, Walter D. 2007. Delinking: The rhetoric of modernity, the logic of coloniality and the grammar of de-coloniality. *Cultural Studies* 21(2–3): 449–514.

Mkandawire, Thandika. ed. 2005. *African intellectuals: Rethinking politics, language, gender and development*. Dakar and London: CODESRIA & Zed Books.

Montero, Maritza. 2007. The political psychology of liberation: From politics to ethics and back. *Political Psychology* 28(5): 517–33.

Nandy, Ashis. 1987. *Traditions, tyranny and utopias: Essays in the politics of awareness*. Delhi: Oxford University Press.

Nandy, Ashis. 2001. *An ambiguous journey to the city: The village and the other odd ruins of the self in the Indian imagination*. New Delhi: Oxford University Press.

Nandy, Ashis. 2003. *The romance of the state: And the fate of dissent in the tropics*. New Delhi: Oxford University Press.

Odora Hoppers, Catherine A. ed. 2002. *Indigenous knowledge and the integration of knowledge systems: Towards a philosophy of articulation*. Claremont, South Africa: New Africa Books.

Patel, Sujata. 2010. *International handbook of diverse sociological traditions*. London: Sage.

Paz, Octavio. 1990 [1950]. *The labyrinth of solitude*. Enlarged edn. London: Penguin.

Pearson, Noel. 1997. The concept of native title at common law. In Galarrwuy Yunupingu, ed. *Our land is our life*. Brisbane: University of Queensland Press.

Plaatje, Solomon T. 1982 [1916]. *Native life in South Africa: Before and since the European war and the Boer rebellion*. New edn. Braamfontein: Ravan Press.

Prebisch, Raúl. 1950. *The economic development of Latin America and its principal problems*. New York: United Nations Department of Economic Affairs.

Pusey, Michael. 1991. *Economic rationalism in Canberra: A nation-building state changes its mind*. London: Cambridge University Press.

Quijano, Aníbal. 2000. Coloniality of power and Eurocentrism in Latin America. *International Sociology* 15(2): 215–32.

Reuter, Julia and Villa, Paula-Irene. eds. 2010. *Postkoloniale soziologie: Empirische befunde, theoretische anschlüsse, politische intervention*. Bielefeld: Transcript.

Rowse, Tim. 2012. *Rethinking social justice: From 'peoples' to 'populations'*. Canberra: Aboriginal Studies Press.

Said, Edward W. 1978. *Orientalism*. London: Routledge & Kegan Paul.

Shariati, Ali. 1986. *What is to be done? The enlightened thinkers and an Islamic renaissance*. Ed. Farhang Rajaee. Houston: Institute for Research and Islamic Studies.

Smith, Dorothy. 1990. *The conceptual practices of power: A feminist sociology of knowledge*. Boston: Northeastern University Press.

Smith, Linda Tuhiwai. 2012. *Decolonizing methodologies: Research and indigenous peoples*. 2nd edn. London: Zed Books.

Sun Yat-sen. 1975 [1927]. *San Min Chu I: The three principles of the people*. Trans. Frank W. Price, ed. L.T. Chen. New York: Da Capo Press.

Walter, Maggie, Pyett, Priscilla, Tyler, Bill and Vanderwyk, Annie. eds. 2006. Beyond the margins/beyond marginality. *Journal of Sociology Special Issue* 42(4): 341–45.

3

Beyond divisions and towards internationalism: Social sciences in the twenty-first century

Sujata Patel

In recent decades, the dynamics of the world have changed. At one level, the world has contracted. It has opened up possibilities of diverse kinds of trans-border flows and movements of capital and labour and of signs and symbols, often organised in intersecting spatial circuits. While in some contexts and moments these attributes cooperate, at other times they are in conflict with and contest one another. Thus, even though we all live in one capitalist world with a dominant form of modernity, inequalities and hierarchies are increasing and so are fragmented identities. Lack of access to livelihoods, infrastructure and political citizenship now blends with exclusions relating to cultural and group identities, and these are organised in varied spatial and temporal zones. Fluidity of identities and their continuous expression in unstable social manifestations and in new geographical regions demand a fresh perspective with which to examine them. Not only do contemporary social processes, sociabilities and structures need to be perceived through new and novel spaces, prisms and perspectives, it is also increasingly clear that these need to be seen through new methodological protocols. As a consequence, social scientists are in search of a new framework that moves beyond the nineteenth and early twentieth-century social science language and addresses the new challenges posed by contemporary processes.

At one level, the social science theories that were promoted to examine modernisation and modernism across the world in the 1950s and 1960s have little or no purchase. Based on a 'convergence' notion, these theories, in both their liberal and/or their Marxist formulations, argued that the structures, patterns and processes associated with modernisation and capitalism and thus industrialisation and urbanisation (emerging earlier in Europe and later extending itself in the Americas and the Antipodes) were universal models of social change and dynamics of the world. The non-Western world, it was thought, would follow a similar path. Such a thesis cannot be accepted today as it is increasingly evident that there are no singular models of growth or change. At another level, this interrogation has also demanded a reframing of the divisions that organise the geographies of the world, such as the neat partitions of the world into three (First, Second and Third worlds) or two (developed and less-developed countries). Increasingly, it has become clear that there are regions, such as Asia, which are evolving in different ways to other regions. In this chapter, I identify and discuss the various discursive practices of social science that need to be dismantled in order to build the new language that contemporary times demand.

I argue that social scientists have to deconstruct and disassemble epistemic and theoretical models at three levels. In the first section, I discuss the parochialisms and ethnocentrisms built into social science scholarship in the form of Eurocentric–Orientalist positions and highlight how the binaries of the universal and the particular have been organised in the context of the geopolitics of global/international/national. In section two, I indicate how this episteme and its binaries continue to organise post–World War II institutional structures such as universities and research institutes both in the global North (including Australia) and in the global South. I discuss how the perspective of methodological nationalism combined with Eurocentrism–Orientalism institutionalised an Atlantic[1] representation of modern society in the disciplines of sociology, political science and economics and a particularistic indigenous one for the nation-states of the global South. In the last section, I discuss the challenges this legacy presents to a country such as Australia, which needs to connect with the territories of its own region.

---

1   The term 'Atlantic' alludes to European and North American social science theories and is used by Walter Mignolo (2002).

Eurocentrism, colonialism and the episteme of the universal–particular

The social sciences emerged in Europe in the context of European modernity. They analysed this birth through a linear conception of time and suggested that it was produced through the values and institutional system that were universalised in Europe in the past 500 years—in its own backyard. This theory incorporated two master narratives: the superiority of Western civilisation (through progress and reason) and the belief in the continuous growth of capitalism (through modernisation, development and the creation of new markets). These master narratives, which Charles Taylor (1995) calls a 'culturist approach', are recognised now as ethnocentric in nature. European social sciences assessed its own growth in terms of itself (Europe) rather than in terms of the other (the rest of the colonised world), which was its object of control and through which it became modern. It was a theory of 'interiority' (Mignolo 2002)—that is, a perspective that perceived itself from within rather than from without.

A notion of linear time affirmed a belief that social life and its institutions, emerging in Europe from about the fourteenth century, would now influence the making of the new world. In doing so, it 'silenced' its own imperial experience and the violence without which it could not have become modern. These assumptions framed the ideas elaborated by Hegel, Kant and the Encyclopaedists and were incorporated in the sociologies of Durkheim, Weber and Marx. No wonder these theories legitimised the control and domination of the rest of the world through the episteme of coloniality (Dussel 1993; Mignolo 2002; Quijano 2000).

This discourse of modernity presented a universal set of axioms, in which time as historicity defined its relationship to space. To put it differently, because it saw its own growth in terms of itself and defined it through its own specific and particular history, that which was outside itself (the place) was perceived in terms of its opposite: lack of history and thus inferior. Henceforth all knowledge was structured in terms of the master binary of the West (which had history, culture, reason and science) and the East (which was enclosed in space, nature, religion and spirituality). This binary linked the division and subsequent hierarchisation of groups within geospatial territories in the world in terms of a theory of temporal linearity: the West was modern because it had evolved to articulate the key features of modernity, compared with the East, which was traditional. Dussel thus says:

> Modernity appears when Europe affirms itself as the 'centre' of a *World* History that it inaugurates; the 'periphery' that surrounds this centre is consequently part of its self-definition. The occlusion of this periphery ... leads the major thinkers of the 'centre' into a Eurocentric fallacy in their understanding of modernity. If their understanding of the genealogy of modernity is thus partial and provincial, their attempts at a critique or defence of it are likewise unilateral, and in part, false. (Dussel 1993: 65)

This binary opposition constructed the knowledge of the two worlds, the West and the East, and placed these as oppositions, creating hierarchies between them and thereby dividing them in terms of 'I' and the 'other'—positing a universality for 'I' and particularities for the 'other'. 'Maintaining a difference under the assumption that we are all human' (Mignolo 2002: 71) was part of the normative project of modernity and subsequently of its sociological theory. These were the 'truths' of modernity and the modern world; these truths were considered objective and universal (Dussel 1993; Mignolo 2002; Quijano 2000).

Thus Eurocentrism and its twin, Orientalism, are interconnected cultural and epistemic logics of capitalist imperialism. They incorporated themselves in the disciplines of history and sociology to make Europe the central point of a narrative and analysis of the growth of modernity. Not only did they argue that Europe's superiority and its control of the world had provided the conditions for Europe's ascendance, but also they created a scientific language that justified and legitimised this perspective and made it a universal truth (Amin 2010).

Eurocentrism was a style of thought that ontologically and epistemologically divided the 'Occident' and the 'Orient' to create knowledge on and of the Occident and the Orient as distinct. Enmeshed in Eurocentrism were two myths: first, the idea of the history of human civilisation as being a trajectory that departed from a 'state of nature' and culminated in the European experience of modernity. Second, it incorporated a view of the differences between Europeans and non-Europeans as natural, though in actuality these were based on racialised differences. Within Eurocentrism, the colonial experience was present in its absence. No wonder Eurocentrism has also been discussed as the episteme of colonial modernity. 'Both myths', according to Anibal Quijano (2000: 542), 'can be unequivocally recognized in the foundations of evolutionism and dualism, two of the nuclear elements of Eurocentrism'.

These seminal assumptions were embodied in the framing of the disciplines of sociology and anthropology in India in the late eighteenth century. Sociology became the study of modern (European, later to be extended to Western) society while anthropology was the study of (non-European and non-Western) 'traditional' societies. Thus, sociologists studied how the new societies evolved from the deadwood of the old; notions of time and history were embedded in this discourse. In contrast, anthropologists studied how space and place organised 'static' cultures that could not transcend their internal structures to be and become modern. This narrative was affirmed by social scientists within the Antipodes, although they were not part of the European geographical territory. As a consequence, a Eurocentric–Orientalist perspective defined the teaching and learning of the West and the East within the universities in the Antipodes (see also Connell in this volume).

These frames also constructed the academic knowledge of India as elaborated by colonial anthropologists and administrators, who further divided the East that they were studying into separate geospatial territories with each territory given an overarching cultural value. In the case of India, it was religion: Hinduism. The discourse of coloniality collapsed India and Hinduism into each other (Patel 2006). The collapse of India into Hindu India is not new. The genealogy of the collapse goes back to nineteenth-century colonial constructs that assumed two principles. The first assumption was geographical and distinguished between groups living in the subcontinent from the spatial-cultural structures of the West, thereby creating the master binary of the West and the East. Later, those living in the subcontinent were further classified geographically in spatial-cultural zones and 'regionally' subdivided.

The second assumption related to the internal division and relationship between these groups within India. All groups living in the subcontinent were defined by their relationship with Hinduism. Those who were directly related to the constructed notion of Hinduism as now understood, such as castes and tribes, were termed the 'majority' and organised in terms of distinct hierarchies (castes were considered superior to tribes, who were thought to be 'primitive'), while those who were not were conceived as 'minorities'—mainly groups who practised Islam and Christianity (Patel 2006). Evolutionist theories were used to make Hinduism the 'great tradition', anchored in a timeless civilisation, and its margins were the folk cultures, the 'little traditions'.

Anthropologists and sociologists researching South Asian religions have often uncritically accepted this logic, and have thereby become trapped in this discourse. The geographically vast subcontinent of South Asia has thousands of communities with distinct cultural practices and ideas who have lived and experienced existence in various forms of unequal and subordinate relationships with each other. In the nineteenth century, anthropological and sociological knowledge dissolved these distinctions and recategorised them into four or five major religious traditions, thereby constructing a master narrative of the majority and the minority. This logic homogenised distinctions between groups but it also naturalised the Orientalist–Eurocentric language as the only language with which to comprehend the unequal distribution of power and resources.

British civil servants and anthropologists, and later Indian anthropologists, placed the debate of identifying and designating these as 'castes' or 'tribes' within the discussion of 'stocks' or 'races' in relation to other 'stocks' and 'races' in the Western world. In order to formulate these categories, they drew on evolutionary theory and Victorian social thought associated with 'race science'. In this they were aided by a theory of the 'Aryan' (white or fair-skinned) invasion of India, which grew out of the discovery of the Indo-European language family in the late nineteenth century. Hence, linguistic classification merged with racial classification to produce a theory of an Indian civilisation formed by the invasion of fair-skinned, civilised, Sanskrit-speaking Aryans, who conquered and partially absorbed the dark-skinned, 'savage' aborigines.

This theory was critical in producing the basic division of groups in India into Aryan and non-Aryan races, now termed 'castes' and 'tribes'. What is of interest is the fact that while 'castes' were defined in the context of Hinduism as groups who cultivated land, had better technology and high civilisational attributes, 'tribes' were defined in contrast to castes, and were said to practise primitive technology, to live in interior jungles and to be animistic in religious practices. Such classifications and categorisations were not peculiar to India. They also found manifestation in the African continent, as British officials used this knowledge to construct categories of social groups in Africa and retransferred these newly constructed classifications back again to India, as happened in the case of the term 'tribe' as a lineage group based on a segmentary state.

In the process, 'caste' (and 'tribe') was made out to be a far more pervasive, totalising and uniform concept than ever before and defined in terms of a religious order, which it had not always been. In fact, ancient and medieval historiographers now inform us that those whom we identify as castes and tribes were groups shaped by political struggles and processes over material resources. In pre-colonial India, multiple markers of identity defined relationships between groups and were contingent on complex processes, which were constantly changing and were related to political power. Thus, there were temple communities, territorial groups, lineage segments, family units, royal retinues, warrior sub-castes, 'little as opposed to large kingdoms', occupational reference groups, agricultural and trading associations, networks of devotional and sectarian religious communities, and priestly cabals. An internal critique has retrieved these sources to argue how these can be deconstructed and analysed as varied and to analyse how colonial knowledge standardised and homogenised them through an Orientalist perspective.

The thesis of Eurocentrism has posed seminal questions regarding the episteme of the social sciences in a fundamentally different manner. The questions are not about what constitutes the boundaries of the 'social' and how to incorporate new voices and areas of study within the existing ways of doing social sciences.

Rather the questions raised are primarily about the nature and construct of the corpus of established knowledge regarding the 'social' as this was formulated in the late nineteenth and early twentieth centuries. These are questions about what constitutes its 'science', its facticity and its truth. It is about the way this knowledge, which is regarded as 'truth', has been designed and devised; it is about the moorings of its perspectives, methodologies and methods—that is, its system of practices. These, it is argued, fail to comprehend and perceive the world in ways that do not and cannot fit in with the episteme of social sciences constituted within and through the Atlantic traditions.

The geopolitics of travelling theory and the two avatars of methodological nationalisms

Contemporary globalisation has led some social scientists to suggest that what needs to be dismantled is not only Eurocentrism but also methodological nationalism. The sociologist Ulrich Beck (2000), for example, has argued that our attention should be focused on dismantling the principles of nation, nation-state and nationalism that have organised the framing of social theory.

What is methodological nationalism? In its most straightforward usage, methodological nationalism implies coevalness between 'society' and the 'nation-state'—that is, it is an argument that a discussion of modern society (which sociology undertakes) entails an implicit understanding of the nation. Or, in other words, the nation is treated as 'the natural and necessary representation of the modern society' (Chernillo 2006). Methodological nationalism is the taken-for-granted belief that nation-state boundaries are natural boundaries within which societies are contained. This ignorance and/or blindness is reinforced through a mode of 'naturalisation'; sociological theories take for granted official discourses, agendas, loyalties and histories without problematising these. Ultimately this error leads sociologists to territorialise social science language and reduce it to the boundaries of the nation-state. When these positions are exported across the world, methodological nationalism becomes embedded in Eurocentric positions (Gutiérrez Rodríguez et al. 2010).

It is my argument that what were considered 'methodological errors' by European sociologists became, in the case of ex-colonial countries, an advantage in the historical moment that defines the decades after independence. Thus, in the case of India, as in other ex-colonial countries, methodological nationalism was a self-conscious embrace of a place/territory to create a set of guidelines with which to confront the colonial discourses of social science. Identification with 'place' allowed 'national' intellectuals to build intellectual solidarity against dominant colonial knowledge. Second, the recognition of this place-bound solidarity facilitated the growth of an 'alternative' discourse. This then became the principle for organising the institutionalisation of knowledge systems through a gamut of policies and regulations. These policies determined the protocols and practices of teaching and learning processes, the establishment and practices of research within research institutes, the distribution of grants for research, the language of reflection, the organisation of the profession and the definitions of scholars and scholarship (Patel 2011a).

For example, the initiation of sociology as a discipline (against anthropology) allowed some departments in India to inaugurate the teaching, learning and research of a modern Indian society rather than a traditional one. In this they were aided by the legacy of nationalist ideologies that wished to see India as a modern nation-state. This advantage received a further fillip with the initiation of a nationalist modernist project by the post-independence state and its use of higher education for creating a new India (Patel 2011c).

This sociological knowledge discussed, debated and represented social changes occurring within one nation and territory: India. Sociologists saw their project as that which analyses one's own society (India) in one's (indigenous) 'own terms', without colonial and now neo-colonial tutelage. This project allowed for the institutionalisation of a particularistic *problematic* in a new way—an assessment of how modernity and modernisation were changing India's characteristic institutions: caste, kinship, family and religion. This particularistic problematic also influenced Marxist perspectives as radical sociologists interrogated and set aside 'revisionist' Orientalist theories and elaborated the distinct nature of class and class relations in India and theorised their differential modes of production (Patel 2011b).

These developments took place in a context wherein social sciences were engendered to play a critical role in conceptualising development and planned change. This agenda entailed a need to professionalise the discipline and organise it within the territory of the nation-state. In this context, the two strands of methodological nationalism mentioned above—'territorialisation' and 'naturalisation'—became, in new ways, symbiotically linked with each other to become an integral part of the traditions of sociological thinking in India. Sociology not only interrogated (even if partially) the received inheritance of colonial theories and methodologies, but also promoted a new language with new perspectives and methodologies that defined itself as Indian sociology (Patel 2011c).

Rather than restricting an understanding of international sociology, nationalist sociologies from ex-colonial countries have enlarged it. Many newly independent countries have used this strategy, such as Nigeria, India and those in Latin America. Raewyn Connell's book *Southern theory* (2007) documents the many positive outcomes that can be realised by attempting this pathway. This type of project has, however, promoted varied but uneven intellectual traditions within different nation-states as scholars discuss, debate and represent social changes occurring in their countries. It has also allowed nationally oriented intellectual infrastructural resources to be created, including universities, research institutes and laboratories, as well as journals, publishing houses and professional norms and ethics. These have asserted alternative ways of assessing contextual processes, thereby underlining the many particularities that have structured the world and, on the other hand, have highlighted the inequalities that structure international sociology. This heritage has relevance today and cannot be washed away (Patel 2011a).

In a large number of post-independent nation-states, however, nationalist social sciences have become closely associated with official discourses and methods of understanding the relationship between nation, nation-state and modernity. As a consequence, other contending perspectives have become marginal. If the social sciences of the Atlantic region promoted Eurocentrism through methodological nationalism, those of newly independent countries valorised the elite notions of nation and the state and, in many instances, the visions of its upper sections became the frames for doing social science. This continues to be true for many intellectual inquiries. Contemporary social science has remained silent on the political moorings of this project, failing to examine its close linkages with the metropolitan (advanced capitalist) hegemonic orientation and consequently the dynamics of capital accumulation on a world scale.

Hountondji (1997) has argued that these remain culturist projects; he refers to 'ethnoscience' and suggests that these projects remain part of the colonial and neo-colonial binaries of the universal–particular and the global–national. Farid Alatas (2003) has proposed that in the post–World War II period social science culture in ex-colonial countries is marked by academic dependencies of six kinds: dependence on ideas, dependence on the media of ideas, dependence on the technology of education, dependence on aid for research as well as teaching, dependence on investment in education, and the dependence of Third World social scientists on demand in the West for their skills.

Social scientists have thus argued that the two avatars of methodological nationalism formulated in the context of post–World War II internationalism have introduced and reproduced academic dependencies in new ways. The Malaysian sociologist Syed Hussein Alatas (1972) and the African philosopher Paulin Hountondji (1997) have discussed these as the 'captive mind' and 'extraversion' respectively. They argue that the syndrome of 'captive mind' and 'extraversion' can be seen in the teaching and learning processes, in the way curriculums and syllabuses are framed; in the processes of research, the designing of research questions and the methods and methodologies used;

as well as in the formulation of criteria for accepting articles for journals and books, and ultimately in defining what and where one publishes, and what is academic excellence.

The two kinds of methodological nationalism have justified and legitimised an intellectual culture wherein Northern social science is held out as a model for the rest of the world. The consequence of this dependence is the 'infantilisation' of scientific practices within non-Atlantic regions. Not only are these at an incipient stage of growth, but this very condition encourages brain drain and further intellectual dependencies. It is backed by the sheer size of Northern social science and its intellectual, human, physical and capital resources—the infrastructure necessary for its reproduction. This includes not only equipment, archives, libraries, publishing houses and journals, but also the evolution of a professional culture of intellectual commitment and engagement that connects the producers and consumers of knowledge, embedded in relationships between Northern and Southern universities and students, as well as Northern nation-states and global knowledge-production agencies.

How does one move forward in this matter given the deeply embedded inequalities that organise the global production of knowledge?

Strategies for creating new discourses

I would like to initiate this discussion by first addressing the two challenges we must confront. The first challenge is of an epistemic nature. Some social scientists have argued that the best way out of this epistemic and methodological difficulty is to particularise the universals of European thought. They suggest that we need to provincialise the hegemonic social sciences of the Atlantic region and understand how deeply structured are the inequalities of academic production (Connell 2010). Some have argued that this is a project for the Atlantic region, which concerns universities and research institutes, publishing houses and journals, scholarship and its professional norms. It involves an interrogation of the syllabuses and curriculums, research questions and methodologies of doing research and involves a self-conscious effort to decolonise its academic moorings. In this context, for example, Immanuel Wallerstein has argued that:

> Europe in the sixteenth to eighteenth centuries did transform the world, but in a direction whose negative consequences are upon us today. We must cease trying to deprive Europe of its specificity on the deluded premise that we are thereby depriving it of an illegitimate credit. Quite the contrary, we must fully acknowledge the particularity of Europe's reconstruction of the world because only then will it be possible to transcend it, and to arrive hopefully at a more

inclusively universalist vision of human possibility, one that avoids none of the difficult and imbricated problems of pursuing the true and the good in tandem. (Wallerstein 2006: 106–7)

Dipesh Chakrabarty, the historian of subaltern studies, has made a similar argument. He coined a new methodology, called 'provincialisation', and explained its quest:

To 'provincialize' Europe was precisely to find out how and in what sense European ideas that were universal were also, at one and the same time, drawn from the very particular intellectual and historical traditions that could not claim universal validity. (Chakrabarty 2000: xiii)

This is indeed a laudable strategy and needs to be juxtaposed with the second challenge, which is to understand how similar universals dominate and determine nation-based projects for creating new social sciences. As mentioned above, these are part of the projects to create nationalist social science in ex-colonial countries, which include many nation-states within Asia. In this context, we need to ask whether its legacy—that of creating and institutionalising a nationalist and an anti-colonialist social science—can be dismissed arbitrarily, especially in the context of the epistemic and institutionally unequal division of academic resources. More significantly, we need to ask how we can ensure and assure the constitution of a critical global social science language once we displace these structures.

Certainly, these challenges need not be seen as independent of each other; they are mutually embedded within each other. If the discursive practices of knowledge institutions have to be interrogated, it has to be done jointly and collaboratively by drawing on intellectual resources from all parts of the region. This is a project for the global social science community within and outside the Atlantic region and can be initiated within the Atlantic region without difficulties. How does one do so?

I suggest this can be done at two levels. The first step is to work out how we can go beyond the contextualising of the particular 'content' that asserts that truth claims are not universal. While it is important to deconstruct the explanations that these universal theories offer and the narratives they construct (which are European in genealogy), there is also a need to analyse their very 'form'—that is, the concepts through which explanations become possible, as well as the very idea of what counts as explanation. I am suggesting that we understand the collective heritage of social sciences and not simply designate them as 'European' or non-Western and then associate truth claims with them. An argument that justifies these divisions has little relevance, given that we remain within one world capitalist system. The task, in contrast, is to recognise that they often provide only partial and sometimes flawed understandings. We need not reinvent the wheel. There is, however, a necessity to generate explanations that are relevant for different contexts.

To do so there is a need to change institutional practices of doing social science and to make it competitive rather than monopolistic as it is now. There is a necessity to open up the market of production, distribution and consumption of knowledge to new audiences, institutions and processes across the region. Social science needs to articulate itself in many expressions at different sites (other than academic) and engage with the ways these define their distinctive culturist oeuvres, epistemologies, theoretical frames, cultures of science and languages of reflection, as well as sites of knowledge production and transmission. In addition to classrooms and departments, together with syllabus formulations and protocols of professional codes, this type of move can also include campaigns, movements and advocacies. Thus, its production involves a creative dialectic within and between activists, scholars and communities assessing, reflecting on and elucidating immediate events and issues that intervene to define the research process, as well as the organising and systematising knowledge of the discipline in long-term institutionalised processes central for teaching and learning.

The second way is to build intellectual networks across institutions and scholarship among and between scholars of the region. This is what the Asian region needs to initiate. Horizontal linkages between localities and nation-states can substitute for existing vertical hierarchical linkages between imperialist and ex-colonial countries or between that of core and periphery in the production, distribution and consumption of knowledge. This type of initiative will help us reflect collectively on the common and relevant themes that structure the experience of being part of the region. Through this type of process and intent, it will be possible to outline an Asian perspective.

References

Alatas, Farid Syed. 2003. Academic dependency and the global division of labour in social sciences. *Current Sociology* 51(6): 599–613.

Alatas, Syed Hussein. 1972. The captive mind in development studies. *International Social Science Journal* 24(1): 9–25.

Amin, Samir. 2010. *Eurocentrism, modernity, religion, and democracy: A critique of Eurocentrism and culturalism*. 2nd edn. New York: Monthly Review Press.

Beck, Ulrich. 2000. The cosmopolitan perspective: Sociology in the second age of modernity. *British Journal of Sociology* 51(1): 79–106.

Chakrabarty, Dipesh. 2000. *Provincialising Europe: Postcolonial thought and historical difference*. Princeton, NJ: Princeton University Press.

Chernillo, Daniel. 2006. Social theory's methodological nationalism: Myth and reality. *European Journal of Social Theory* 9(1): 5–22.

Connell, Raewyn. 2007. *Southern theory: The global dynamics of knowledge in social science*. Cambridge: Polity.

Connell, Raewyn 2010. Learning from each other: Sociology on a world scale. In Sujata Patel, ed. *The ISA handbook of diverse sociological traditions*. London: Sage.

Dussel, Enrique. 1993. Eurocentrism and modernity. *Boundary 2* 20(3): 65–76.

Gutiérrez Rodríguez, Encarnación, Boatcâ, Manuela and Costa, Sérgio. eds. 2010. *Decolonizing European sociology: Transdisciplinary approaches*. Surrey: Ashgate.

Hountondji, Paulin J. 1997. Introduction. In Paulin J. Hountondji, ed. *Endogenous knowledge: Research trails*. Dakar: CODESRIA.

Mignolo, Walter D. 2002. The geopolitics of knowledge and the colonial difference. *South Atlantic Quarterly* 101(1): 57–96.

Patel, Sujata. 2006. Beyond binaries: A case for self-reflexive sociologies. *Current Sociology* 54(3): 381–95.

Patel, Sujata. 2011a. Against cosmopolitanism. *Global Dialogue* (4). International Sociological Association. URL: www.isa-sociology.org/globaldialogue/2011/05/challenging-cosmopolitanism/. Consulted 31 December 2012.

Patel, Sujata. 2011b. Lineages, trajectories and challenges to sociology in India. *Footnotes* March. American Sociological Association. URL: www.asanet.org/footnotes/mar11/intl_persp_0311.html. Consulted 31 December 2012.

Patel, Sujata. 2011c. Ruminating on sociological traditions in India. In Sujata Patel, ed. *Doing sociology in India: Genealogies, locations, and practices*. New Delhi: Oxford University Press.

Quijano, Anibal. 2000. Coloniality of power, Eurocentricism and Latin America. *Nepantla: Views from South* 1: 553–800.

Taylor, Charles. 1995. Two theories of modernity. *The Hastings Centre Report* 25(2): 24–33.

Wallerstein, Immanuel. 2006. *European universalism: The rhetoric of power*. London: New Press.

PART II: REGIONAL ISSUES IN THE SOCIAL SCIENCES

4

Inter-Asia referencing and shifting frames of comparison

Chua Beng Huat

Even today, in some quarters of academia in Asia, we can still hear laments about the intellectual domination of the West. For example, it has been pointed out that local Asian scholars are often read by Western scholars as though they are anthropological local informants. The substantive local knowledge that Asian scholars generate is then reconfigured as empirical input to concept and theory formation by Western academics (who are consequently depicted by their critics as former and neo-colonisers). This hierarchical division of academic labour therefore recuperates past colonial domination (see also Chapter 2 in this volume). Conversely, scholars in Asia, who are trained in the Euro-American academies, pluck ready-made concepts from existing literature generated in the latter contexts, and apply them to local conditions in Asia. Local complexities often have to be severely trimmed to fit 'neatly' into the selected Euro-American concepts. The richness of the local is sacrificed to reaffirm an idea for which its original context has been erased, abstracted and 'universalised'. According to this logic, if what was found in the United States is also to be found in an Asian location, the universalising claim of a Western-originated concept is thus (re)affirmed. In these instances, intellectual domination is self-inflicted. Both processes—the neo-colonial appropriation of Asian scholarship by Western academics and the uncritical application of Euro-American concepts by scholars in Asia—are unhappy ones. There are, however, strategic reasons for such bad practices: both afford a better chance of publication in privileged, internationally refereed journals edited in the West and published by English-language book publishers with international reach.

Energy is still being spent on contesting this domination through different modes of conceptualising the difference between 'Asia' and the West. Methods of contestation include critiquing Western cultural imperialism, provincialising the West, enunciating a corrective discourse of the local point of view and conceptualisations of different or alternative modernities (Chakrabarty 2000; Gaonkar 2001). Such contests, however, are essentially futile after 200 years of European presence, largely as colonising powers, in Asia. The education undertaken in Western institutions by Asian scholars and the paradigms and concepts from the West cannot be excised from scholarship formation in Asia by Asians. A more fruitful way forward is suggested by Chen Kuan-Hsing (2010). Chen advocates that Asian scholars should multiply their points of reference, especially those in Asia, and treat Euro-America as one reference point equal to other possible points of reference. Aihwa Ong also called for 'inter-referencing' Asia, referring 'broadly to practices of citation, allusion, aspiration, comparison and competition' (2011: 17). In some sense, both suggestions are simply articulating and catching up with the actual practices in governance and enterprise in Asia, as I shall argue in this chapter.

Emerging inter-Asian referencing

At the beginning of the twenty-first century, Asian studies as a discipline has to confront the palpable rise of capitalism across the region. One of the consequences of this rise, in contrast with the current financial crisis in Europe and the continuing economic depression in the United States, is an increased confidence in the way things are done in Asia. The idea that the nominal West can be a model for or guide to economic development for the future has been displaced and replaced with Asian references in several areas of economic, social and political practice. The earliest example of this referencing of Asia was the case of export-oriented industrialisation.

Export-oriented industrialisation was pioneered by Japan, and was instrumental in the rapid reconstruction of its devastated post–World War II economy, propelling Japan to become the world's second-largest economy by the 1990s. This industrialisation model was replicated by South Korea, Taiwan, Hong Kong and Singapore, in that order, from the mid-1960s, with equally palpable capitalist economic successes. At the academic level, this model has given rise to various conceptual innovations—for example, a Japan-centred theory of 'flying geese', whereby Japan leads the way in labour-intensive export industries. As it moves up the technology and capital-intensive industrial chains, it casts off its labour-intensive industries to the next set of industrialising economies, which in turn do the same as their respective economies develop: from Japan to South Korea, Taiwan, Hong Kong and Singapore, and subsequently to Indonesia, Thailand and Vietnam, and so on (Ozawa 2005). The developing economies of the last four countries in turn generated conceptual and theoretical work on several fronts: the new international division of labour, the newly industrialising economies and the developmental state.

A more recent development is in the area of urban and regional planning. One defining characteristic of cities in Asia is high population density, which, with a few exceptions, is way beyond the imagination of American and European city dwellers. Densities such as those of Hong Kong, Shanghai and Mumbai are seldom seen in Euro-America. In view of the rapid urbanisation process in all Asian countries, the planning guidelines of European cities—where the old city is retained and new developments can maintain relatively low height and low density—hold no lessons for urban planners in Asia. Increasingly, urban planners in Asia have to turn to urban developments in other Asian locations as models. Singapore, for example, has served as a reference point for many Asian city governors and urban planners, often rhetorically to drive their development plans rather than concretely to 'reproduce' or clone Singapore in their own cities. This was the case with Bangalore looking towards Singapore in the early 2000s (Nair 2005: 123–24). There are, however, instances where practices in Singapore are concretely replicated, such as the attempt to 'green' Dalian City in China (Hoffman 2011: 55–76), and the residential development of Surabaya, Indonesia, where even the statue of the 'founder' of Singapore, Sir Thomas Stamford Raffles, has been replicated (Idawati 2010). Referencing Singapore has also generated significant urban development cooperation between Singaporean and Chinese state-owned enterprises, and business opportunities for Singapore-based architectural and urban planning consultancies (Chua 2011: 29–54). Meanwhile, Singapore is studying the public transport system of Hong Kong; Hyderabad is studying the infrastructure development of Shanghai; and Bangalore has itself become a reference point for cities aspiring to attract investment in high-tech industries (Goldman 2011).[1]

A third area where inter-referencing between Asian locations takes place is in the regionalisation of the media and popular culture. There is a historically well-established network of production, distribution and consumption of Chinese-language pop music, opera and films within the ethnic-Chinese-dominated locations of China, Taiwan, Hong Kong and Singapore and in other smaller 'diasporic' ethnic-Chinese communities throughout Southeast Asia. At different

---

1   For more cases of inter-referencing of Asian cities, see the other essays in Roy and Ong (2011).

periods in the past, Japanese film and pop music made forays into this network and achieved intermittent popularity for some singers and actors. In the 1990s, Japanese television dramas became a staple of audiences throughout East Asia. This success encouraged the Korean television industry, where dramas are the mainstay of daily programming, to learn from the high-quality production values of Japan and to actively export its own dramas regionally. As a consequence of the liberalisation of the media industries in Taiwan and China, satellite and cable stations in these locations were quick to import Japanese and Korean dramas to fill the excess slots in their programming schedules, first by pirating the programs and later by legally importing them. Imported Japanese and Korean programs are either dubbed or translated for redistribution throughout the Chinese-language media network, thus expanding the market for producers and their importers. The creation of a regional transnational audience has led to tentative attempts at co-production between one or more locations, involving actors and other production professionals from different places, to produce 'pan–East Asian' films and dramas with the hope of expanding the audience and market for such products. All of these processes—concentrated in the past two decades—have resulted in a loosely integrated regional media/cultural industry in East Asia. As for the regional transnational audiences, different Asian locations seen on television have become locations of cultural interest, promoting intra-Asian tourism and cultural exchanges. Locations that show evidence of greater development in terms of capitalist consumer modernity have come to represent aspirational futures for audiences in less-developed economies and, for locations that are coeval in development, examples for mutual cultural learning and emulation. On the academic front, these developments have engendered a new field of individual and collaborative research in East Asian popular culture (Chua 2012; Chua and Iwabuchi 2008).

The first of the above three instances of inter-referencing is an example of Japan's long-standing tendency to place itself as 'being in but not a part of Asia', by positioning itself as the leader taking along the rest of Asia. This tendency contributed to Japan's imperialist ambitions, expressed in regional aggression in the Pacific War. Unfortunately, such illiberal tendencies persist in some segments of Japanese society (Iwabuchi 2002a: 547–73). The second instance is a straightforward attempt at reproducing a model locally or, more importantly, of invoking another Asian location as a provocation to local government to act towards an aspirational future. The last is of integration of the region through working out the historical and cultural differences that not only characterise the region but also often act as obstacles to regional collaboration. Beneath the noisy and quarrelsome international political discussions between the East Asian neighbours, an integrative cultural exchange network is being developed.

Shifting frames of comparison

Instances of inter-Asian referencing exemplify a significant epistemological shift in the generation of knowledge in Asia. In 200 years of development of capitalism and liberal democracy in Euro-America, many kinks have been ironed out along the way. For example, the process of the enfranchisement of all citizens passed through stages of discrimination and restrictions on individuals of different gendered and racialised positioning. The exploitation of labour has a long history—from the horrendous conditions of early industrialisation in the seventeenth century to the institutionalisation of postwar social democracy and other forms of welfarism. In contrast, rapid capitalist development is a postwar phenomenon in most parts of Asia, with the exception of Japan. Asian nations, with few exceptions, are still struggling to institutionalise some, if not most, aspects of electoral democratic politics in political and economic governance. With such great historical temporal distance, in any comparison of Asia with Euro-America, the Asian location will (not unexpectedly) come up short on a whole constellation of political and economic dimensions. That is why, in an Asia–Euro-America comparison, Asia is permanently in a state of catch-up, as Chakrabarty (2000) puts it, placing Asia in the 'prison house of history'.

In contrast, all the nations in Asia have emerged from either imperial dynasties, such as China and Japan, or colonialism after World War II. In most cases, democratic political processes were introduced to the newly independent Asian nations only after World War II. With the exception of Japan, the first wave of capitalist industrialisation was not initiated in Asia until the 1960s. This was the case in South Korea, Taiwan, Hong Kong and Singapore, followed subsequently by others in Southeast Asia, with the most recent entrants being the post-socialist economies of China, Vietnam and, to a significant extent, India. The span of time between the early movers and the later entrants into electoral democratic politics and economic industrialisation is no more than three decades. The success or failure of any state in instituting democracy and capitalist economic growth remains within the horizon of imaginable possibilities for the other states in the region. Thus, as Chen (2010) suggests, inter-referencing Asia shifts the frame of comparison to a temporally coeval, horizontal plane between locations in Asia—in contrast with the temporally and historically unequal comparison of Europe and Asia.

Comparative political economy

Let us take political development as an illustration. In the postcolonial states in South and Southeast Asia, with the possible exception of India, immediate attempts after independence to institutionalise electoral democratic politics generally failed, often resulting either in dictatorship, as in South Korea, the Philippines and Indonesia, or in some less than fully democratic form of electoral politics, such as the one-party-dominant state of Singapore or the Malay-first multi-party alliance in Malaysia. In the case of the respectively post-dynastic and postcolonial communist states of China and Vietnam, very limited village-level elections have been instituted only since the 1990s. Furthermore, most of these nations are still struggling with different modes of repressive government. There is also endemic corruption by self-interested politicians and other members of the elite, taking turns to put their hands in the nation's till under the veil of 'democratic' elections, as electoral processes become the *sine qua non* to claims of being democratic, regardless of the substance. Political education of the citizenry in modern democracy is in many ways still in its infancy. The comparative analysis of these Asian examples holds significant lessons for understanding the differences and the complexities of trajectories within the region.[2] By contrast, there is an analytic stance that holds Western liberal democracy as the endpoint of democratic development and thus as the 'critical' mirror that, unsurprisingly, constantly finds Asian examples wanting. The result is ideologically laden labelling of the Asian examples as 'authoritarian', 'illiberal' (Bell et al. 1995), 'electoral autocracy' (Diamond 2002) or, perhaps more generously, 'semi-democratic' (Case 1993). Each of these comparisons is driven, implicitly or explicitly, by an ahistorical teleology of 'sameness', towards an endpoint already achieved by the contemporary West, without pausing to ask whether Asia wants to be the same as the West.

In the economic dimension, the relatively temporally coeval patterns of economic development of Asian countries can definitely be fruitfully compared with one another. Within the generalised concept of the 'developmental state', the current comparative configuration of the different states in East Asia can be shown to be largely determined by the different ways that state and capital were conjoined at the early stages of export-oriented industrialisation in each country. The Korean government, for example, first transferred the industries that were handed over by the defeated Japanese colonial administration to the few extant Korean industrial families and subsequently provided significant financial advantages to encourage the family capitalist class to spearhead export-

---

2   See the special issue of *Democratization* (2007), 'Beyond hybrid regimes', guest edited by Garry Rodan and Kanishka Jayasuriya.

oriented industrialisation, creating what are now known as the *'chaebols'* (comparable to the Japanese *zaibatsu* or *keiretsu* companies). Since the 1980s, these families have effectively sustained their dominance in the respective *chaebols* with a system of complicated cross-share ownership and executive positions, as the *chaebols* as a group progressively monopolised the national economy. Consequently, they have attracted public criticism for the corrupt and illegal manipulation of company finances for selfish family benefit and for stifling domestic entrepreneurial initiatives by acquiring successful business start-ups or setting up competing companies and forcing start-ups out of business. By the end of the 1990s, *chaebols* had become political liabilities for all elected presidents, with each promising reform of the system. The *chaebols*, however, have grown to be global corporations and have become independent of the state; they have become a relatively autonomous interest group that actively lobbies for their preferred electoral candidates. Dependency on electoral support has blunted the politicians', and hence the state's, ability to act against the *chaebols*.[3]

In Singapore, by contrast, at the point of launching industrialisation, there were no industrial capitalists. This forced the newly elected, independent government to rely on foreign capital investment to power its industrialisation. In enterprises where foreign capitalists were risk-averse, the state established its own corporation to take up the business. The state also invested heavily in so-called natural monopolies rather than transferring such enterprises to private capital. The result is a state with a high degree of economic autonomy; not only is it not dependent on local capitalists, it is also able to continue to chart the direction of its industrial policies. Meanwhile, its investments in state enterprises have reaped huge returns, as many of these enterprises have become successful globalised corporations, with the Singapore government continuing as the majority shareholder and manager. Finally, the accumulated profits generated by state enterprises have been used to set up a sovereign wealth fund that invests globally on behalf of the Singapore state—a process that is being emulated by emerging economies, such as China, when they are able to do so.

Asian models

Perhaps the most practical aspect of referencing Asia is in how locations in the region are trying to learn from one another's experiences, to take lessons from ostensibly successful examples and to find so-called best practice in different aspects of social, economic and political governance. A significant example is the way China, the biggest country in Asia, studies Singapore, one of the smallest, for potentially useful lessons in many aspects of governance, in spite

---

3   For a comprehensive review of the political economy of *chaebols*, see Chang (2011: 101–28).

of the vast difference in scale. Singaporean architecture and urban planning consultants, for example, in both private and government-linked companies, are receiving large urban planning contracts in different cities in China, starting with the Suzhou Industrial Park outside Shanghai—the first cooperation between state-owned companies and relevant state authorities. Since 1992, this model of cooperation between the two countries has multiplied to include several other large urban planning projects, including the Tianjin Eco-City Project and the Guangzhou Knowledge City Project. The Nanyang Technological University in Singapore runs a 'Chinese mayor' program for would-be mayors and other city bureaucrats from China to learn about the urban management systems of Singapore. Finally, in 2012, the state-owned China Central Television began making a 10-part documentary series on different aspects of Singaporean life, including the political system, to be aired in China as public education. The reason for China's referencing of Singapore is obvious. China would like to replicate, if possible, despite the difference in scale, Singapore's success in capitalist development while maintaining a non-corrupt, elected single-party-dominant state power with a high degree of electoral popularity, and hence legitimacy to govern. Apart from China, Singapore has regularly been mentioned in other Asian locations, including the newly independent Timor-Leste, as an example for emulation, and as an icon of successful economic development and improvement of material life of its citizens—rather than for its anti-liberal polity under the long-ruling People's Action Party (PAP). Other examples of Asian references can be found: Shanghai as a model for Hyderabad; and Malaysia as a model for Islamic capitalist development.

From an academic angle, what is interesting about 'modelling' Asia is the conceptual and critical research this process might generate. First, such modelling is a process of knowledge and expertise transfer, which involves a significant amount of intergovernmental traffic, which shapes regional international relations. Second, processes and practices of governance are developed in a particular location as consequences of local historical contingencies and are often conceived and executed as interconnected activities. In the process of transfer across space and time, this historically determined assemblage of practices is disassembled and only selective aspects are picked up and applied in the new environment. The result is often contrary to the achievements of the original model. Third, while there are instances in which the modelling process has led to mimicry, more often than not the model is evoked rhetorically as a trope to criticise local authorities and, hopefully, to provoke them into greater accountability and accomplishment in bettering local citizens' lives. We could paraphrase, for example, the late Deng Xiaoping (1904–97), initiator of the marketisation of the Chinese economy, who exhorted Chinese bureaucrats to look to Singapore because 'they are doing something right and we ought to be able to do better' (see further Fook 2010: 175). Each of these areas of intergovernmental, commercial and political activities that resulted from referencing Asia constitutes a site of theoretical and applied research.

Pop-culture regionalism

Globally, there is no doubt that the United States, especially Hollywood, is the dominant producer and distributor of transnational popular culture. Juxtaposed against this, however, is the emergence of regional networks of production, distribution and consumption of popular culture in Asia. This has been facilitated by new communication technologies and the liberalisation of the once nationalised or tightly controlled media industries in the region. Each geographically identifiable region has its own networks. There is usually one dominant player (some more than others depending on the relative economic conditions among the member countries in a region) in each network. This is the primary producer and exporter of the pop culture that is distributed, legally or otherwise, and consumed regionally. In the case of South Asia, the dominant player is Bollywood (Rajadhyaksha 2003). In mainland Southeast Asia, Thai pop culture is well received in Laos and areas bordering Myanmar (Jirattikorn 2008) and Cambodia. In island Southeast Asia, among the Muslim/Malay-language communities, Indonesia is marginally dominant; and in East Asia, the regional network is much more complicated, with shifting dominant players according to different popular culture genres (Chua 2012). Such networks might peripherally exceed their respective regional boundaries and appear in other parts of Asia, but they do not reach the global market, despite frequent claims by the producers and other grandiose claims infused with nationalism. Despite occasional breakthroughs to the global market, more than 95 per cent of Korean pop culture exports are destined for East Asia, with Japan taking more than 80 per cent and the rest going to Taiwan, Hong Kong and China, and, via these three locations, to the rest of the small diasporic ethnic-Chinese communities around the world. What is interesting about these regional popular culture networks is that they exist beneath the noisy international relations among the quarrelling nations who are constantly provoking antagonism over historical events to bolster nationalism. As armed conflicts increasingly become something to avoid, competition between the quarrelling nations has also led to the export of popular culture as an instrument of 'cultural diplomacy'.[4] Of these regional networks, the one that has received the most academic investigation is the East Asian Pop Culture Network. The political, economic, social and

---

4   There is a significant body of literature on East Asian popular culture, which includes films, pop music and television dramas. For a comprehensive survey of this literature, see Chua (2012).

cultural processes in the transnational production, distribution and reception/ consumption of regional popular culture investigated in the East Asian Pop Culture Network can readily serve as points of reference for the other regional networks in Asia.

Concept formation

Scholars of Asia, especially social scientists, have often trimmed local complexities to fit into existing concepts whose origin in Euro-American studies has been erased, with the concepts apparently being universalised. The point here is not to reject such concepts out of hand simply because they are generated in the West, nor to deny scholars in the West the right to theorise with whatever empirical material they have to hand. The problem is one of adequate conceptualisation and understanding of the local. A concrete example will clarify the issue.

One of the common practices among Huaren (ethnic-Chinese) in Singapore is for working children, including those married with families of their own, to voluntarily give money to their parents monthly, even when the parents are not in need, as is the case in most middle-class families. There are no written agreements, of course, and the quantum given is flexible. Locally, it is generally regarded as an expression of filial piety, of Confucianism as a 'little' tradition. One young Scandinavian scholar radically simplified this practice as a 'contract' in English. Contract, unfortunately, implies a formal legal financial transaction, suppressing completely the symbolic and emotive complexities that are embedded in the practice, including the self-worth and self-image of not only the children but also the parents. The scholar was well aware that this was an unhappy choice of terms. During an oral presentation, the scholar freely admitted, and apologised for, the inadequacy of the concept of contract. This unfortunate slippage is, perhaps, the result of focusing too much on the financial aspects of the idea of filial piety because giving money to parents monthly is the most concrete and therefore the most-mentioned activity that materialises the fuzzy and complex concept for young Chinese research respondents.[5] This is not an uncommon example; the messiness of the local empirical material has been trimmed to fit awkwardly into an existing concept developed elsewhere.

---

5   This overemphasis on the financial aspect of filial piety is evident in her book, where the term 'contract' is also used (Goransson 2009: 103).

Concepts are shorthand ways of representing an inexhaustible volume of descriptive empirical information. Each concept is a decontextualised, abstracted lexical item with its own contextual origin and a history that has been suppressed or erased. Consequently, the existing concept never captures new empirical material without slippage, distortion, reduction or excess. Modification is unavoidable if a concept is to be used in a new context. Additionally, working in different language contexts in Asia, local practices often cannot be represented by existing concepts, as seen in the example above. Local concepts are not always translatable into English terms without severe loss of richness. Faced with both conditions, one should preserve the richness of the local and develop concepts that are adequate to its complexity, including, if necessary, by using local terminology. Again, a concrete example will clarify.

A Korean cultural studies scholar, trained in Australia, in her analysis of the mode through which the Korean pop culture industry exports its products internationally, uses the term '*mugukjeok*' to characterise what makes their products globally mobile. The term has its equivalents in both Chinese (无国籍 / *wu guo ji*) and Japanese (無国籍 / *mukokuseki*). This scholar credited Koichi Iwabuchi with introducing this term in his analysis of Japanese media culture exports (Jung 2011: 17–18). Western scholarly attention to Iwabuchi's (2002b) work, however, has picked up the term 'culturally odourless' for Japanese cultural exports as opposed to Jung's appropriation of the term *mukokuseki*. The reason is quite simple.

In English, *mugukjeok* would likely be translated into 'stateless', a common negative term in the politics of citizenship. A stateless person is one without citizenship, and therefore no civil rights, in a world constituted by nation-states. The term *mukokuseki* therefore does not denote transnational boundary crossing as a positive value; hence, the preference for the term 'odourless'. However, Jung has nuanced the term in Asian languages in the context of cultural exports by turning 'statelessness' into a positive quality of mobility, of being unbound by nations, erasing the reference to nations, as in the term 'transnational'. For me, this is a better term to characterise culture that travels than any 'trans' words in English. This is an example of what I think of as the process of new concept formation that is a consequence of inter-Asia referencing. In this instance, the proximity of the Chinese, Korean and Japanese languages, which contain traces of the past, and maybe even a continuing, shared culture, has facilitated the development of the concept.[6] Such shared cultural affinities,

---

6   The use of compounds derived from Chinese characters in these East Asian languages facilitates such inter-referencing.

however, are not a necessary condition: a new concept could be formulated in the English language in one Asian location and provoke nuanced resonance in another.

Conclusion

I have demonstrated above that one consequence of the rise of Asia in global capitalism is the stimulation of concrete and practical instances of one location in Asia using another as a reference point for its own ongoing social, economic and political governance. Following such concrete activities, there has been a similar shift in Asian studies, especially among scholars based in Asia, to call attention to the process of referencing Asia. This has resulted in an epistemological shift from the temporally hierarchical Asia–Euro-America comparison, which places Asia permanently in a position of 'catch up', to one of a horizontal comparison of inter-Asian locations among relatively comparable equals, thus generating different forms of knowledge and, perhaps, knowledges of greater utility for Asian development, intellectual and otherwise. The shift to inter-Asia references also engenders an opportunity for the development of new concepts, facilitated by regional language affinities and, perhaps, deeper structures in shared culture that still resonate in contemporary capitalist life.

Such inter-Asia referencing, however, is not and should not be the end of the process. There is often a tendency among 'local' scholars to emphasise the 'non-transferability' of local concepts, usually as a rearguard strategy to preserve the uniqueness of the local. This is also because of an abhorrence of 'universals'—a sentiment grounded in a postcolonial suspicion of universalisation as a mode of subjugation of the colonised. While such postcolonial cautions are necessary, one should also realise that, ironically, to overemphasise the non-transferability of local concepts is to condemn local scholarship to the fate of being 'unique' and, therefore, 'interesting' in an exotic way, but ultimately, irrelevant to others.[7] The universalisation of concepts is necessary if the knowledge is to be communicated across spatial and cultural boundaries; one might say that universalisation is the logic of knowledge production and there can be no provincialisation of knowledge. Scholars in Asia, therefore, have a responsibility to situate local scholarship as part of the global archive and to add universalising concepts developed in Asia.

---

7   As one who writes often on Singapore, I am constantly faced with such comments regarding the 'uniqueness' of Singapore because it is an island nation or a city-state and, therefore, holds no lessons for 'normal' countries.

References

Bell, Daniel A., Brown, David, Jayasuriya, Kanishka and Jones, David Martin. 1995. *Towards illiberal democracy in Pacific Asia*. London: Macmillan.

Case, William. 1993. Semi-democracy in Malaysia: Withstanding the pressures for regime change. *Pacific Affairs* 66(2): 183–205.

Chakrabarty, Dipesh. 2000. *Provincializing Europe: Postcolonial thought and historical difference*. Princeton, NJ: Princeton University Press.

Chang, Kyung-Sup. 2011. *South Korea under compressed modernity: Familial political economy in transition*. London: Routledge.

Chen, Kuan-Hsing. 2010. *Asia as method*. Durham, NC: Duke University Press.

Chua, Beng Huat. 2011. Singapore as model: Planning innovations, knowledge experts. In Ananya Roy and Aihwa Ong, eds. *Worlding cities: Asia experiments and the art of being global*. Chichester: Wiley-Blackwell.

Chua, Beng Huat. 2012. *Structure, audience and soft power in East Asian cinema*. Hong Kong: Hong Kong University Press.

Chua, Beng Huat and Iwabuchi, Koichi. eds. 2008. *East Asian pop culture: Analysing the Korean wave*. Hong Kong: Hong Kong University Press.

Diamond, Larry. 2002. Thinking about hybrid regimes. *Journal of Democracy* 13(2): 21–35.

Fook, Lye Liang. 2010. Singapore's involvement in China's reform. In John Wong and Bo Zhiyue, eds. *China's reform in global perspective*. Singapore: World Scientific Publishing.

Gaonkar, Dilip Parameshwar. ed. 2001. *Alternative modernities*. Durham, NC: Duke University Press.

Goldman, Michael. 2011. Speculating in the next world city. In Ananya Roy and Aihwa Ong, eds. *Worlding cities: Asia experiments and the art of being global*. Chichester: Wiley-Blackwell.

Goransson, Kristina. 2009. *The binding tie: Chinese intergenerational relations in modern Singapore*. Honolulu: University of Hawai'i Press.

Hoffman, Lisa. 2011. Urban modeling and contemporary technologies of city-building in China: The production of regimes of green urbanisms. In Ananya Roy and Aihwa Ong, eds. *Worlding cities: Asia experiments and the art of being global*. Chichester: Wiley-Blackwell.

Idawati, Dyah E. 2010. Imagining Surabaya's new image: to be another Singapore? Global urban frontiers: Asian cities in theory, practice and imagination workshop. September 8–9, Asia Research Institute, National University of Singapore.

Iwabuchi, Koichi. 2002a. Nostalgia for a (different) Asian modernity: Media consumption of 'Asia' in Japan. *positions: east asia cultures critique* 10(3): 547–73.

Iwabuchi, Koichi. 2002b. *Recentering globalization: Popular culture and Japanese transnationalism*. Durham, NC: Duke University Press.

Jirattikorn, Amporn. 2008. Pirated transnational broadcasting: The consumption of Thai soap operas among Shan communities in Burma. *Sojourn* 23(1): 30–62.

Jung, Sun. 2011. *Korean masculinities and transnational consumption: Yonsama, Rain, Oldboy and K-pop idols*. Hong Kong: Hong Kong University Press.

Nair, Janaki. 2005. *The promise of the metropolis: Bangalore's twentieth century*. New Delhi: Oxford University Press.

Ong, Aihwa. 2011. World cities, or the art of being global. In Ananya Roy and Aihwa Ong, eds. *Worlding cities: Asia experiments and the art of being global*. Chichester: Wiley-Blackwell.

Ozawa, Terutomo. 2005. *Institutions, industrial upgrading, and economic performance in Japan: The 'flying-geese' paradigm of catch-up growth*. Northampton, MA: Edward Elgar.

Rajadhyaksha, Ashish. 2003. The 'Bollywoodization' of the Indian cinema: Cultural nationalism in a global arena. *Inter-Asia Cultural Studies* 4(1): 25–39.

Rodan, Garry and Jayasuriya, Kanishka. 2007. Beyond hybrid regimes. *Democratization* 14(5): 773–94.

Roy, Ananya and Ong, Aihwa. eds. 2011. *Worlding cities: Asia experiments and the art of being global*. Chichester: Wiley-Blackwell.

5

Beyond the culturalist problematic: Towards a global social science in the Asian Century?

Kanishka Jayasuriya

Introduction

This volume engages with debates about research and study on Asia and engaging with the knowledge produced in the Asian region in the next few decades.[1] My argument is simple: the advent of the so-called Asian Century is not simply about making us knowledgable about Asia or developing institutional capacities for such knowledge. Rather, it also challenges some of the fundamental assumptions of the social sciences. This has become problematic for some of the key assumptions driving Asian studies. It has also become problematic, in the Australian context, for some of the public policy assumptions about 'Asia literacy', or 'Asia capability' as it is called in its latest incarnation (Asialink 2013; Department of Education 2014; see also Heryanto in this volume). In turn, this has a number of implications for the way we do research on Asia as well

---

1   As noted in the introduction to this volume, the terms of debate shift between focusing on 'Asia', the 'Asia-Pacific', the 'Indo-Pacific', the 'Pacific' or the 'Pacific Rim'.

as broader public policy implications for research investment—particularly in which research programs to invest, as well as the kinds of skills and expertise we need to 'study Asia'.

In short, my argument is not about how we respond to the Asian Century, but more about the way the Asian Century challenges us to move beyond some of the defining assumptions of mainstream social sciences as well as area studies. In the Australian context, if we want to make the study of Asia central to our basic research mission in the social sciences, we have to transcend the modernisation framework and the culturalist problematic that have been the basis of so much of the public policy discussion of social science and area studies. The key question is not about producing knowledge about Asia, but how, and in what way, the study of Asia can contribute to determining the parameters of a truly global social science. I argue in this chapter that the rise of Asia poses the possibility of building a 'global social science', but constructing this requires more than adding Asia to the social science pot. Building a global social science requires us to transcend some of the fundamental assumptions that have guided social science and area studies in Australia and elsewhere (see also the introduction to this volume and chapters by Connell and Patel).

The culturalist problematic is central to the way in which area studies have been conceived and organised. The area studies paradigm incorporates a configuration of research problems based on an attempt to understand a particular geographical 'area'. It lies outside the conventional discipline-centred perspective of academia. It is defined in terms of the distinctive characteristics and circumstances of the area itself. Even postcolonial or postmodernist responses—such as the search for alternative pathways of modernity (Gaonkar 2001)—are trapped within these unhelpful binaries of the West and Asia.

I will come back to this point in relation to Australian public policy on research and teaching on Asia, but there is a broader point to be made about the dominant ways of understanding Asia. Here, the implicit assumption of much of the social science research on Asia and various area studies work is that 'Asia' is benchmarked against European experience, whether in terms of being exceptional or deviant, or of replicating some kind of previous social, political and economic trajectory in Western Europe or North America.

There is now a discussion about the future of area studies, and Asian studies in particular. In the United States, of course, the emergence and growth of area studies were marked by the Cold War (see also Chapter 7 in this volume). The end of the Cold War has not seen the end of area studies, but there is an epistemic anxiety about 'what it is' and how and what we should do, even as the emphasis has shifted to studying Asia for trade and economic reasons. As I argue below, such an area studies focus has had a particular resonance in Australia. It has been based on an underlying assumption that Australia needs to be literate about the region 'out there', which at the same time helps to reproduce a cartographic boundary.

In this chapter, I identify and contextualise the key elements of this culturalist problem. I argue that this culturalist paradigm has shaped public policy strategies structured around notions of Asian literacy and capability. In the final section of the chapter, I chart a new problem-oriented strategy that avoids some of the pitfalls of the culturalist problematic, and that responds to the changing social and political circumstances that have made the Asian literacy model increasingly ineffective in the Asian Century. Such a problem-solving approach offers us a path towards building a global social science.

The culturalist problematic and Asia literacy and capability

While notions of Asia capability or Asia literacy central to Australian educational strategies are carefully framed in technocratic policy language, they carry the cultural binaries of Western and non-Western societies (Mamdani 1996). The implicit 'modernisation' framework and the associated binaries are what account for a surprisingly resonant culturalist definition of the region that is visible in so many public policy attempts to invest in research and engagement on Asia. This culturalist understanding is evident in the White Paper *Australia in the Asian Century* released by former prime minster Julia Gillard (Commonwealth of Australia 2012). This report—though written by a formidable team of technocrats—adopts the notion of Asia capability to explain how the public sector, including universities, and the private sector can drive engagement with the region. In this context, the report recommends significant investment in five priority Asian languages. It is not language training per se that is at issue here but the way these public policies reinforce a particular culturalist understanding of the region. While this report has been placed in political cold storage since the election of the Abbott Liberal government, some of its underlying assumptions continue to frame current government policies, particularly in relation to the 'New Colombo Plan' to facilitate Australian student mobility in Asia (see also the introduction to this volume).

Culturalism in this context refers to a set of institutional and intellectual practices that separate the cultural process from underlying social and political relationships. The cultural process is then reduced to a set of abstract traits (linguistic, religious, and so on), which become, in turn, the basis for understanding the social and political processes in a particular geographical area. It is useful, I think, to view culturalism as a kind of problematic that we are able to understand in a range of different and often diverse approaches to the region, not in the form of their content, but in terms of the presence of a set of underlying problems that these approaches attempt to resolve. These problems often revolve around explaining why a particular culture or area is not like 'us', thereby producing a very specific problem of 'literacy'. At the core of this 'culturalism' is the way that social and political relations—issues of power and conflict—are displaced or replaced with cultural understandings of political and social problems. Nevertheless, the crucial point here is how non-material ways of understanding social and political change come to dominate the study of Asia in ways reminiscent of what Sternhell (2009) has recently illuminated as a powerful strain within conservative and liberal strands of counter-Enlightenment political theorising.

It is in the social sciences and area studies that these notions of culturalism have had a deep impact on the study of non-Western societies and, in particular, the study of Asia. In fact, the culturalist problematic continues to impact on the way social sciences are organised in the region. Patel (2006; and in this volume) has argued that these notions of culturalism have roots in colonial practices of rule—defining and ordering notions of custom that lent themselves to a technology of rule that extensively utilised notions such as 'caste' and 'tribe' for organising political rule—a point that is central in the work of scholars such as Mamdani (1996) and Dirks (2001). In the post–World War II period, these culturalist understandings emerged in the guise of modernisation theory—an emergence that has now been well documented (Higgott 1983). Moreover, these culturalist ideas have continued to resonate in the development and organisation of social sciences in postcolonial countries where Orientalist 'binaries were now reframed to incorporate the traditional–modern dichotomies and legitimize the colonial project of modernity that divided the peoples of the world into two groups, the traditional and the modern' (Patel 2006: 388).

The influence of this culturalism is felt not just in mainstream social sciences but also in various postmodernist guises. In an insightful analysis of the influential work of Ashis Nandy, Bonnett (2011), for example, argues that Nandy's notion of authentic tradition—as a site of political resistance—is paradoxically framed by a notion of Occidentalism that in turn diminishes the critical potential of this notion of tradition as political resistance. The point is that, even though the Orientalist boundaries that we have identified earlier might change, situating the problem in terms of the 'resistance of tradition' is still within the culturalist problematic. An analysis of this tradition of work is beyond the scope of this short essay, but the broader argument is that even some postcolonial theories frame questions of social and political transformation in terms of conflict over 'cultural' stakes and boundaries, with 'the cultural' having its own distinctive set of dynamics.

Certainly, modernisation has been challenged by the rapid social and economic transformation of Asia, but culturalism as an intellectual and institutional practice remains a powerful influence in both area studies and social sciences. It is especially pronounced in the analysis and understanding of the rise of China, which is often seen in terms of notions of a return to civilisational practice. To take an example from international relations, Kang (2007) has contested—in my view, persuasively—the idea that Asia will mirror Europe's past. He then, however, reinserts an essentialised notion of East Asian history to explain the rise of China in terms of Asia's cultural past. According to this view, the rise of China needs to be understood in the context of the East Asian version of informal and hierarchical relationships between states. The Asian Century heralds a return not just to China's past, but also to a past seen in terms of a reassertion of underlying cultural practices. Social and political processes—in Kang's case, the relationships between states—are understood in terms of the unfolding of a set of non-material values. It is this culturalist glue that binds older strands of modernisation theory with notions of Chinese or East Asian civilisational practice.

In an illuminating article, Callahan proposes what he terms a new 'Sino speak'— reflected, for example, in the work of Kang or the more popular writing of Martin Jacques—which frames the arguments of several public intellectuals and scholars working on China. This is, of course, a strand of work on China and is not meant to include the whole body of social and political studies of Chinese social and political transformation. Nevertheless, it is a vein of thinking that is particularly influential within policymaking communities. On this basis, Callahan argues that Sino-speak is founded on the idea that 'China' is exceptional, and is therefore forging an alternative modernity shaped by its distinctive cultural trajectories. Sino-speak, Callahan notes, employs 'a set of distinctions—convergence/divergence, East/West, tradition/modernity, civil/ military and inside/outside—to make sense of China's future and the world's future' (Callahan 2012: 36). This depoliticises the material context of social and political transformation to privilege a particular form—to use Mamdani's words—of 'culture talk'.

Australian public policy and the culturalist problematic

These culturalist ideas have had a distinctive impact on Australian public policy strategies for teaching and research on Asia. The decision to invest a substantial multi-million dollar award to the China Studies Centre at The Australian National University neatly illustrates this argument. Geremie Barmé (2005), the Director of the China Studies Centre, has sought to articulate what he calls 'a new Sinology' as a mode of managing Australia's engagement with a rising China and, indeed, with the broader Sinophone world. This approach affirms a conversation and intermingling that also emphasise strong scholastic underpinnings in the classical and modern Chinese language and studies. In line with the culturalist problematic that we have identified, in this new Sinology, Barmé emphasises the distinctive cultural foundations—in almost Orientalist fashion—on which we need to engage with a newly ascendant China. It follows that understanding and engaging with this cultural distinction requires the development of 'cultural competence'. In fact, the politics of engagement is seen in terms of a broader transcultural civilisational dialogue between Australia and the Sinic world. Obscured in this culturalist analysis is the fact that Chinese 'modernity' is shaped by its engagement with the global capitalist economy and forms the foundations of its compressed capitalist development.

The more significant feature of this new Sinology is the way it fits with the broader thrust of Australian investment in research and teaching in Asia. The China Studies Centre at The Australian National University was the beneficiary of a generous research grant from the Commonwealth to pursue its research agenda. There is a link between the politics of Australian engagement with the region and the public investment in teaching and research on the program of 'cultural' literacy. The implicit rationale of many proponents of increased research investment in the region is underpinned by an amorphous notion of Asia literacy linked to an engagement with, and an understanding of, the distinctive cultural and civilisational foundations of Australia's key neighbours—such as Japan, Indonesia, China and India—depending on the flavour of the era. Accordingly, this logic suggests that in order to engage more effectively with the region, we need to become more Asia literate. As such, this Asia literacy strategy for building research capacity implicitly favours an area studies approach with an emphasis on the importance of language and culture. Centres for Asian studies, as well as more specific country-oriented institutes, are creatures of the political and institutional circumstances that led to their establishment in the past few decades.

The Asian Century White Paper (Commonwealth of Australia 2012) is preoccupied with a broad-ranging interest in the institutional and governance reforms of public as well as private institutions for the Asian Century. This is the rub: governance reform is seen in terms of the technocratic engineering of governing institutions to make them more capable of competing in the region. This capability, however, is seen in cultural terms. For example, the White Paper advocates getting senior executives of public and private institutions to speak an Asian language. The report recommends an extensive program of student mobility—a policy adopted by both the Gillard–Rudd governments and the

Abbott government—but this mobility is seen in terms of expanding the cultural competence of Australian students. In essence, the White Paper argues that the crucial problem lies in building a set of cultural capabilities that it deems as Asia capability—a concept influenced by the business-backed Asialink centre at the University of Melbourne. The White Paper argues for an increase in 'the number of workplaces that can attract, use and retain Asia-capable talent—people who have the "knowledge, skills and mindset" for successful engagement in Asia' (Commonwealth of Australia 2012: 180). The report suggests that, in tandem with this rationale, public investment in teaching and resources is governed by these Asia capability objectives.

None of this is new in Australian public policy. This 'culturalist problematic', as Walker (1999), Jayasuriya (2010) and Beeson and Jayasuriya (2009) have argued, has a much longer provenance in twentieth-century Australia. A consistent theme running across various mission statements and public policies has been the idea of Asia literacy on research and teaching of Asian studies dating from the Auchmuty Report (Auchmuty 1971), followed by those of FitzGerald (1980) and Ingleson (Asian Studies Council 1989). Aligned with the broad thrust of the Garnaut Report on Australia–Asia relations (Garnaut 1989), this led to repeated calls for research capacity to help Australia understand the distinctive cultural and social characters of the region as part of its engagement strategy.

In fact, notions of Asia literacy have been prevalent for much of the twentieth century. For example, this culturalist problematic found a sympathetic reception within the Institute of Pacific Relations (IPR) based in the United States, with branches in New South Wales and Victoria (Akami 2002). A notable work of the IPR was the study by Jack Shepherd—an Australian based at the IPR in New York—entitled *Australian interests and policies in the Far East* (1939). In some ways, this remarkable work foreshadowed the Garnaut Report (1989) in highlighting Australia's emerging role as a Pacific power in a culturally distinctive East Asian region with growing developmental potential. Like many others in the IPR, Shepherd sought to understand development and international relations through newly emerging social science techniques. The work of those such as Shepherd reflected an attempt to understand economic development in non-European contexts, which in some ways anticipated the modernisation theories of the 1950s and 1960s, albeit without the Cold War underpinning. These early studies sought to understand economic development as an experiment in how 'to secure cultural integrity while also engineering economic modernity' (Brown 1990: 81). Hence, the Asia-Pacific region provided some clear lessons for Australia's own political and economic development. Another key intellectual in the IPR in the interwar period was Frederic Eggleston, an influential public intellectual and politician who played an influential role in the formation of the

Research School of Pacific Studies (later the Research School of Pacific and Asian Studies) at The Australian National University (Akami 2001: 101–31; see also the introduction to this volume).

It is evident that this culturalist problematic has had considerable impact on shaping public policies towards the study and teaching of Asia. How, though, do we explain the relationship between public policy on Asian engagement and this culturalism? One reason for this relationship is that there is a curious symmetry between the technocratic politics of engagement and culturalism. The Garnaut Report and the Asian Century White Paper were both strongly influenced by the idea that Asian engagement needed the right set of economic policies, but the extra economic dimensions of the engagement were often seen in cultural terms. There is much in the White Paper about the need for productivity and growth in order to compete in the Asian Century, but these objectives are seen in depoliticised terms as requiring the right 'cultural fix'. On this basis, the politics of engagement is dislocated from the economic and social relations of power and conflict. Consequently, when the White Paper grapples with the key problem of institutional collaboration and partnership of business and government—which it sees as vital for engagement—it frames these problems as one of developing the cultural skills, such as language, which are seen as essential for collaboration. Institutional reform, in this view, is depoliticised in favour of a narrative of cultural engagement divorced from the messy political and social conflicts of institutional transformation in Australia.

For this reason, there is an affinity between the technocratic politics of engagement or institutional reform and the culturalist problematic. To the extent that institutional reform becomes a central plank of technocratic projects, the 'extra economic' problems associated with it are seen in depoliticised terms as failures of cultural adaptation. Stoler (2008) argues that epistemic anxieties arise when technocrats face circumstances and problems for which their analytical skills prove to be a poor fit for the policy or regulatory objectives they seek to manage. In the case of Asian engagement, this failure leads to the use of culturalist frameworks to manage new problems or issues, but in a way that avoids the analysis of political and social conflict. It is this affinity between the culturalist and technocratic analyses that then becomes a significant driver of policy investment in teaching and research in Asia. This is seen in the priority given to language in the White Paper. More generally, it is evident in the general bias towards the humanities disciplines, and the corresponding neglect of social sciences.

The other key issues relating to the relationship between public policy on Asian engagement and the effects of the culturalist problematic are the insulation and demarcation of the region from Australia. Walker (1999) has argued that there is a 'cartographic anxiety' in Australian engagement with the region. He argues that the 'powerful masculinising and racialising impulse in Australian nationalism would have been a great deal less intense, had it not been for the geo-political threat attributed to awakening Asia from the 1880s' (Walker 1999: 5). As I have observed elsewhere (Jayasuriya 2010), these cartographic notions of Asian engagement have become central to political projects of economic modernisation after the Hawke–Keating reforms of the 1980s and 1990s. In this political project, 'Asia' was seen in terms of the economic benefits—manifested in a growing middle class—that it could provide as the basis of continued Australian prosperity. This would only occur, however, if Asia could modernise and adapt its institutions to take advantage of the region's economic growth. These politics of modernisation were a core element of the statecraft of the Labor governments. Engaging with Asia is not only central to economic modernisation, it is also related to the social modernisation of Australia—associated with policies of Asia literacy and multiculturalism.

It is here that public investment in the study and teaching of Asia has become a central component of the political project of Asian engagement. This is best summed up by Kevin Rudd, in his first incarnation as prime minster, when he hoped that 'we become not just the most Asia-literate country in the collective west but also the most China-literate country, because it's going to be such a huge impacting factor for Australia's future' (quoted in Walker 2013: 28). This quote is revealing, in that programs of Asia literacy are core elements not only of the engagement policy, but also of the way in which it serves to demarcate cultural boundaries between Australia and the region. It is for this reason that public investment in the teaching and study of Asia, underpinned by the culturalist problematic of Asia literacy or Asia capability, has been a pivotal component of statecraft projects of economic modernisation in Australia.

Towards a problem-solving approach

These Asia capability approaches propose that it is necessary to become literate about a region 'out there' rather than generating an in-depth knowledge of a common set of problems pertaining to the region as a whole. It is not area studies per se that is problematic here but the fact that these approaches are located within an Asia literacy strategy that rests on a particular set of assumptions about the mainsprings of social and political change. These assumptions effectively depoliticise or marginalise economic and social problems, while downplaying the fact that challenges in the region are often of a trans-boundary nature. Consequently, this focus on the understanding of the distinctiveness of cultural arrangements sidelines the analysis of common trends, problems and processes.

To overcome the limitations of the Asia literacy model research strategy, which has been dominant in recent times, I suggest that we adopt a 'problem-oriented research strategy' (PORS) based on the new social and political circumstances of the region. This strategy will mould the research around key issues, problems and puzzles of social, economic and political transformation pertaining to the region as a whole. These are rooted in tangible real-world problems, but their analysis has broader theoretical relevance for social science and humanities disciplines. As such, this orientation will enable us to move beyond simplistic distinctions between applied and basic research, and involve the participation of a broader range of actors—stakeholders, if you like—in the research enterprise.

Increasingly, the governance challenges confronting the region, such as the issue of climate change or financial governance, are the same as those confronting Australian policymakers. Clearly, we need to focus much more on confronting and dealing with these common sets of issues that are often transnational rather than national in origin, while at the same time understanding how they are contested within particular contexts. For this reason, it is imperative that we understand the specificities of countries within our region in a way that locates social, cultural and political change in the broader context of capitalist transformation in the region.

One interesting example of such an approach is what the World Bank calls a 'problem-driven' approach to governance reform and political economy analysis, where it is argued that studies of governance and institutional reform have much to gain by adopting a problem-driven approach. This approach to governance and political economy analysis 'focuses on particular challenges or opportunities, such as analysing why reforms in the power or health sector or those aimed at improving urban development might not have gained traction and what could be done differently to move forward' (World Bank 2009: viii).

Adopting such a perspective enables a specific approach to research on issues of governance reform that focuses on the specific vulnerabilities and problems for reform. This also enables the identification of specific institutional and political economy drivers of both successful and failed reforms. While we may quibble with conclusions reached by this approach—and I certainly do—it has much to warrant serious consideration of a problem-oriented rationale for research on governance reform, and provides an example of a PORS, which differs from the standard approach hitherto operative in the Asia literacy mode of research.

This new approach has a strong trans-disciplinary focus in examining the nature of research problems in its purview. At the same time, it places emphasis on the transnational nature of many contemporary problems, which simply cannot be dealt with in Asia literacy research models. While I do not intend to buy into what has come to be known as the broader debate on Mode 1 and Mode 2 knowledge, the PORS advanced here clearly has affinities with the so-called

Mode 2 forms of knowledge production that emphasise real-world problems and notions of trans-disciplinarity (Gibbons et al. 1994). Mode 1 knowledge is discipline-based in basic research while Mode 2 knowledge places emphasis on problem solving and an inter-disciplinary approach to knowledge production.

The recent emphasis on the Asian Century coincides with this significant shift in the sites and forms of knowledge production. In contrast with the discipline-based focus on knowledge in Modes 1 and 2, knowledge is not rigidly limited to academia, but is located in various webs of strategic alliances and collaborations and includes multiple stakeholders. The crucial point here is that this approach deals with problems within a 'specific and localised context' (Gibbons et al. 1994: 3). While it may be stretching this shift towards a new form of knowledge, it may be useful to consider this as a shift in the balance between Mode 1 and Mode 2 knowledge within the social sciences.

It is clear that the preoccupation with Asia literacy or Asia capability fails to recognise the broader shifts in the nature of social science knowledge. Indeed, the failure of some of our main social science organisations to recognise these shifts has meant that they have not been able to present a persuasive case for the importance of investing in social science research as a means of dealing with pressing social and economic problems in the region. A striking contrast here is the Social Science Research Council (SSRC) in the United States, which has been active in promoting the kind of problem-solving strategy advocated here. Nevertheless, the rationale advanced here for a PORS does not depend on arguments about changing notions of knowledge production. Neither do we argue for abandoning country-focused studies or area studies—an expertise that is also crucial to our strategy. These are situated, however, within an orientation that departs from outdated notions of Asia literacy.

Key features of this approach

Let me summarise this model. The key features are:

- an issue or problem-oriented strategy that bypasses the country-focused or area studies Asia literacy models
- a research enterprise that gives weight to the transnational and trans-disciplinary nature of contemporary problems such as inequality or climate change and, as such, calls for work across the disciplines
- an emphasis on the importance of solving problems as a way of advancing basic social science, and the potential to build partnerships with actors—academic and non-academic—in the formulation and organisation of projects, so that the funding of research needs to be couched in non-instrumental ways.

No doubt, this approach is not devoid of problems—such as issues of academic autonomy—which will need to be properly managed and organised. There is also a serious danger of research becoming instrumental and driven by short-term considerations. In thinking about these issues, however, we need to connect the idea of problem solving with a more general concern about the challenges of providing funding and distributing public and collective goods. The challenge for the social scientist is to conceive of these goods beyond the 'national frame' and, at the same time, to consider how to engage with multiple groups and interests in the formulation of these global societal challenges.

The final advantage of this problem-oriented strategy is that there is much that we can learn from Asia-based social scientists dealing with contemporary challenges and problems that are not simply universal. To provide a few examples: Chinese scholar Cui Zhiyuan (2005) has emerged as one of the key thinkers of the Chinese New Left. We might disagree with the framework he has developed in his writing—namely, to theorise the notion of property as a bundle of rights in Chinese economic reforms. Nonetheless, his framework allows him to move beyond a simple identification of Chinese enterprises as either private or state. He forces us to think about the nature of state enterprise and the possibilities of market reform in a more complex and sophisticated way. This has significant implications for the increasingly hybrid nature of property in the West, as much as in China. It also has implications for Western, including Australian, attempts to regulate foreign investment by state-owned Chinese enterprises. In a different context, Thai scholar Pasuk Phongpaichit has worked extensively on the informal economy—sex work and gambling—and the way it shapes not just the formal economy but also structures of politics (Phongpaichit et al. 1998). Her work on the informal economy is of interest not just in Thailand, but also has wider ramification for countries like Australia, where the gambling and sex industries have become key economic players. One final example: the Indian political scientist Neera Chandhoke has written perceptively and critically on issues of civil society organisation and the state, particularly around partnership with the state. She argues that recent moves towards partnership have blunted the political edge of civil society. This is a point that applies not just to India but also to the broader changes in the relationship between civil society and the state in other countries (Chandhoke 1995).

Conclusion: A global social science?

This chapter has touched on only one dimension—the culturalist problematic—of the difficulty of constructing a global social science. Equally important—and this is really the subject for another essay—is to move beyond the methodological nationalism of the social sciences. Methodological nationalism takes for granted the nation-state and society as its frame of reference (see also Patel in this volume). Methodological nationalism is ingrained in the social sciences. Certainly, given that the nation-state and society are more visible in the postcolonial era, the process of nation-state formation remains a prominent feature of area studies. Nevertheless, the dominant focus of area studies continues to be territorially bounded within the nation-state and society.

A critical issue relating to methodological nationalism is its failure to recognise that many of the pressing concerns—such as the provision of public goods, inequality and migration—can no longer be isolated within a national context. The source and transformation of global forces have challenged some of these national elements. This clearly suggests that one of the defining features of global social science is likely to be the adoption of a transnational perspective, denoting a close examination of the social and political mechanisms that link various parts of the globe. It is more useful to consider the entanglement of the United States and China in the emerging Asian economy than to concentrate on unproductive debates over the demise of the United States or the rise of Asia. It seems to me that the connections and linkages are precisely what make the rapid capitalist transformation of China more explicable. The fact that party capitalism in China feeds on the debt of private consumption in the United States is just one example of how a focus on transnational linkages enhances our understanding of the great transformation now under way in Asia.

These transnational processes have always been with us, but it is clear that the nature of these interconnections and mechanisms has intensified in a way that challenges some of the methodological, nationalist assumptions of the culturalist problematic. Again, none of this should be surprising for those who study Asia seriously. It needs to be acknowledged that the very concept of Asia itself is a product of these changing connections and networks. Scholars of Asia are ideally placed to exploit the advantages of such a transnational perspective. To this end, however, we need to shift away from the area studies approach that defines so much of the research on Asia.

Finally, and most importantly, this requires building a real set of institutional partnerships and linkages with the rapidly developing social science community in Asia. This illustrates the need for a pivotal shift in the nature of the production of knowledge on Asia that will impact on the methods and priorities of research in countries such as Australia and the United States. No doubt, scholars in Asia, Australia and the United States work within very different political constraints, but here is the opportunity to build a more global as well as a more equitable social science community. All of this requires that we move beyond the culturalist problematic and the associated notions of Asia literacy and Asia capability that have shaped Australian public policy.

References

Akami, Tomoko. 2001. Frederic Eggleston and Oriental power, 1925–1929. In Paul Jones and Vera Mackie, eds. *Relationships: Japan and Australia, 1870s–1950s*. Melbourne: History Monographs and RMIT Publishing.

Akami, Tomoko. 2002. *Internationalizing the Pacific: The United States, Japan, and the Institute of Pacific Relations in war and peace*. Oxon: Routledge.

Asialink. 2013. Media release. National Centre for Asia Capability, Melbourne. URL: asialink.unimelb.edu.au/media/media_releases/media_releases. Consulted 4 December 2014.

Asian Studies Council. 1989. *Asia in Australian higher education*. Canberra: Asian Studies Council.

Auchmuty, James J. 1971. *The Teaching of Asian languages and cultures: Report of the Commonwealth Advisory Committee*. Canberra: Commonwealth Government Printing Office.

Barmé, Geremie. 2005. The new Sinology. *Chinese Studies Association of Australia Newsletter* 31 (May 2005). URL: ciw.anu.edu.au/new_sinology/index.php. Consulted 4 December 2014.

Beeson, Mark and Jayasuriya, Kanishka. 2009. The politics of Asian engagement: Ideas, institutions and academics. *Australian Journal of Politics and History* 55(3): 360–74.

Bisley, Nick. 2012. China's rise and the making of East Asia's security architecture. *Journal of Contemporary China* 21(73): 19–34.

Bonnett, Alastair. 2012. The critical traditionalism of Ashis Nandy: Occidentalism and the dilemmas of innocence. *Theory, Culture and Society* 29(1): 138–57.

Brown, Nicholas. 1990. Australian intellectuals and the image of Asia, 1920–1960. *Australian Cultural History* 9: 80–92.

Cui, Zhiyuan. 2005. Liberal socialism and the future of China: A petty bourgeoisie manifesto. In Cao Tianyu, ed. *China's model for modern development*. Oxon: Routledge.

Callahan, William A. 2012. Sino-speak: Chinese exceptionalism and the politics of history. *Journal of Asian Studies* 71(1): 33–55.

Chandhoke, Neera. 1995. *State and civil society: Exploration in political theory*. New Delhi: Sage.

Commonwealth of Australia. 2012. *Australia in the Asian Century*. White Paper. Canberra: Commonwealth of Australia. URL: asiancentury.dpmc.gov.au/white-paper. Consulted 7 October 2013.

Department of Education (Western Australia) 2014. *What is Asia literacy?* Perth: Department of Education. URL: det.wa.edu.au/curriculumsupport/asialiteracy/detcms/navigation/what-is-asia-literacy. Consulted 4 December 2014.

Dirks, Nicholas B. 2001. *Castes of mind: Colonialism and the making of modern India*. Princeton, NJ: Princeton University Press

FitzGerald, Stephen. 1980. *Asia in Australian education: Report of the Committee of Asian Studies to the Asian Studies Association of Australia*. Canberra: ASAA.

Gaonkar, Dilip Parameshwar. ed. 2001. *Alternative modernities*. Durham, NC: Duke University Press.

Garnaut, Ross. 1989. *Australia and the Northeast Asian ascendancy*. Canberra: Australian Government Publishing Service.

Gibbons, Michael, Limoges, Camille, Nowotny, Helga, Schwartzman, Simon, Scott, Peter and Trow, Martin. 1994. *The new production of knowledge: The dynamics of science and research in contemporary society*. London: Sage.

Higgott, Richard. 1983. *Political development theory: The contemporary debate*. London: Routledge.

Jayasuriya, Kanishka. 2010. Building citizens: Empire, Asia and the Australian settlement. *Australian Journal of Political Science* 45(1): 29–43.

Kang, David C. 2007. *China rising: Peace, power and order in East Asia*. New York: Columbia University Press.

Mamdani, Mahmood. 1996. *Citizen and subject: Contemporary Africa and the legacy of late colonialism*. Princeton, NJ: Princeton University Press.

Patel, Sujata. 2006. Beyond binaries: A case for self-reflexive sociologies. *Current Sociology* 54(3): 381–95.

Phongpaichit, Pasuk, Piriyarangsan, Sungsidh and Treerat, Nualnoi. 1998. *Gangs, gambling, gaming: Thailand's illegal economy and public policy*. Bangkok: Silkworm.

Shepherd, Jack. 1939. *Australian interests and policies in the Far East*. New York: Institute of Pacific Relations.

Sternhell, Zeev. 2009. *The anti-Enlightenment tradition*. New Haven, CT: Yale University Press.

Stoler, Ann Laura. 2008. *Along the archival grain: Epistemic anxieties and colonial common sense*. Princeton, NJ: Princeton University Press.

Walker, David. 1999. *Anxious nation: Australia and the rise of Asia 1850–1939*. Brisbane: University of Queensland Press.

Walker, David. 2013. *Experiencing turbulence: Asia in the Australian imaginary*. New Delhi: Readworthy.

World Bank. 2009. *Problem driven governance and political economy analysis*. Washington, DC: World Bank.

6

Voices and choices in reproductive rights: Scholarship and activism

Sylvia Estrada-Claudio

There has been a long struggle for reproductive health in the Philippines. In this chapter, I reflect on the process leading up to the passage of the Reproductive Health Bill in the Philippines in December 2012. Although there is much to be dissatisfied with in the implementation of the Bill, the process leading up to its passage in 2012 is instructive. This prompts reflection on the role of academics in promoting social change, the possibility of coalitions between academics and activists, and the importance of transnational solidarity, even in campaigns focused largely in a particular national context. Opposition to the Bill, on the part of the Catholic Church of the Philippines, also drew on international connections and communication between conservative lobby groups. Furthermore, policies on reproductive health and human rights issues have international repercussions where they weaken the efficacy of international agreements on such issues.

On 13 December 2012, the House of Representatives (HOR) of the Republic of the Philippines passed, on second reading, House Bill 4244,[1] better known as the RH (Reproductive Health) Bill. The passage in the HOR on second reading gave

---

1   The full title is *An Act Providing for a Comprehensive Policy on Responsible Parenthood, Reproductive Health, and Population and Development, and for Other Purposes*. Hereinafter, 'Reproductive Health Bill' or 'RH Bill'.

President Benigno Simeon Aquino III the necessary political capital to certify the Bill as urgent. This paved the way for the Philippines Senate to set aside the mandated three-day waiting period between second and third readings of its own version, *An Act Providing for a National Policy on Reproductive Health and Population and Development*, and vote the Bill into law on 17 December 2012. On that same day, the HOR voted to pass the Reproductive Health Bill into law on third reading. President Aquino subsequently signed the consolidated version of both houses of the Philippine Congress on 21 December 2012 into law as the *The Responsible Parenthood and Reproductive Health Act* of 2012 (hereinafter, the RH law). Subsequently, on 16 March 2013, the RH law's implementing rules and regulations were also signed, in a working-class community in Manila.

The certification of the RH Bill as urgent was necessary because the last weeks of 2012 were also the last few weeks before the adjournment of the Fifteenth Congress. After 12 years,[2] beginning with the Twelfth Congress, the Philippines finally had a law that mandated the provision of reproductive health services[3]— that is, until 19 March 2013, when, in response to petitions alleging the law to be unconstitutional, the Supreme Court issued a *status quo ante* order (SQAO) stopping implementation for 120 days (*Republic of the Philippines, Supreme Court En Banc Notice*, 19 March 2013). On 8 April 2014, the Supreme Court ruled that the law was 'not unconstitutional' but struck down eight provisions partially or in full (Bernal 2014). Advocates of the Bill (now referred to as the law) believe that the provisions struck down do not prevent the implementation of an effective reproductive health program by the Philippine government.

Interest in the struggle for the passage of the law has long extended beyond Philippine society.[4] The long struggle of reproductive health advocates has touched on many themes relevant to this volume: struggles and solidarities across national borders, and the roles of different academies and social science traditions.

The main opposition to the law comes from the Catholic Bishops' Conference in the Philippines (CBCP). The CBCP opposes what it refers to as 'DEATH' legislation, which, according to them, is an acronym for 'divorce, euthanasia,

---

2   Other actors would say that the count actually began in the Eleventh Congress and therefore took 16 years. The difference in dating is in itself indicative of the various views of those who advocated for the law. Advocates who were uncomfortable with what they perceived as a mix of both health and demographic targets in the bills filed in the Eleventh Congress begin their 'count' from the Bill filed during the Twelfth Congress.

3   The law does not change other laws that make abortion illegal under all circumstances. It does, however, mandate the prevention and management of abortion complications and the humane care of women who seek care after a miscarriage or abortion.

4   See, for example, Rina Jimenez David's comments at the 'Women Deliver' international conference on reproductive health, which was held after the issuance of the Supreme Court's *status quo ante* order. Despite this, Jimenez David reports, 'Women Deliver co-organizer Dr. Raj Karim said it was time "to celebrate" in the Philippines, the passage of the RH Law' (Jiminez David 2013).

abortion, total reproductive contraception and homosexuality' (GMA News Online 2008). The Philippine situation reflects closely the social policy positions of the Roman Catholic Church on sexual reproductive rights (CBCP 2000). Thus, the Philippines is the last country in the world that does not allow divorce (after Malta passed a divorce law in 2011) (BBC 2011). It is part of a small minority of countries that penalise abortion under all circumstances, prompting the UN Human Rights Council (UNHRC 2012: 4), in its concluding remarks in its last review of Philippine commitments, to recommend that the government ensure that exceptions be made to protect the life of the mother and in cases of incest and rape. The Philippines is also part of a diminishing number of countries that do not have an explicit policy on non-discrimination against lesbian, gay, bisexual and transgender (LGBT) peoples—a matter also noted by the UNHRC (2012: 3).

This position is not merely that of the Philippine clergy. The CBCP repeatedly cites its allegiance to Catholic theology as espoused by the curia. The well-known opposition of the Vatican to divorce, euthanasia, abortion, contraception and homosexuality has been a mark of its contemporary theology (Cochrane 2004).

The Philippines is the last bastion of Catholic conservatism in Asia. Through the centuries, since the time of Spanish colonisation, when the Philippines was run like a Catholic theocracy, politicians have been afraid to alienate the church. An oft-cited saying is that 'Philippine politics is addition'. This means that politicians will always welcome the support of any large, organised group like the Catholic church. The previous administration, of Gloria Macapagal Arroyo, is illustrative. During the regime of her successor, Arroyo has been in and out of jail or house arrest because of several court cases against her, relating to election sabotage and plunder (Salaverria 2012). Her presidency survived repeated corruption scandals. The most serious threat, however, was a crisis in which there was credible evidence that she had cheated in order to win the presidency. In the cases of former presidents Ferdinand Marcos (1979–89) and Joseph Estrada (1988–2001), the church had been a factor in their ousting. In the case of Arroyo, the church has proven to be her saviour (Rufo 2013: 123–27). During her administration, Arroyo and most of her allies in the legislature ensured the defeat of reproductive health bills. She has also consistently de-emphasised and defunded reproductive health programs in the country (Estrada-Claudio 2010).

The Philippines has become increasingly important to the Vatican because Catholicism is waning in Europe and in areas where the church had influence as a result of colonialism, such as Latin America. Hagopian (2009: 2) cites several challenges to the Catholic church's power in Latin America, including centre-left and leftist politicians who are 'responsive to new demands for social and family policy reform and reproductive rights that run counter to the church's teachings'. Hagopian further cites several examples of the increasingly libertarian laws around homosexuality, divorce and abortion in Latin America (2009: 2). Thus, the outcome of reproductive health legislation in the Philippines is significant to the Vatican. It is also, of course, significant to the individuals, institutions and movements who seek to strengthen women's rights.

The connivance of the Philippine government with the Vatican plays out in the international arena as well, where the Philippines has often served as a Vatican ally in struggles in forums such as the UN International Conference on Population and Development (UNICPD) (Danguilan 1997). Women's rights activists working in the United Nations have waged decades-long battles with the Vatican because of its fundamentalist positions. Indeed, in 2006, UN secretary-general Kofi Anan stated that the 'politicization of culture in the form of religious "fundamentalisms" in diverse geographic and religious contexts has become a serious challenge to efforts to secure women's human rights' (UN 2006: 30).

In the case of Catholic fundamentalism or extremism, therefore, I would argue that the Philippines is on the front line. The struggle for reproductive health legislation is a local struggle that has global repercussions for all societies seeking to establish an effective human rights regime in the international arena. The international arena has permissive or restrictive effects for many national contexts, even for those in the developed world.

The logistical and ideological support for the anti-RH position from forces outside the Philippines is another example of the transnational nature of certain local struggles. The websites of the organisations which petitioned the Supreme Court to declare the RH law unconstitutional show that they either are affiliates of international organisations or have links to organisations in other countries— notably, the United States.[5]

The arguments used by anti-RH advocates in the Philippines not only echo the Vatican line that contraception is sinful, they also echo quasi-scientific arguments that can be found among US-based fundamentalist groups. Those who petitioned the Supreme Court of the Philippines to invalidate the RH law argue that it violates a constitutional provision that 'equally protects the rights of the mother and the unborn from the moment of conception'. They argue that some hormonal preparations and the intrauterine device

---

5   The Supreme Court petitioner, Alliance for the Family Foundation Philippines, is linked to the American Life League. On the American Life League, see Alliance for the Family Foundation Philippines (n.d.). Another petitioner, Pro-Life Philippines (2015), notes in its history that it began with its founder Sr Pilar Verzosa meeting the founder of Human Life International (HLI). HLI is a US-based organisation that lists Dr Ligaya Acosta as its Regional Director for Asia and Oceania. See Human Life International (n.d.). Dr Acosta is a Filipina who is one of the main spokespeople of the anti-RH movement. The website of HLI (www.hli.org) also has several features on the RH struggle in the Philippines. See Footnote 7 for the link to the Supreme Court *en banc* decision to consolidate petitions. Petitioners are listed on the first page of that document.

(IUD) work to prevent the implantation of the fertilised ovum, and that these contraceptives therefore cause abortion. This is the very same argument we see coming from the American Association of ProLife Obstetricians and Gynecologists (Colliton n.d.). It would seem that the Vatican itself knows the importance of the link between local struggles and the international arena, as it has worked with other fundamentalist governments and forces to turn back human rights work at the United Nations.[6]

Another theme is the relationship between the academy, society and nation-building. Many of the academics who became involved in the campaign for the RH Bill considered involvement in the effort part of their scholarship. This kind of engagement continues a tradition of academic involvement in nation-building and in postcolonial struggles. This type of engagement is also nuanced by the particular history of the academic institution and its own engagement with colonialism, anticolonial struggles and nation-building, as I will discuss below. To do so, it is necessary to give a short description of the universities that became players in the national debate on the RH law. I shall begin by describing two universities that, as institutions, are polar opposites: the University of the Philippines (UP) and the University of Santo Tomas (UST).

At the time of its establishment in 1908, UP was the showcase for the libertarian and Enlightenment ideals of the American occupiers. The leading academic institution at that time was the Pontifical UST (de Dios 2008: 1). Established in 1611, the UST became a symbol of theocratic abuses in education under Spanish colonialism. This is epitomised in the description of a physics class at the UST in the novel *El Filibusterismo* (The Filibuster) by the Philippines' national hero, José Rizal (1861–96). The UST had resisted a decree in 1868 by the Spanish revolutionary government to secularise and be renamed the University of the Philippines. That resistance lasted until the restoration of the monarchy, making the decree moot (Abinales and Amoroso 2005: 93). UST was bestowed the title of 'Pontifical University' in 1902 and 'The Catholic University of the Philippines' in 1947 (UST n.d.). Thus, UP and UST have been perceived by historians and many present-day members of these institutions as contrapuntal.

---

6   It must be noted that fundamentalism and intolerance are not confined to Roman Catholicism but are seen in all religions. Thus, in the United Nations, alliances are formed between conservatives from various religious groups. Such alliances caught the world's attention in 1994 during the UN International Conference on Population and Development in Cairo, as noted by Freedman (1996). Ten years later, in November 2004, Catholic, Muslim and US-based Christian fundamentalists met in Doha to discuss a united opposition to feminist interventions in the United Nations. Designated Muslim and Christian groups and individuals who organised the first meeting have since cooperated on joint actions, which have been particularly troubling in the United Nations, where the alliance has worked through the governmental delegations of several Arab countries. For example, a week after the Doha conference, the Government of Qatar put forward a conservative resolution on the family to the UN General Assembly, which was approved without a vote. This dismayed European countries and several others (Whitaker 2005).

While both institutions, especially the secular and rambunctious UP, had both pro-RH and anti-RH adherents, the UP, through various university council resolutions, college positions and individual statements by its faculty and staff, had been a bastion of support for the RH Bill. UST, on the other hand, had served as a bastion of support for the anti-RH position.

The UP, through its various experts, had also served as technical support for the authors of the Bill in both chambers of the Philippine Congress. The technical support that the UP contributed to the RH struggle involved demographers, economists, development specialists, psychologists and health experts, to name a few. Demographers from the UP Population Institute, for example, provided the research and analysis that allowed a 'good enough' estimate of the country's maternal mortality rates.[7] These high rates were then cited by health experts to underscore the need for access to contraceptives and to trained personnel and health facilities—key measures mandated in the law.

Two points need to be made here: first, scholars engaged in national events find that their scholarship, disciplinary interests and explorations are guided by what they feel their people need in order to live in dignity. Second, such engagement, however, is not merely one that extracts ideas such as research agendas from social movements. Rather, it gives back to these social movements. For it to be truly helpful, it requires the full application of scholarly discipline and rigour because the statements that were made during the course of the national debates were subject to the strongest contestation and scrutiny. In this sense, the UP faculty who supported the passage of the law were fulfilling UP's role as the secular and scientific voice for the nation.

The UST, on the other hand, consistent with its character as a Catholic university, firmly and officially opposed the passage of the RH law. Many of its faculty members would confront their pro-RH counterparts (many from UP) in debates, forums, roundtables and the like. Typically, while UP professors stuck to mainly scientific arguments, UST faculty would often refer to Catholic doctrine.

The academic fisticuffs between the UP and UST would eventually turn into a barroom brawl. In 2008, 14 professors from the Jesuit-run Ateneo de Manila University called for the immediate passage of the RH Bill.[8] The professors stated clearly that the call was made in their capacity as individuals and was not that of the Ateneo. Nevertheless, the statement could not but carry the institutional cachet of the Ateneo. More importantly, however, the Ateneo

---

7   See, for example, the report by the Guttmacher Institute (2009). The report is co-authored by the UP Population Institute and Likhaan, a non-governmental organisation (NGO). The report itself illustrates the nature of the RH struggle in which an international and US-based private entity (Guttmacher) worked with an academic institution (UP) and an NGO.

8   See the position paper on the RH Bill by Individual Faculty of the Ateneo de Manila University (2008).

professors challenged the hegemony of the anti-RH position within Catholic doctrine and argumentation. Citing the church's own teachings, they stated that Catholics could support the RH Bill in good conscience.

Voices against the RH Bill also came from within UP, with some professors[9] circulating a position paper questioning certain demographic premises of the Bill and what these professors claimed were mistaken notions about population and the environment espoused in the Bill. Typical of UP, however, the position paper posed secular arguments rather than scientific ones.

The differences among the UP professors did not generate as much heat as the differences between the faculties of the Catholic universities of UST and Ateneo. While it is difficult to speculate on the reasons, it is typical and expected of the secular UP to contain divergent voices. The pro-RH position, representing as it does the position of mainstream scientific institutions such as the World Health Organization (WHO), had perhaps established a comfortable hegemony in UP. The Ateneo position, however, disrupted the hegemonic position of the anti-RH stance in the Catholic schools.

Anyone who is familiar with church history would not be surprised that a Jesuit-run institution would play such a role. In the Philippines, too, José Rizal was said to have remarked as he walked by the Ateneo on his way to his execution: 'All that the Jesuits taught me was good and virtuous' (National Historical Commission of the Philippines n.d.). This contrasts with his caustic portrayal of the UST physics classroom in *The Filibuster*.

The academic intramural debates over the RH Bill intensified in the final years of the campaign to pass the Bill into law. In March 2011, more than 200 professors from UP and Ateneo released a joint statement supporting the RH Bill.[10] By this point, the original 14 professors who had signed the 2010 statement had increased their ranks several-fold. In August 2012, 192 professors from the Ateneo released yet another statement in support of the Bill. This produced the strongest backlash against these professors yet, with anti-RH forces, including

---

9   One cannot ascertain the number. As an advocate, I scrutinised the initial paper posted on the Internet, but it is no longer available. I could not verify the identities of most of the signatories. Many were clearly not UP faculty and some seemed to be alumni. I subsequently met two UP professors at a televised debate who claimed to be members of the group and responsible for the statement. They refused to state the number of faculty backing their statement. The only available source for this effort that I could find is a Facebook page with the name 'UP Students, Faculty and Alumni Against the RH Bill'. One clear arena for this struggle is new social media, but this is beyond the scope of this essay. There is also a Facebook page, 'Ateneans for RH'.

10   The number would have been higher if the Ateneo professors had not urged the release of the statement in March 2011. Many more from the UP had wanted to sign but the institutional context of our colleagues in Ateneo was such that we deemed it wise not to prolong the process of gathering signatures.

some Catholic bishops, calling for their resignation or dismissal (Alave 2012). This also prompted the Ateneo leadership to officially state (yet again) that they supported the official position of the CBCP in opposing the RH Bill.

The following month, September 2012, 45 faculty and staff of De La Salle University (DLSU), a Catholic university founded in 1911 by the Brothers of the Christian Schools (DLSU n.d.), issued a statement of support for the RH Bill. This produced a similar backlash, with calls for their resignation or dismissal. In this case, too, the leadership of De La Salle had to issue a statement of clarification about the university's official position.[11]

An editorial in the *Varsitarian*, the student paper of UST, in October 2012 castigated the pro-RH professors for their refusal to obey official Catholic precepts (*Varsitarian* 2012). The editorial also accused the professors of not telling the truth about contraceptives. This caused a controversy in itself because the editorial was deemed by many to have overstepped the bounds of reasoned discussion, degenerating into name calling. The editorial was the only public indication of 'cracks' in the anti-RH position of UST (Suller 2012).[12] The furore over the editorial eventually caused UST to dissociate itself from the editorial (Rappler 2012).[13]

In October 2012, a day after the release of the UST editorial, UP's Institute for Human Rights and the Center for Women's Studies hosted professors from Ateneo and DLSU in a forum. While the professors who served as speakers were some of the leading voices for the RH struggle, the topic of the forum was not the RH Bill. It was about the threats to academic freedom posed by those calling for the investigation of the professors of DLSU and Ateneo who had supported the Bill.

The threat to academic freedom from conservative religious movements is not merely a threat to educational institutions; yet academia is most vulnerable to fundamentalist movements because free thought is a necessary condition

11   In wonderfully nuanced statements, both DLSU and Ateneo nonetheless upheld the value of the differing voices of their faculty despite reiterating the church's position on the RH Bill.
12   The article cites one tweet from a UST student, @mashi_carigms: 'To every person who found the Varsitarian article derogatory & offensive, as a Thomasian, I apologize for the blatant display of disrespect.' The article also reports the editorial of the Ateneo student paper, the *Guidon*, reacting to the UST editorial. The reaction echoes two tropes: the first being the claim to scientific authority by pro-RH advocates, and the second, an echo of Rizal's condemnation of the church's educational approach. The article quotes the *Guidon* as saying, 'Time and again, statistics have been disregarded and research has been misrepresented—not to mention plagiarized—in the effort to fight the bill. Ignorant and condemnatory statements have been made, invoking a rigid kind of Catholic theologizing completely out of touch with temporal realities.' The article goes on to report that '[t]he *Guidon* editorial said it was unsettling how some members of the Catholic Bishops' Conference of the Philippines "seem to believe that universities are merely channels of indoctrination rather than institutions that foster intelligent discourse"'.
13   When the UST 'dissociated itself' from the statement, it also adverted to more secular values, saying that the *Varsitarian* was an independent student publication.

for real scholarship. The strengthening of secular values through the defence of academic freedom as a means to counteract these threats is important. Additionally, in the course of the struggle for the RH Law in the Philippines, activist scholars in and out of academia have become increasingly convinced of the value of secularism in defence of sexual and reproductive rights.

Indeed, among the most important voices in the later part of the RH struggle were those of organisations whose main concern is secularism. These provided a counterpoint to the CBCP's attempt to make its religious stance appear to express the morality of the Philippine majority. This is exemplified by the organisation Filipino Freethinkers, which held the first 'excommunication party' on 26 November 2010. In the light of the CBCP's threat to excommunicate President Aquino for his support of the RH Bill, the party celebrated with the theme 'if supporting the RH Bill means excommunication, excommunicate me' (Filipino Freethinkers 2012).[14]

In the light of the resurgence of fundamentalisms, as noted by Anan (UN 2006), the Philippine case may present scholarship practices and traditions of value to cross-cutting transnational issues related to social development. Wezel (2006) argues that secularist values are important to social development. Using survey data from the World Values Survey, Wezel notes that, despite wide variations in people's orientations, these can be reduced to just two basic dimensions: weak versus strong secular-rational values and weak versus strong self-expression values. Secular-rational values include less emphasis on religion and national pride, more emphasis on independent thinking rather than respect for authorities, and the acceptance of divorce (as a marker for less emphasis on 'familism'). Self-expression values include liberty aspirations (that is, the enjoyment of civil and political rights), the acceptance of homosexuality (as a marker of tolerance of non-conformity), a strong sense of self-direction, participation in petition signing (used as a marker of the public expression of sentiments) and the ability to trust others. Wezel argues that where self-expression and secular-rational values are strong, there is a move towards choice. When the two dimensions are weak, there is a move towards constraint. Wezel concludes that moving from constraint to choice is necessary to human development because it makes people mentally free and allows them to develop their potential. Wezel also notes that at a social level, the move towards choice generates potential for democratic

---

14   As my position is important to one of the themes of this paper, I will add that I am a senior adviser of this young (in terms of membership and number of years of establishment) organisation. Red Tani, one of the founders of the organisation, has noted in several public talks as well as personal communications to me that they were not focused on the RH Bill until I spoke at the first Filipino Freethinker Forum on secularism and reproductive health on 2 March 2009. That talk is available on YouTube (www.youtube.com/watch?v=BAyCZJYc0K0. Consulted 23 September 2013).

reform. Wezel's data also chart countries along the two dimensions, revealing a trend towards choice and democracy in countries that achieve higher levels of economic well-being.

It is this inextricable link between the work of the scholar and the society in which he or she is embedded that is also illustrated by the struggle to pass the RH law. When not toiling in academia, I work with a non-governmental organisation (NGO) called Likhaan (Likhaan n.d.). Our core work has been to provide reproductive health services for women in poor urban communities using principles of participation and organisation. We have been at this work for almost two decades.

Likhaan decided to embark on legislative advocacy because we saw massive violations of women's rights. This has included bans on all forms of modern contraceptives in various local government units. The most notorious of these is a ban in the capital city of Manila imposed by its former mayor from 1998 to 2007 (Demeterio-Melgar et al. 2007). Likhaan has also documented other violations, including the denial of emergency obstetric care and post-abortion care to women. The RH law would, among other things, be an important step towards addressing the unacceptably high maternal mortality rate in the country. Similarly, HIV/AIDS activists see the law as part of a set of measures that would address our still-rising incidence of new infections (Department of Health-National Epidemiology Center 2012).

When we first filed proposed legislation on reproductive health more than a decade ago, it did not pass out of the congressional committee on health— one of the earliest of numerous steps towards passage into law. By the time the Bill was passed by both houses of the Philippines Congress, survey after survey had shown large majorities of our people knew of the provisions of the Bill and supported its passage. That support spans all socioeconomic classes (Social Weather Stations 2011).[15] On the eve of the Supreme Court decision on the constitutionality of the Bill, Social Weather Stations (2014) released the results of a survey showing that 77 per cent of respondents agreed that 'the RH Law follows what the Constitution should stand for, so it is only proper for the Supreme Court to allow it'.[16]

---

15   Other notable findings are that 68 per cent say government should fund all means of family planning, whether artificial or natural. A plurality, 46 per cent, disagree that youth would be promiscuous if family planning were included in sexuality education. These statements were the most controversial aspects of the law because the CBCP and other anti-RH religious groups objected particularly to these provisions.

16   It is interesting that the level of support for contraceptive provision—the heart of the anti-RH argument that the law was unconstitutional—had increased from the 2011 survey. At this point, 84 per cent agreed that the government should provide free contraception.

The importance of this support by the general public cannot be overemphasised. I am not aware of any piece of social legislation in recent Philippine history that has been so thoroughly discussed. It is a testament to the capacity of social movements and allies in other social institutions (media, the academy, certain government agencies) to undertake mass education leading to attitudinal change. Such a phenomenon must surely be of interest to many in the social sciences, including in my own areas of development studies, women's studies and social psychology. Regardless of whether the RH law will be fully implemented (legality being only one step towards full access), it will be interesting to track whether the general public, made aware of its reproductive health rights by the legislative struggle, will demand services from government. Certainly, the Department of Health and related agencies (for example, the Philippine Population Commission) have long registered support for the RH Bill—a change in attitude attributable in part to the advocacy for and passage of the law.[17]

Peculiar to my position as an academic at UP, I cannot but hark back to the university's mandate as stated in its charter: one of UP's functions is to 'lead as a public service university by providing various forms of community, public and volunteer service as well as scholarly and technical assistance to government, the private sector and civil society while maintaining its standards of excellence' (*An Act to Strengthen The University of the Philippines as the National University*, 2008).

As the reader may have guessed, UP's institutional context made it relatively easy for its faculty and staff to advocate for the RH Bill, including undertaking research on the matter. This does not, however, exempt those advocates from having to pay the price of this kind of engaged academic scholarship. In this chapter, I have presented an example of academic engagement that, although by no means the only formula for knowledge generation, is validated by its genuine effect on people's lives and dignity. Yet much of the work has not led to the type of knowledge products and activities given weight by recruitment, tenure and promotions systems (Commission on Community Engaged Scholarship in the

---

17   Dr Esperanza Cabral, for example, the predecessor of the current Department of Health (DOH) secretary, broke ranks with her boss, President Arroyo, in a series of public pronouncements backing both the RH Bill and the principles of reproductive health. On her becoming DOH secretary, a newspaper article stated: 'It will be recalled that Cabral stated her support for a national modern family planning program when she was Department of Social Welfare and Development secretary, going against the Malacañang line of backing only the Catholic Church-approved natural family planning as a national program. She said that there are many members of the Arroyo Cabinet who support the RH bill, but it was she who, by chance, opened up to members of the media. Cabral's predecessor in the Department of Health, Francisco Duque III, strictly toed the Malacañang line during his tenure' (Llaguno 2010). Malacañang is the official residence of the Philippine president and is often used as a synonym for the Office of the Philippine President.

Health Professions 2005).[18] While some knowledge products such as research were necessary for the advocacy, much of the work has been technical support to lawmakers, public statements, primers, newspaper articles, fact sheets, lobbying and organising—activities that would not be classified as scientific publications or as prestigious teaching activities. Indeed, the 'knowledge product' that I would be most proud of in this context is the RH Bill itself. Unfortunately, I cannot claim single, joint or main authorship of this document. Anecdotally, I might add that a number of my colleagues tend to scoff at the various international university ranking systems precisely because ranking criteria do not take into account knowledge products and activities that emerge from our mode of engaged scholarship.

Finally, the experiences of women struggling for sexual and reproductive rights in the Philippines speak to another theme of this volume: the increasing interconnectedness of nations as evidenced in the many efforts towards various forms of regional and transnational integration, and the threats to and possibilities for global solidarity and well-being that this brings. One such threat from the increasing interconnectedness of economic systems involves the current global economic crises that continue to haunt Europe and the United States and which affect large numbers of the world's population. Religious fundamentalisms and other undemocratic political projects are fed by the insecurity and alienation brought about by globalisation, with resultant struggles around the national, tribal and religious identities that often affect women's rights (Estrada-Claudio 2010: 38). Such struggles again take particular national forms of expression, which nonetheless have global implications.

Like feminists in other parts of the world, those of us who have struggled for sexual and reproductive rights have been accused repeatedly of trying to impose Western interests and values.[19] It is not within the purview of this chapter to discuss the disjunctures and conjunctures within the various feminisms. A simple but cogent summary of these nuances, however, can be found in Rabar (2013):

> Many people argue that feminism is a Western ideology and therefore has no place in the Middle Eastern societies. The term feminist and feminism might have been coined in the West, but its goals are worldwide because patriarchy has no language or colour, and female subjugation is a global issue, not just a Western

---

18   Several professor emeriti, university professors and full professors of various universities made public statements in support of the RH Bill, and contributed time to the campaign, including writing informative and persuasive articles for communities and the general public. This fact must be stated because those of us who question current criteria for what is 'academic' are either accused of not being able to live up to these standards or patronised with advice as to how we can get ourselves published in peer-reviewed and reputable scientific and preferably international journals.

19   I direct readers' attention to another *Varsitarian* article in order to reinforce my contention above that the UST served as a bastion of support for the anti-RH forces (*Varsitarian* 2013).

one. If people were to follow this logic, it is akin to saying that Islam belongs to Arab societies because it was created in the Arabian Peninsula. There are dozens of feminist organisations in the Middle East that aim to eradicate inequality within the society. They are not Western organisations but have been initiated by local people with an interest in protecting and promoting the rights of women.

Feminism in the Middle East has its own narratives and differs from the Western feminism in many regards. It is a category in its own right. There are differences between Black feminism, European feminism, Arab feminism and many other types of feminism. It is a unique movement because it encompasses different cultures, and countries, but has only one goal to create egalitarian societies where women are given equal rights and opportunities.

I have often countered the argument that feminists are captured by Western individualistic modes of sexual expression by noting that current conceptions of female sexuality are also foreign impositions. As Melencio (2009) notes, Catholicism and the peculiar sexual mores now touted by conservatives as Philippine tradition were actually imposed on the Philippines by the Spanish colonists.

What these debates highlight is that approaches such as what has been called 'area studies' (Jayasuriya 2012) can often limit the understanding of certain issues within a particular nation. Philippine feminists working for the RH Bill have had to balance the contingencies of various identity positions and struggles. They have managed to balance the demands of Philippine citizenship, the problematics of racism and elitism within feminist movements, and the necessity for cross-border solidarity movements. Like feminists in other locales, they live the contradictions of a desire to preserve the uniqueness of their national culture and identity without sacrificing an allegiance to a human rights regime that sees rights as inalienable and indivisible. I would contend that these strategies, which have been forged within social movements, can be a paradigm for just and equitable forms of integration and globalisation.

First, social science research looking at cross-border issues needs to take into consideration the increasing porousness of national/political barriers as the world becomes even more intertwined and globalised. This calls for a reconsideration of traditional approaches that assume greater homogeneity within nations and a clearer demarcation of national boundaries and processes. Our experiences, therefore, support Jayasuriya's (2012) proposal for a problem-oriented approach in social science research. Such a problem-oriented approach best captures the transnational nature of the significant social struggles that we are undertaking.

Second, despite the increasing interpenetration of national cultures, we must acknowledge the diversity that local contexts bring. For example, let me point out that in the context of our struggle to pass the RH Bill, Philippine academia continues to refresh a very long tradition of academic engagement in national political concerns. Such an engagement works in two ways. On the one hand, our engagement is an attempt to use our expertise in service of our people's desires for social justice and human rights. On the other hand, this engagement deepens our scholarship and directs its parameters. In other words, the Philippine academic tradition that I have discussed here is influenced by its location historically in a postcolonial nation that has remained in a position peripheral to industrial and post-industrial development. In the highly politicised arena of what is considered a 'world-class' institution of higher learning, this particular tradition demands a set of criteria for determining the quality of scholarship different from those that are currently accepted as global criteria. Differing traditions such as these need to be valued if there is a future for regional integration that will benefit the peoples of Asia.

Third, as the White Paper on *Australia in the Asian Century* (Commonwealth of Australia 2012: 3) notes, 'Australia's future is irrevocably tied to the stability and sustainable security of our diverse region'. As citizens and particularly as academics, we need to take a very nuanced and, I would add, a politically informed view of 'diversity'. The engaged scholarship that we are called on to undertake in the Philippines may be very different from the intellectual engagements of academia in other countries in the region. Certain principles such as human rights and freedoms, however, remain matters of cross-cutting concern for academia as well as the larger society.

Regional integration needs to balance the need to preserve cultural diversity and richness with the goals of economic equity and people-to-people solidarity within and across nations. As I have discussed in this essay, some of the practices that can guide this effort arise from social movement actors who lead multiple identities as academics and national citizens who are nonetheless conscious of the demands of being global citizens in an increasingly integrated world.

References

Abinales, Patricio N. and Amoroso, Donna J. 2005. *State and Society in the Philippines*. Lanham, MD: Rowman & Littlefield.

Alave, Kristine L. 2012. Catholic bishop goes after Ateneo professors for heresy. *Philippine Daily Inquirer* 21 August. URL: newsinfo.inquirer. net/254188/catholic-church-wants-pro-rh-bill-ateneo-professors-sacked. Consulted 4 April 2015.

Alliance for the Family Foundation Philippines. n.d. alfi.org.ph/links/. Consulted 28 September 2013.

An Act Providing for a Comprehensive Policy on Responsible Parenthood, Reproductive Health, and Population and Development, and for Other Purposes. House Bill 4244. URL: www.congress.gov.ph/download/basic_15/HB04244. pdf. Consulted 22 July 2013.

An Act Providing for a National Policy on Reproductive Health and Population and Development. SB 2865. URL: www.senate.gov.ph/lisdata/115029777!. pdf. Consulted 22 July 2013.

An Act Providing for a National Policy on Responsible Parenthood and Reproductive Health. RA 10354. URL: www.gov.ph/2012/12/21/republic-act-no-10354/. Consulted 22 July 2013.

An Act to Strengthen The University of the Philippines as the National University. Republic Act No. 9500. 2008. URL: www1.up.edu.ph/wp-content/ uploads/2013/04/RA_9500.pdf. Consulted 24 August 2013.

BBC. 2011. MPs in Catholic Malta pass historic law on divorce. *BBC* 25 July. URL: www.bbc.co.uk/news/world-europe-14285882. Consulted 11 August 2013.

Bernal, Buena. 2014. SC declares RH law constitutional. *Rappler* 8 April. URL: www.rappler.com/nation/54946-supreme-court-rh-law-constitutional. Consulted 5 December 2014.

CBCP [Catholic Bishops' Conference in the Philippines]. 2000. *That they may have life and have it abundantly.* Manila: CBCP. URL: cbcponline.net/v2/?p=449. Consulted 11 August 2013.

Colliton, William, F., jr. n.d. Birth control pill: Abortifacient and contraceptive. URL: www.aaplog.org/position-and-papers/oral-contraceptive-controversy/ birth-control-pill-abortifacient-and-contraceptive/. Consulted 29 September 2013.

Commission on Community Engaged Scholarship in the Health Professions. 2005. *Linking scholarship and communities: Report of the Commission on Community Engaged Scholarship in the Health Profession.* Seattle: Community Partnerships for Health.

Cochrane, Donald. 2004. *The Vatican, sexuality, and homosexuality.* California: University of Saskatchewan. URL: www.usask.ca/education/people/ cochraned/the_vatican.pdf. Consulted 11 August 2013.

Commonwealth of Australia. 2012. *Australia in the Asian Century.* White Paper. Canberra: Commonwealth of Australia.

Danguilan, Marileen J. 1997. *Women in brackets: A chronicle of Vatican power and control*. Manila: Philippine Center for Investigative Journalism.

de Dios, Emmanuel S. 2008. *Secular morality and the university*. Discussion Paper No. 2008, 05. Manila: School of Economics, University of the Philippines.

Demeterio-Melgar, Junice Lirza, Pacete, Jocelyn C., Aguiling-Pangalangan, Elizabeth, Lu, Anna Victoria M. and Sabundayo, Maria Lourdes. 2007. *Imposing misery: Manila's ten year ban on contraceptives*. Pardiss Kerbai, ed. New York: Likhaan, ReproCen and Center for Reproductive Rights. URL: www2.ohchr.org/english/bodies/cescr/docs/info-ngos/CRR_ReportPhilippines.pdf. Consulted 16 November 2012.

Department of Health-National Epidemiology Center. 2012. *Philippine HIV and AIDS registry*. Manila: Department of Health-National Epidemiology Center. URL: aidsdatahub.org/dmdocuments/NEC_HIV_July-AIDSreg2012.pdf. Consulted 12 November 2012.

DLSU [De La Salle University]. n.d. About DLSU. Manila: DLSU. URL: www.dlsu.edu.ph/inside/. Consulted 24 November 2013.

Estrada-Claudio, Sylvia. 2010. Sanctifying moral tyranny: Religious fundamentalisms and the political disempowerment of women. In Claudia Derichs and Andrea Fleschenberg, eds. *Religious fundamentalisms and their gendered impacts in Asia*. Berlin: Friedrich-Ebert, Stiftung.

Filipino Freethinkers. 2012. *Excommunicate me*. 26 November. URL: filipinofreethinkers.org/excommunicateme/. Consulted 23 September 2013.

Freedman, Lynn. 1996. The challenge of fundamentalisms. *Reproductive Health Matters* (8): 55–69.

GMA News Online. 2008. CBCP head scores 'DEATH' bills in congress. *GMA News Online*. URL: www.gmanetwork.com/news/story/106120/news/nation/cbcp-head-scores-death-bills-in-congress. Consulted 12 November 2012.

Guttmacher Institute. 2009. *Meeting women's contraceptive needs in the Philippines*. New York: Guttmacher Institute. URL: www.guttmacher.org/pubs/2009/04/15/IB_MWCNP.pdf. Consulted 21 August 2013.

Hagopian, Frances. 2009. Introduction. In Frances Hagopian, ed. *Religious pluralism, democracy, and the Catholic church in Latin America*. Notre Dame, IN: University of Notre Dame Press.

Human Life International. n.d. Web page. URL: www.hli.org/news/1095-ligaya-acosta. Consulted 29 September 2013.

Individual Faculty of the Ateneo de Manila University. 2008. Catholics can support the RH bill in good conscience. *abs-cbnNEWS.com* 23 October. URL: www.abs-cbnnews.com/views-and-analysis/10/22/08/catholics-can-support-rh-bill-good-conscience-0. Consulted 17 August 2013.

Jayasuriya, Kanishka. 2012. *Building Australian research capacity on Asia: A new problem-oriented strategy*. Indo-Pacific Research Center Policy Brief No. 1. Adelaide: University of Adelaide.

Jiminez David, Rina. 2013. Cheers for RH law at 'Women Deliver'. *Philippine Daily Inquirer* 30 May. URL: opinion.inquirer.net/53639/cheers-for-rh-law-at-women-deliver. Consulted 22 July 2013.

Llaguno, Frankie. 2010. New DOH chief backs reproductive health bill. *ABS-CBN News.Com* 26 January. URL: www.abs-cbnnews.com/lifestyle/01/26/10/new-doh-chief-backs-reproductive-health-bill. Consulted 23 August 2013.

Likhaan. n.d. Likhaan Center for Women's Health Inc. URL: www.likhaan.org/. Consulted 16 November 2012.

Melencio, G. 2009. Historical markers on Filipino women's sexuality during Spanish colonial times. URL: philippinehistory.ph/historical-markers-on-filipino-women%E2%80%99s-sexuality-during-spanish-colonial-times/. Consulted 16 November 2012.

National Historical Commission of the Philippines. n.d. *The life and writings of Dr Jose Rizal*. Manila: National Historical Commission of the Philippines. URL: joserizal.nhcp.gov.ph/Biography/man_and_martyr/chapter17.htm. Consulted 7 August 2013.

Pro-Life Philippines. 2015. *History*. Manila: Pro-Life Philippines. URL: www.prolife.org.ph/?page_id=74. Consulted 15 March 2015.

Rabar, Ruwayda Mustafah. 2013. Five myths about feminism in the Middle East. *Arabian Gazette* 1 February. URL: www.arabiangazette.com/5-myths-about-feminism-in-middle-east/. Consulted 10 October 2013.

Rappler. 2012. UST disowns *Varsitarian*'s stance vs 'lemons, cowards'. *Rappler* 9 October. URL: www.rappler.com/nation/13905-ust-disowns-varsitarian-s-stance-vs-lemons,-cowards. Consulted 20 August 2013.

Republic of the Philippines, Supreme Court En Banc Notice. 19 March 2013. URL: sc.judiciary.gov.ph/jurisprudence/resolutions/2013/03/204819.pdf. Consulted 22 July 2013.

Rufo, Aries C. 2013. *Altar of secrets*. Manila: Journalism for Nation Building Foundation.

Salaverria, Leila B. 2012. Arroyo charged with plunder for misuse of PCSO funds. *Philippine Daily Inquirer* 17 July. URL: newsinfo.inquirer.net/229539/arroyo-slapped-with-plunder-case. Consulted 5 December 2014.

Social Weather Stations. 2011. *Second quarter 2011 social weather survey: 82% say family planning method is a personal choice; 73% want information on legal methods available from government*. 11 August. URL: www.sws.org.ph/pr20110811.htm. Consulted 15 March 2015.

Social Weather Stations. 2014. *SWS confirms survey on RH Law for The Forum for Family Planning and Development*. 7 April. URL: www.sws.org.ph/pr20140407_SWS%20Confirms%20Survey%20on%20RH%20Law%20for%20T he%20Forum%20(media%20release).pdf. Consulted 4 April 2015.

Suller, Erika. 2012. UST student paper calls Ateneo, La Salle lemons and cowards. *Philippine Daily Inquirer* 9 October. URL: newsinfo.inquirer.net/285548/ust-student-paper-calls-ateneo-la-salle-lemons-and-cowards. Consulted 5 December 2014.

UN [United Nations]. 2006. *In-depth study on all forms of violence against women*. Report of the Secretary-General. A/61/122/Add.1 New York: UN. URL: daccess-dds-ny.un.org/doc/UNDOC/GEN/N06/419/74/PDF/N0641974.pdf?OpenElement. Consulted 15 August 2013.

UNHRC [United Nations Human Rights Council]. 2012. *Concluding observations on the fourth periodic report of the Philippines, adopted by the Committee at its 106th session, 15 October to 2 November*. Advanced and unedited copy. New York: UNHRC. URL: reproductiverights.org/sites/crr.civicactions.net/files/documents/crr_Philippines_Concluding_Observations.pdf. Consulted 10 August 2013.

UST [University of Santo Tomas]. n.d. *History*. Manila: UST. URL: www.ust.edu.ph/about-us/history/. Consulted 15 March 2015.

Varsitarian. 2012. Of lemons and cowards. 30 September. URL: www.varsitarian.net/editorial_opinion/editorial/20120930/rh_bill_ateneo_and_la_salle_of_lemons_and_cowards. Consulted 12 October 2012.

Varsitarian. 2013. RH exposed as an imperialist tool. 8 April. URL: www.varsitarian.net/news/20130408/rh_exposed_as_us_imperialist_tool. Consulted 5 December 2014.

Wezel, Christian. 2006. A human development view on value change trends 1981 to 2006. PowerPoint Presentation. World Values Survey. URL: www.worldvaluessurvey.org. Consulted 4 December 2014.

Whitaker, Brian. 2005. Fundamental union. When it comes to defining family values, conservative Christians and Muslims are united against liberal secularists. *The Guardian*, 25 January.

7

Beyond Consumasia:
The neglected challenges

Tessa Morris-Suzuki

Which Asia?

The issue of engaging with Asia raises a question posed by Mahatma Gandhi almost 70 years ago: 'Which Asia?' In March 1947, the first major postwar Asian gathering, the Asian Relations Conference, was held in New Delhi to 'foster mutual contact and understanding' among the nations of the region. One of the speakers was Gandhi, who addressed the closing session. When first invited to this meeting of representatives from all over Asia, though, Gandhi's characteristic response had been to pose a question: which Asia, he asked, would be present at the conference (cited in Samaddar 1996: 40). Reading the White Paper on *Australia in the Asian Century*, I found myself recalling Gandhi's question. The White Paper's executive summary begins with a series of ringing declarations:

> Asia's rise is changing the world. This is the defining feature of the 21st century—the Asian century … Asia's extraordinary ascent has already changed the Australian economy, society and strategic environment … Australia is located in the right place at the right time—in the Asian region in the Asian century. (Commonwealth of Australia 2012: Executive Summary 1)

Yes, but ... which Asia?

The answer is not difficult to discern. The White Paper's executive summary goes on to tell us that

> within only a few years, Asia will not only be the world's largest producer of goods and services, it will also be the world's largest consumer of them. It is already the most populous region in the world. In the future, it will also be home to the majority of the world's middle class. (Commonwealth of Australia 2012: Executive Summary 1)

These words—growth, consumers, middle class—run like a mantra throughout the White Paper. Little boxes in the text give us glimpses of the Asians with whom Australia (but which Australia?) will interact: the stockbroker in Ahmedabad who owns a washing machine, a refrigerator, a television, a DVD player and two mobile phones, 'all of which, with the exception of the refrigerator, are international brands' (Commonwealth of Australia 2012: 64); the Chinese, Indian and Thai tourists who enjoy 'personal experiences customized for customers from Asian countries' at Tangalooma Island Resort (Commonwealth of Australia 2012: 97); the 33,000 accountants across the Asian region who are certified practising accountants with CPA Australia; the highly educated Asian migrants whose technical expertise is boosting Australian economic growth.

In as far as it goes, this is, of course, all true. Many (though not all) countries of Asia are experiencing remarkable rates of economic growth. In many, the size of the middle class is expanding rapidly. Australia's economic fortunes are profoundly dependent on those of the region, and efforts to improve Australian education about and understanding of Asia are to be applauded. The problem is that, in the end, the reader of the White Paper is left with an image of 'Asians' that is utterly different from, but in some ways as one-dimensional as, the images that abounded in Australian, European and US writings about Asia at the height of the Cold War. Then, Asians were poor, hungry, downtrodden and susceptible to the dangerous allure of communism. Now they are upwardly mobile and possessed of marketable skills and an apparently insatiable appetite for the globalised allure of consumerism. Cold War Orientalism presented us with Asians entangled in the ancient bonds of patriarchal families and traditional communities. The White Paper offers us 'Consumasians'—their identities defined by their shopping list of brand-name goods and their folio of graduation certificates.

While the White Paper was being debated in the Australian media, the media was also reporting concerns over the health of 170 asylum-seekers who were on hunger strike in the detention centre on Nauru, having been sent there by an Australia which refuses to abide by its Geneva Convention obligations to process the refugee claims of boat people on its territory. As of January 2015, there were more than 1,800 asylum-seekers detained in overcrowded conditions on Nauru and Manus Island detention centres, many of them from Iran, Afghanistan, Sri Lanka, Myanmar, Bangladesh and other Asian countries, and these detainees were just the tip of a very large iceberg (Australian Customs and Border Protection Service 2015; Hall 2012).

The refugees detained on Nauru and Manus Island should not be seen as representing a separate, poor and suffering Asia to be considered alongside the White Paper's Consumasia. Rather, they are the same people. Many of the detainees, too, are highly educated and in search of upward mobility; almost all of them want a better material life for themselves and their families. They too want to participate in the material abundance of consumer society. To recognise this is not to deny that many have also genuinely suffered fear, violence and persecution in their home countries. The people detained indefinitely in inhumane conditions on Nauru and Manus Island are not the 'other' of the globalised, economically expanding Asia depicted in the White Paper; they are an integral part of that Asia, another dimension of the same complex region, a dimension that complicates the picture.

Which face of 'Asia' do we recognise? With which dimension of Asia will we interact, and how?

The other Cold War

The White Paper, to be fair, does acknowledge some of the complexities. It notes that rapid growth in Asian economic powerhouses such as China and India comes with costs, which include widening gaps between rich and poor and deepening environmental challenges. However, by placing the rise of Asia so squarely in an economic framework—by viewing it almost exclusively through the prism of free-market globalisation—the White Paper obscures some important dimensions of regional change and regional interaction, which become clearly evident if we use other prisms for considering events in the region.

For social scientists and other researchers engaging with various parts of Asia, it is (I would suggest) important to consider the region though a different prism: that of the end of the Cold War and the creation of a post–Cold War order. It is interesting that the White Paper makes only the most fleeting references to the Cold War as an event of a vague and seemingly rather distant past. Reading it with no prior knowledge, you would not guess that there had ever been such things as communism or Maoism. The Vietnam War gets just one mention in the context of migration to Australia, and there is also a single reference to the 'Korean War wool boom'. Yet it could be (and often has been) argued that the economic rise of Japan, South Korea, Taiwan and other economies was closely related to the structures and events of the Cold War. It could also be argued that what is happening in Asia today is all about the uncertain end of the Cold War. Looking at events through this prism, though, requires us to rethink some aspects of conventional wisdom about the Cold War as well as about 'the rise of Asia'.

As Cambridge-based Korean scholar Kwon Heonik observes in his book *The other Cold War*:

> In the media and across academic communities, it is widely assumed that the cold war era ended when the Berlin Wall fell in November 1989. In the subsequent decade, 'after the fall' became the most popular means to express what was then perceived to be the new, hopeful spirit of the time and to contextualize contemporaneous events and developments on the basis of a radical rupture in time … The general consensus about the end of the cold war in chronological terms relates to a broad consensus about the moral implications of the great End. The Cold War ended because the Communist system ran out of steam to compete with the capitalist economy and liberal democracy. (Kwon 2010: 4–5)

As Kwon also points out, however, things look very different if you view the Cold War from the perspective of East Asia, particularly (perhaps) from the perspective of Korea. There, of course, despite all the massive transformations of the past three decades, the Cold War has never really finished. The peninsula remains divided by a line even more impenetrable and fiercely guarded than the erstwhile Berlin Wall. Sixty years after the Panmunjom Armistice, no peace treaty has ever been signed to conclude the Korean War. Indeed, North and South Korea do not even have an armistice, since the South Korean government of the day refused to sign the Panmunjom agreement. More broadly, traces of Cold War thought and structure remain embedded in many parts of the region, whether in the US bases that still occupy much of the territory of Okinawa; in the Cold War military alliances that still, virtually unchanged, link Japan and South Korea to the United States; or in the spectres of Mao Zedong and Ho Chi-Minh, whose presences, albeit often in disconcertingly twenty-first-century commodified forms, still haunt the physical and mental alleyways of significant parts of the region.

Looking at things from this perspective, we might tell a different story of the history of the Cold War. In this alternate narrative, the Cold War did not end abruptly in and around Berlin in 1989. Instead, the events that took place in Europe from the late 1980s to early 1990s were just the beginning of a long, slow ending—a gradual and uncertain transition to a post–Cold War order. The end of that ending is being played out here in our region—in East Asia and the Pacific—as we speak. This alternative geography and chronology produce a different, less comforting and more challenging set of moral implications.

For example, they cast into question the moral narrative of the triumph of liberal democracy. The rise of China, and also of other smaller Asian economic powerhouses like Vietnam, shows no clear sign of being accompanied by the triumph of traditional Euro-American forms of liberal democracy, although it is being accompanied by a proliferation of complex and fascinating forms of local activism, and by a churning up of established political ideas. Engaging seriously with this churning of ideas is likely to require something much more profound than 'Asia literacy'. It may require a willingness to rethink some of our most deeply seated assumptions about the nature of political debate and even about the meaning of politics itself.

Viewing Asia (and particularly East Asia) through the prism of a transition to a post–Cold War order, rather than through the prism of globalised market liberalism, does not necessarily produce a pessimistic view of our region's future, but it does produce a more conjectural view. It casts a sharp spotlight on the uncertainties. How will rising powers such as India and China relate to one another, to the old Cold War great powers Russia and the United States, and to less rapidly growing neighbours such as Japan? Are the economic forces drawing the region together strong enough to resist the political forces that sometimes threaten to pull it apart? The answers to these questions cannot be extrapolated from the present in the way that the White Paper extrapolates future demographic and even economic growth rates, for they depend on political and human contingencies. The region stands finely balanced on the cusp of history, and whether it tips in the direction of a new age of integration or (as some East Asian commentators have suggested) into a second Cold War depends on the choices that regional governments, including the Government of Australia, are making today.

A focus on the difficult and uncertain search for a post–Cold War order reminds us of the great social and conceptual challenges that confront the region. Consider, for example, one analogy. Since the fall of the Berlin Wall in 1989, some 4.3 million people from the former East Germany have left their homes to resettle in the western half of the reunited Germany or in other parts of Western Europe. Although 2.7 million westerners have moved into the east, the area that was once East Germany has lost about 10 per cent of its population. This mass migration has had huge social effects, not only on the receiving regions, but also on the towns and villages that the migrants left behind. The social effects are not experienced uniformly, not least because the migrants are drawn disproportionately from certain sections of the population. They are, by and large, younger and more educated than those who remain behind, and more than two-thirds of them are women. On top of problems of readjustment and sometimes of discrimination in the migrants' new home communities, the outflow of people has left serious age and gender imbalances in the communities they have left behind. One major study of the phenomenon suggests that the concomitant feelings of insecurity have contributed significantly to the rise of neo-Nazism in the former East Germany (Berlin Institut für Bevölkerung und Entwicklung 2007).

The social challenges of a transformation on the divided Korean Peninsula are vastly greater than those that were faced by Germany. East German gross domestic product (GDP) per capita on the eve of German reunification has been estimated to be about 59 per cent of West German GDP per capita. As of 2011, North Korean per capita GDP is estimated to be less than 6 per cent of the South Korean level (Bennett 2013: 26; de Groot et al. 2004: 71). Now imagine what will happen when North Korea, even if it is not reunited with South Korea, starts seriously to open its doors to the rest of the region, as it is almost certain to do with the gradual melting of the last fragments of the region's Cold War ice.

East Asia's impending refugee crisis

I highlight the Korean crisis, both because it is one of the most significant crises facing our region in the Asian century and because it provides one vivid illustration of a crucial regional dilemma that the White Paper does little to address. Of course, there is no particular reason to think that the division between the two Koreas will collapse dramatically, as did the division between the two Germanies. If it did, though, such a collapse would have drastic and indeed almost catastrophic implications for South Korea. Ultimately, in whatever way, greater integration of North Korea into the region will take place, and the effects of this on neighbouring countries—particularly, but not exclusively, South Korea—will be enormous.

The situation in North Korea (the Democratic People's Republic of Korea, DPRK) today is widely misunderstood and misreported in the international press, and is barely mentioned in the White Paper. A particularly widespread misconception is that North Korea is somehow frozen in an unchanging state of communist dictatorship. This view arises from the fact that, at the level of the national leadership, very little has changed in recent years. The reins of power have passed from the founding father, Kim Il-sung (1912–94), to his son Kim Jong-il (1941–2011), and then to his grandson Kim Jong-un. Following the massive famine of the mid-1990s, in which about one million North Koreans are believed to have died, there were some signs of efforts to relax controls on the economy in the late 1990s and the first years of the twenty-first century. Thereafter, though, the government has returned to a repressive policy of attempting to maintain tight controls on any market activity, and in 2009 the state enacted a disastrous re-denomination of the currency, which in effect amounted to a confiscation of the savings of ordinary North Koreans. Initial hints of impending economic liberalisation under the new leader, Kim Jong-un, have yet to produce noticeable effects.

If you look not at the state leadership but at what is happening at a grassroots level, though, a very different, but no less disturbing, picture emerges. Despite repeatedly enacted restrictions and prohibitions on market activity, the market is in fact flourishing and is, in a fascinating way, rising up from below to permeate and devour the structure of the official system. Ironically, then, North Korea provides a vivid example of the flourishing of Asian market economies, which the White Paper commends. The reason for this development in North Korea, however, is very simple: the official system does not work any more. Officially, North Korea has a planned economy in which all significant businesses and all land and real estate are owned by the state. All adult men, having finished a period of universal conscription that lasts for up to six years, are provided with jobs by the state, and the state distribution system (in theory) provides rations of basic foodstuffs to all families on the basis of their consumption needs. In practice, this system has been in a state of collapse for at least the past 15 years. The state distribution system barely functions, and jobs allocated in state-owned enterprises quite often involve very little work and no pay.

One consequence of this collapse is economic catastrophe. North Korea is the only part of our region that stands on the brink of large-scale famine. According to a 2012 UN nutritional survey, some 28 per cent of North Korean children under the age of five show signs of chronic malnutrition that will stunt their future growth and development (Agence France-Presse 2013). A key factor behind the nutritional crisis is a chronic energy shortage. Since the fall of the Soviet Union and other communist regimes, which were major economic supporters and trade partners of the DPRK, North Korea has lacked the energy needed for industry and domestic use, and particularly to produce the fertilisers that are needed to sustain the scientifically selected breeds of rice and other crops introduced in its earlier attempts to boost food production. Fertiliser shortages result in poor yields and soil exhaustion. Meanwhile, fuel shortages lead to the cutting of forests, resulting in massive deforestation, soil erosion, landslides and flooding, further reducing crop yields. Malnutrition is linked to the spread of disease— particularly tuberculosis (TB). The World Health Organization (WHO) estimates the DPRK's rate of TB infection at 345 in 100,000—one of the highest levels outside sub-Saharan Africa. Multi-drug-resistant TB is spreading particularly fast (Perry et al. 2011: 263).

The North Korean government, for all its many faults and failings, is neither ignorant of nor indifferent to these problems. Major reforestation programs are being attempted in various parts of the country. North Korean medical experts work with those from other countries and from organisations like WHO to try to tackle issues of malnutrition and disease. Gradual shifts in policy are leading to the modest expansion of a 'middle-class' consumer society centred on Pyongang. By early 2013, North Korea's mobile phone provider Koryolink had almost two million subscribers (Mirani 2013). As elsewhere, however, such developments also reflect growing gaps between rich and poor, city and country.

Meanwhile, the other side of the crisis is economic and social change, as people do what they have to do to survive. This means cultivating illegal plots of land on mountainsides, crossing the border illegally to buy goods in China in illegal street markets, making handicrafts to sell, and sometimes even setting up small enterprises illegally employing others. It is believed that during the famine of the 1990s, up to 300,000 North Koreans may have crossed into China in an attempt to find a means of survival, most of them subsequently returning to North Korea. At present, the number of North Koreans in China is well below the level of the late 1990s, but may well rise again if famine conditions persist. Within North Korea, meanwhile, the expanding illegal economy now extends surprisingly far. There are numerous reports of a flourishing real estate market in North Korea. North Koreans increasingly pay to exchange state-owned houses or apartments—some seeking to 'trade up' to more desirable residences while others supplement inadequate incomes by 'trading down'. Brokers act as intermediaries in this market. The spread of black or grey market activities is inevitably accompanied by growing corruption. According to one well-informed source whom I interviewed, payments (preferably in foreign currency) are an important part of the process of acquiring membership of the ruling Korean Workers' Party, which is itself a necessary prerequisite for many of the country's most prestigious jobs.

Whatever happens at the leadership level, the massive problems that beset the country are not going away, and they have profound implications for North Korea's neighbours and for the Asia-Pacific region as a whole. Any attempt to reintegrate North Korea into the region will require an effort to address the vast problems—including poverty, malnutrition and energy shortages—that beset the country's people. Indeed, the more North Korea is reintegrated and opens its doors to the region, the more these problems will also affect surrounding countries. Left unaddressed, the massive wealth gap between North Korea and the rest of Northeast Asia will become an ongoing source of future social and economic insecurity.

Human flows and human security

One result of extreme wealth gaps between neighbouring countries is the flow of people from poorer to richer countries. In Australia, recent very unproductive debates about refugee problems have focused on refugees from the Middle East, Afghanistan and Sri Lanka, but any opening of North Korea's doors, however this occurs, is going to lead to new mass movements of people (both within and across the borders of North Korea), which will affect the region, as well as affecting the society of the DPRK itself. Even now, when the Cold War dividing line remains as heavily guarded as ever, cross-border flows are substantial.

The largest group of North Korean emigrants and refugees is almost certainly in China, but the total number of North Koreans currently living in China is unknown. Some South Korean non-governmental organisations (NGOs) cite figures as high as 300,000. However, many scholars put the post-famine number at about 30,000–50,000 (Kim 2012: 45). China responds to the problem in essence by having no policy. It does not recognise undocumented migrants from North Korea as refugees, and officially has a policy of returning those apprehended to the DPRK (where they face imprisonment in terrible conditions). There is, however, abundant evidence to suggest that Chinese authorities do not pursue North Korean undocumented migrants vigorously unless expediency encourages them to do so. Meanwhile, as many as 40,000 North Koreans, including garment workers, mechanics and construction workers, have been encouraged to enter China legally under guest labour schemes (Demick 2012).

China has rightly been criticised by the outside world for its policy, which results in North Korean migrants living in fear, often in hiding, and vulnerable to extreme economic and often also sexual exploitation. It must be said that China is right in pointing out that a large number of North Koreans who cross the border do so primarily for economic rather than for political reasons, and are therefore not strictly speaking 'refugees' in the narrow definition of the Geneva Convention on the Status of Refugees. On the other hand, the Geneva Convention also prohibits 'refoulement'—that is, the practice of sending people (whether recognised as refugees or not) back to home countries where they are liable to persecution. China's practice of returning undocumented entrants to North Korea clearly flies in the face of this provision.

While human rights groups have been vocal in the criticism of China's treatment of North Korean emigrants, there have been few serious efforts by other countries of the region to engage China in dialogue on constructive responses to the problem—particularly on the possibility of creating strategies of 'orderly departure', which would enable North Korean refugees in China to leave for other countries where they could be resettled. An orderly departure program, if nothing else, might at least reduce the number of refugees relying on people smugglers to take them on long, arduous and extremely dangerous onward journeys from China to countries such as Laos, Mongolia or Burma, from where most seek to enter South Korea.

As of August 2012, South Korea had accepted more than 24,000 emigrants from the north, more than half of them arriving since the beginning of 2005 (Republic of Korea Ministry of Unification n.d.). South Korea treats all Koreans as its citizens. There is, therefore, no need for North Koreans who seek refuge in the south to go through a refugee recognition process. Major problems of adjustment, however, face many North Korean 'newly settled people' (*saeteomin*), as they are sometimes called in the south. The South Korean system continues to be based on a structure set in place at the height of the Cold War, when the small numbers of defectors from the north were almost all relatively high-ranking officials, military officers and so on, who were defecting for overtly ideological reasons. The system therefore begins by placing refugees, generally for about a month, in a closed facility for debriefing and identification checks. They are then transferred to a closed residential educational centre, the Hanawon, where they receive education in civics and life skills, designed to turn them into good South Korean citizens (O 2011). Some critics argue that a new approach is needed to assist today's generation of North Korean emigrants to adjust to life in the south. After they leave the Hanawon, refugees can continue to receive support at 30 local Hana centres, and also receive reasonably generous financial assistance from the state. Yet there is abundant evidence that North Korean refugees struggle with problems of social and cultural adaptation. Many suffer from post-traumatic stress disorder (PTSD), which often goes untreated. Unemployment is widespread, and their average wages are far below the South Korean norm. In January 2011, only about 50 per cent of North Korean refugees in the south were in paid employment, and most of those had manual labouring jobs. A study by Emma Campbell at The Australian National University notes that surveys show widespread negative views of North Korean refugees among South Koreans, including those of the younger generation. A 2008 national survey showed that more than half of young South Koreans were opposed to marrying someone from the north, and interview research has also shown that many South Koreans see migrants from the north as likely to be law-breakers or troublemakers (Campbell 2011).

A rapidly growing number of North Korean contract workers—probably now about 20,000—are working on projects in the Russian Far East. There are also believed to be more than 1,000 North Korean refugees in Thailand, several hundred in Laos and Cambodia, an unknown number in Mongolia and about 200 in Japan. Further afield, the United Kingdom has accepted 280 North Korean refugees, Germany more than 200 and the United States 86. Australia does not accept North Korean asylum-seekers because, like many other countries, it accepts South Korea's official definition of all Koreans as being South Korean citizens, and therefore argues that North Korean refugees have a natural place of refuge in the south. As we shall see, however, this view raises serious problems and is likely to become increasingly untenable over time.

An important point to emphasise about the refugee flow from North Korea is that, even more than the movement of people that followed the fall of the Berlin Wall, it appears to be a gendered movement: of 20,407 North Korean refugees in South Korea in 2010, 14,030—or almost 70 per cent—were women (ICG 2011). No reliable figures for North Koreans in China are available, but anecdotal evidence suggests that there, too, women substantially outnumber men.

The role of Australia

Is there a role for Australia in addressing this pressing human security crisis? I believe Australia could potentially play an extremely valuable and positive role, but is currently failing to do so. Although Australia is one of the countries that has a diplomatic relationship with North Korea, this relationship is entirely inactive, and has been for a number of years. In essence, we have put North Korea in the too-hard basket. Australia has continued to contribute to the World Food Program's projects in the DPRK, but otherwise has no aid or development relationship with North Korea and, since 2006, as part of sanctions related to North Korean nuclear testing, has refused to issue visas to North Koreans wishing to come to this country.

In this, we are out of step with many European countries, which have recognised the need for a more positive response to the humanitarian and human security crisis in North Korea. The European Union, for example, cooperates with a number of European governments in providing technical transfer and training programs to assist North Korea to overcome its massive problems of energy and food shortages, soil degradation and deforestation. Although direct food aid of the sort provided by the World Food Program is obviously important in times of crisis, agricultural development projects are likely to be of greater long-term benefit to North Korea's long-suffering people. Development and technical transfer projects are also less susceptible to aid diversion than donations of food.

A few examples can serve to indicate the possibilities. The Dutch government has a program with EU support to provide training for North Korean agricultural technicians in Wageningen University, and also to introduce disease-resistant potato varieties to North Korean agriculture. The Polish government also works with agricultural specialists in North Korea to develop improved methods of crop storage. One particularly interesting example of development support is a Swiss government scheme, developed in cooperation with the North Korean government, to help restore degraded mountainside using new agroforestry practices. An important reason for deforestation in North Korea is that food shortage has driven farmers into remote mountain areas where they secretly create their own private plots to grow food, in the process cutting or burning the natural tree cover. A key feature of the Swiss–North Korean project is that it works with local communities whose members have created illegal private plots, allowing them to continue farming the land on condition that they adopt new recommended soil conservation practices (Xu et al. 2012).

Even the United States, North Korea's most vocal critic, seems to be engaging more closely with North Korean society than does Australia. Although there are no US government schemes to compare with the European ones just mentioned, there are significant examples of non-governmental development assistance. One of the most significant is the long-running project by the American Association for the Advancement of Science, Syracuse University and the US Civilian Research and Development Foundation to work with universities in North Korea to share resources and give lectures about issues including reafforestation, soil quality, river reclamation and agriculture (Taylor and Manyin 2011).

Because of its close economic integration with Northeast Asia, Australia is far more directly affected by events in North Korea than are countries like the Netherlands and Switzerland, and Australia also has a particularly rich store of expertise in areas such as agricultural research, soil regeneration and erosion control. Yet the Australian government and research establishment have completely failed to contribute to these initiatives. Given the current North Korean government's evident moves to attempt some cautious form of opening to the outside world, I would argue that now is the time for Australia to become actively involved in addressing North Korea's human security crisis through well-targeted training, technology transfer and agricultural development projects. The difficulties of running such projects cannot be denied. Careful planning would be needed to make sure that they are effective. Projects should start as small-scale pilots, and be expanded if they show promise. A move away from the too-hard-basket mentality towards cautious but active engagement would not only help to ease one of our region's most pressing humanitarian crises, but also help to make Australia better informed about North Korea and better prepared to respond to future transformations.

At the same time, Australia should not neglect the plight of North Korean refugees, who often struggle to cope even if they are given an opportunity to resettle in South Korea. Other countries, including the United Kingdom and Canada, have shown some degree of willingness to allow limited numbers of North Korean refugees to resettle in those countries, while the United Kingdom also assists North Korean refugees in South Korea by sponsoring English-language courses for them, run through the British Council. Since English-language skills are hard to obtain in North Korea, and are almost essential for career success in the south, this is a measure that is greatly appreciated by many former North Koreans in South Korea. Australia could also take similar initiatives, granting visas selectively to North Korean refugees who find it difficult to adapt to life in South Korea and wish to start a new life elsewhere. There is also obvious scope for Australia to develop schemes, either in South Korea or here in Australia, to provide English-language training for North Korean émigrés.

Huge movements of people—both within and across the boundaries of the rapidly changing nations of Asia—are an inescapable part of the region's future. The twenty-first century is not an age when simple lines can be drawn between the good Consumasians whom we will welcome to our shores to boost our economic growth and the bad 'illegals' who can be kept in their places by tough cross-border policing. The ability to put forward imaginative, long-term and just approaches to tough problems like the North Korean crisis and mass movements of people will be the test of Australia's capacity to contribute to our region's difficult journey into a post–Cold War world.

References

Agence France-Presse. 2013. UN food body approves $200 million food aid to N. Korea. *Agence France-Presse* 8 June. URL: reliefweb.int/report/democratic-peoples-republic-korea/un-food-body-approves-200-mn-food-aid-n-korea. Consulted 17 March 2015.

Australian Customs and Border Protection Service. 2015. *Operation Sovereign Borders: Monthly operational update, January 2015.* Canberra: Australian Customs and Border Protection Service. URL: newsroom.customs.gov.au/channels/Operation-Sovereign-Borders/releases/monthly-operational-update-january-3. Consulted 7 March 2015.

Bennett, Bruce W. 2013. *Preparing for the possibility of a North Korean collapse.* Santa Monica and Washington, DC: Rand Corporation.

Berlin Institut für Bevölkerung und Entwicklung. 2007. *Not am Mann: Von Helden der Arbeit zu neuen Unterschicht?* Berlin: Berlin Institut für Bevölkerung und Entwicklung.

Campbell, Emma. 2011. Changing South Korea: Issues of identity and reunification in formulating the Australia–Korea security policy, foreign policy and wider relationship. *Korea Observer* 42(1): 117–43.

Commonwealth of Australia. 2012. *Australia in the Asian Century.* White Paper. Canberra: Commonwealth of Australia. URL: asiancentury.dpmc.gov.au/white-paper. Consulted 7 October 2013.

de Groot, Henri, Nijkamp, Peter and Stough, Roger. 2004. *Entrepreneurship and regional economic development: A spatial perspective*. Cheltenham: Edward Elgar.

Demick, Barbara. 2012. China hires tens of thousands of North Korea guest workers. *Los Angeles Times* 1 July. URL: articles.latimes.com/2012/jul/01/world/la-fg-china-workers-20120701. Consulted 17 March 2015.

Hall, Bianca. 2012. Hunger strikers slam 'hell hole' camps on Nauru. *Sydney Morning Herald*, 6 November.

ICG [International Crisis Group]. 2011. *Strangers at home: North Koreans in the south*. Asia Report No. 208. Washington, DC: International Crisis Group.

Kim, Mikyoung. 2012. *Securitization of human rights: North Korean refugees in East Asia*. Santa Barbara: ABC/Clio.

Kwon, Heonik. 2010. *The other Cold War*. New York: Columbia University Press.

Mirani, Leo. 2013. Mobile phones are booming in North Korea, of all places. *Business Insider* 26 April. URL: www.businessinsider.com/mobile-phones-are-booming-in-north-korea-of-all-places-2013-4#ixzz3UcwVaE7R. Consulted 17 March 2015.

O, Tara. 2011. The integration of North Korean defectors in South Korea: Problems and prospects. *International Journal of Korean Studies* 15(2): 151–69.

Perry, Sharon, Linton, Heidi and Schoolnik, Gary. 2011. Tuberculosis in North Korea. *Science* 331(21 January): 263.

Republic of Korea Ministry of Unification. n.d. *Humanitarian settlement*. Seoul: Ministry of Unification. URL: www.unikorea.go.kr/eng/default.jsp?pgname=AFFhumanitarian_settlement. Consulted 27 July 2009.

Samaddar, Ranabir. 1996. *Whose Asia is it anyway? Region and nation in South Asia*. Calcutta: Pearl Publishers.

Taylor, Mi Ae and Manyin, Mark E. 2011. *Non-governmental organizations' activities in North Korea*. Washington, DC: Congressional Research Service.

Xu, Jianchu, van Noordwijk, Meine, He, Jun, Kim, Kwang-Ju, Jo, Ryong-Song, Pak, Kon-Gyu, Kye, Un-Hui, Kim, Jong-Sik, Kim, Kwon-Mu, Sim, Yong-Nam, Pak, Je-Un, Song, Ki-Ung, Jong, Yong-Song, Kim, Kwang-Chol, Pang, Chol-Jun and Ho, Myong-Hyok. 2012. Participatory agroforestry development for restoring degraded land in DPR Korea. *Agroforestry Systems* 85 (24 March): 291–30.

8

Rethinking economics in the Asian Century: The market and the state in China

Leong H. Liew

Introduction

A key focus of this book is the importance of intellectual engagement with Asia. Particular emphasis is placed on the new theoretical and practical insights that can be gained by doing so that are relevant to a range of social scientists, regardless of their regional specialisation. In that context, the performance of the Chinese economy in the past 30 years provides a smorgasbord of food for thought (and rethought) about the role of the state in economic development and in the economy more generally. The insights to be gained from examining the Chinese case can be used to reflect on the specificities of the relationship between state and market in other national contexts and the resulting implications for economic theory.

China's post-Mao economic transition has drawn eclectically from economic theory in opening the nation to the market, and has recast the state's role as a selective actor in the marketisation of the economy 'with Chinese characteristics'. The economic results are spectacular. China's purchasing power gross domestic product (GDP) overtook Japan's in 2010 to make China's economy the world's second largest after the United States. Assuming steady reform and no major shock, by 2030 the size of China's economy is projected to exceed that of the United States (WB and DRC 2012: 6).[1] If this is achieved, economic reform will have lifted China from being one of the world's poorest countries to the world's largest economy in roughly 50 years.

The economic reform process has steadily decentralised state administration and eroded the Chinese state's role as central planner with its hand tightly on the economy. The state has not, however, simply retreated to make way for the market. From the start of the economic reform period, the state has played a vital role in strategically steering the nation from a centrally planned to a market economy. The state's role in economic management continues to evolve alongside that of the national economy within a dramatically changing global context. By first 'enhancing' and then 'overriding' the market, the state has contributed significantly to post-Mao economic growth and deserves credit for its role in China's 'economic miracle'.[2]

In this chapter, I examine the role of the state in steering China's post-Mao economic transition, which effectively created conditions for market development and then, with an underlay of the market economy in place, overrode the market to maximise not the usual comparative advantage recognised in neoclassical economics but the economic advantage of the size of China's domestic market and the guarantee that the Chinese Communist Party's monopolistic hold on power would continue. I explain how early post-Mao leaders initially created a constituency for market reform and then proceeded with policies to steer the economy towards a structure compatible with the country's comparative advantage given its relative factor endowments. From the mid-1990s, the state shifted its role to overriding the market in order to build 'national champions' in strategic industries. Here, China began to pursue state-led macroeconomic planning along the lines of the so-called developmental state economic policies that had driven impressive economic growth in Japan and South Korea from the 1960s through the state's strong intervention and extensive regulation and planning.

Yet China's state-led economic development policies mirror those of Japan and South Korea only superficially. Two key differences in particular make the Chinese example *sui generis*. One is size. China's huge landmass and population make the country that much more difficult to govern. Central authority is fragmented and subnational governments can subvert and undermine central

---

1   Subramanian (2011) claimed that China's economy in 2010 was already almost as large as the US economy.
2   Many analysts and officials have referred to East Asia's post–World War II and China's post-Mao economic development experiences as 'miracles'. See, for example, The World Bank and Development Research Center of the State Council, the People's Republic of China (2012: 3).

government industry policies. Size also, however, confers the advantage of a large internal market that can well support industry policy. The other key difference is political structure. In the absence of competition from other political parties, the Chinese Communist Party (CCP) can play a distinctive politico-economic role in shaping the evolving market economy. Yet, as is inevitable in any market economy, the development of markets has given birth to sources of economic power that influence political power and policy and have a huge bearing on the marketisation process. Interest groups have resources to contest official policies[3] and political players can compete for the hearts and minds of the polity, as the example of fallen political star Bo Xilai well illustrates.[4] Hence, sectors of the economy that the party perceives to be strategically significant need to be not only granted favourable treatment but also placed under the control of people who are seen to be at least sympathetic to the party. These factors shape the extent and style of the role of the party/state in China's state-led market reform.

Market-enhancing industry policy

Many neoclassical economists, though not neoliberals, consider state industry policy to be potentially compatible with market reform. Chinese former World Bank chief economist Justin Yifu Lin[5] in his *New structural economics* (Lin 2012), for example, advocates industry policy in developing countries to facilitate economic development. In Lin's perspective, industry policy is appropriate when used to help the private sector to produce according to comparative advantage since industry policy is in this case market enhancing. Lin considers that early post-Mao industry policy was clearly 'comparative advantage following'.

The party/state began China's economic reform with decollectivising the agricultural sector. This did not lead to the immediate freeing of agricultural prices since industry could not afford to pay free-market prices for agricultural inputs while receiving planned prices for outputs. The success of agricultural reform depended on the success of industrial reform, but reforming industry was difficult since introducing the market would create winners and losers, with the latter largely concentrated in the state sector. So, in order to build the

---

3   Interest groups in developing countries often buy their preferred outcomes through bribes.

4   Bo Xilai was removed as party chief of Chongqing in March 2012 and suspended from the Politburo. He was later stripped of all official positions and eventually expelled from the party. On 22 September 2013, he was found guilty of corruption and sentenced to life imprisonment.

5   Justin Lin was born in Taiwan and was a captain in the Republic of China Army before defecting in 1979 to the People's Republic of China. He is a member of the Standing Committee, Chinese People's Political Consultative Council.

necessary constituency of reformers within the party and the state bureaucracy, China's leaders started to develop the market around the planned economy rather than replacing the planned economy altogether.

This plan guaranteed a fixed size of the economy for state-owned enterprises (SOEs), but made the remainder of the economy contestable. State and non-state enterprises were allowed to compete for the non-plan segment. By retaining the plan and allowing the market to operate around it, the party hoped the economy would benefit from the advantages of the market while the state sector would be cushioned from market forces. The competition that the state sector would be exposed to in the market was restricted to sales of non-plan output and purchases of non-plan inputs. This approach would enlarge the economy without harming the state sector (Chen 1987; CPC 1984). This two-track price system is a Pareto-improving strategy, which, by guaranteeing the interests of both the state sector and the officials who managed it, was able to develop a constituency of party and state officials to support this economic reform (Liew 1995). The objective was to arrange for growth out of the plan (Naughton 1995) by first reducing the relative size of the state sector. Only later when the non-state sector had grown sufficiently large enough to absorb underemployed resources of the state sector would attempts be made to shrink the state sector's absolute size.

China's early industry reforms concentrated on developing township and village enterprises (TVEs) and establishing special export zones (SEZs) with tax incentives and other concessions that would attract foreign investment to promote the country's exports. These early efforts were spectacularly successful. The TVEs helped to absorb much of the underemployed labour in the countryside and the export zones laid the foundation for China's later success as a global export powerhouse.

Over the years, China's export structure has been transformed, with a significant shift from agriculture and soft manufactures like textiles and apparel to hard manufactures like consumer electronics, appliances and computers. By 2010, two-fifths of manufacturing exports from developing countries originated from China (Razeen 2011: 5). Transformation of the export structure has not, however, changed the factor intensity of exports, which remain labour intensive. Growth in China's export of hard manufactures is largely due to growth in the processing trade, with Chinese labour assembling high-technology intermediate inputs (Amiti and Freund 2008). Foreign multinational investors in China dominate this processing trade, accounting for 84 per cent of global exports and imports in the trade (Zhou and Latorre 2013).

In the decade after China joined the World Trade Organization (WTO) in 2001, its share of imports in major world markets doubled and accounted for more than 20 per cent of manufacturing imports. Imports from China accounted for 30 per cent of manufacturing imports into the European Union, 35 per cent into Japan and 25 per cent into the United States. In the most protected sectors in these countries, China's import penetration is even more spectacular. Its share in these sectors in 2009 was about 50 per cent in the European Union, the United States and Canada, and about 55 per cent in Brazil, more than 60 per cent in South Korea, and more than 70 per cent in Japan (Mattoo and Subramanian 2011: 4). The most protected sectors are those in which these importing countries do not enjoy comparative advantage. Both China and India are relatively well endowed in labour, but it is China that has successfully used this comparative advantage to become a global powerhouse in manufactures. China's advantage is so large in certain manufactures that its General Agreement on Trade in Services (GATS) commitments to reduce government support to these manufactures are even more generous than those committed to by developed countries. China's trade liberalisation focuses on sectors where China enjoys comparative advantage and it has reduced tariff rates significantly. China's average tariff rate has been reduced from 40 per cent in 1985 to less than 10 per cent in 2011, and tariff revenue was only 2.5 per cent of total tax revenue in 2009 (Razeen 2011: 4–9).

At the opposite end from manufactures are services. According to neoliberal economists following Lin's categorisation, China's industry policy in services is comparative-advantage defying. China has ranked second in the world in the value of inward foreign direct investment (FDI) since 2000, with most flowing to the manufacturing sector. The service sector is attracting an ever larger share—by 2010, accounting for more than 40 per cent of total FDI. According to Chinese government estimates, foreign investors have invested more than US$160 billion in more than 90,000 foreign-invested enterprises (FIEs) in the service sector (Razeen 2011: 5). No doubt China's large domestic market is a major attraction for the huge increase in FDI in the service sector. The additional pull for this FDI, however, is China's protection of its service sector. Although China has opened its service sector to foreign competition and investment (Chen et al. 2011), the sector is still largely internationally uncompetitive so the state is reluctant to commit to further liberalising services under the GATS (Razeen 2011: 9). A clear example is its support for the finance industry. China favours the Chinese bankcard association's UnionPay bankcard over MasterCard and Visa, and allows it to monopolise domestic renminbi-denominated transactions. MasterCard cannot process credit card transactions in renminbi and the central bank, the People's Bank of China (PBC), has prevented ePay Links from partnering with MasterCard to issue renminbi-settled credit cards (Rabinovitch and Anderlini 2013: 20).

Strategic industry policy[6]

The strategy to grow out of the plan had outlived its usefulness by the 1990s. 'Enhancing' the market had served its purpose well in providing the essential underlay of economic reform; the nation was now ready for the next stage (Hua et al. 1988). Underemployed resources in the non-state sector were fast diminishing and the SOE sector was becoming a drag on the overall economy. China's leaders now concluded the SOE sector was ready to be reformed (CPC 1993; DRC 1999). Substantial reform of SOEs was begun in the mid-1990s and, by 2004, the number of SOEs had been reduced by almost three-quarters—from 120,000 to 32,000. Employment in SOEs fell by 28 million, or half of the SOE workforce. In 2007, SOEs employed 18 per cent of the urban workforce compared with 50 per cent in 1995 (Xia et al. 2013: 18).

The CCP described its strategy to reform the SOEs as 'zhua da, fang xiao' ('grasp the big and release the small') (Jiang 1995). Small and medium-sized SOEs were privatised while large firms in key industries were converted into conglomerates styled on Japanese keiretsu or Korean chaebols, in a move to build 'national champions'. Industry policy no longer limited the state to helping the private sector produce according to comparative advantage. The state would now also seek to make Chinese firms globally competitive in state-designated industries where China lacked comparative advantage—that is, industries in which neoliberals deemed China to be uncompetitive. Here the state would override the comparative advantage principle and the market. A key plank of this new policy was to promote indigenous innovation, particularly to help build advantage and offset disadvantage for Chinese ventures in global markets.

In designing and implementing China's new strategic industry policy, Chinese policy advisers consulted many of their current and retired Japanese counterparts (Heilmann and Shih 2013). In 2006, the CCP designated seven industries as 'strategic'—defence, electricity generation and distribution, petroleum and petrochemicals, telecommunications, civil aviation, water transport, and coal—which the state would control. It also targeted machinery, automobiles, electronics and information technology, construction, steel, base metals and chemicals as 'pillar' industries, over which the state would exercise strong influence. While entry barriers into 'pillar' industries are informal and low compared with the barriers to strategic industries, they are high compared with other non-targeted industries and are designed to accept some private operations but discourage private-sector competition (WB and DRC 2012: 26). In 2012 the state owned 30 of the biggest 42 corporations in China and controlled 85 per cent of assets of the 39 sectors that the state considers to be most important (Kurlantzick 2013).

---

6   Parts of this and the next two sections draw on Liew (2005).

Lin (2012) considers national strategic industry policies to be 'comparative-advantage defying': industries that the state chooses to develop are advanced beyond the country's level of economic development or are otherwise beyond what neoclassical economic theory recognises to be the country's comparative advantage. China's strategic industry policy, though, has its own economic logic. The relative factor endowments model of trade (which involves the relative labour force, capital and the available land) behind the free-trade policy prescription favoured by the Washington Consensus[7] assumes constant returns to scale in production technology (that is, a doubling of inputs will double output) and the presence of competitive markets with many sellers. The relative factor endowment model's evaluation that the economic outcome of state intervention in trade is negative depends very much on these assumptions. Changing these assumptions to better accommodate the realities of China's large domestic market and the oligopolies in the world market can make state intervention in trade economically beneficial.

Krugman (1984) showed that with increasing returns, technology and an oligopolistic market structure, import protection can help make a firm competitive in export markets. Import protection can allow the firm to compete at home, which enables it to realise economies of scale, lower its production costs and hence improve its competitiveness in preparation for entry into the global market. Krugman's and other similar trade models provide a rigorous economic justification for developmental state-type industry policies. The prerequisite is a large domestic market, which enables the domestic firm to initially exploit economies of scale in production from import protection alone, without having to rely on exports right from the start.

Another factor that can justify state intervention in Chinese industry is the nation's great regional variation. To apply economic theory, China is more effectively treated as a country comprising several economies that range from the least developed to the most advanced instead of one homogeneous developing economy. Underdeveloped regions in China that are well endowed with unskilled labour should specialise in low-technology products while developed regions well endowed with skilled labour should specialise in high-technology products. Hence, short-term state assistance to high-technology industries in China's advanced economic regions could actually be construed in Lin's terminology as following comparative advantage through a market-enhancing industry policy rather than adopting a comparative-advantage defying strategic industry policy.

---

7   Ramo (2004) labelled China's state-guided development model the 'Beijing consensus'.

China's strategic industry policy is likely to have a much longer life than the few decades during which Japan, South Korea and Taiwan maintained their strategic industry policies. All three have much smaller populations than China and have successfully carried out strategic industrialisation. The pinnacle of their success, though, was during the Cold War when the United States helped what it saw as its strategically important allies to industrialise through accepting their trade subsidies. The United States kept its domestic market open to their subsidised exports and acquiesced to their protection of domestic industries. The United States no longer sees strategic need to help these three trading partners economically and sees them more as economic competitors even though they are still strategic partners.

Today, strategic industry policy and even market-enhancing industry policy are highly contentious. The global economy is weak and in the European Union, United States and other industrialised countries where unemployment has become a recognised problem, the prospect of further job losses fuels domestic opposition to imports from competitive emerging economies that displace local industrial production. China is the most competitive emerging economy in many sectors. Its large domestic market confers advantages in international bargaining over market access and makes the nation less vulnerable to trade retaliation against its exports when it uses import barriers and export subsidies to exploit economies of scale in domestic production. China is not the first country to exploit its market size in trade conflicts. The White House in 2004 lifted trade restrictions against steel imports into the United States from the European Union—a move taken not because of a WTO ruling but because the European Union had threatened to impose restrictions on imports from the United States, which would have harmed states where President George W. Bush was vulnerable politically. A similar threat from a trading partner with a small domestic market would have carried no weight.

China's huge market size clearly also empowers it to use the principle of divide and conquer in accessing overseas markets. A recent example is the lack of a uniform EU voice on how to deal with China in trade disagreements over China's exports of solar panels and telecommunications products. The EU Trade Commission has accused China of dumping solar panels on the European market, but member countries are split over EU Trade Commissioner Karel de Gucht's plan to impose an import tariff of 47 per cent on solar panels from China. France and Italy support the plan but Germany, Britain, Sweden and the Netherlands oppose it. In a similar vein were the European Union's divided responses to Chinese telecommunications giants Huawei and ZTE. Some European manufacturers were alarmed by cheaper Chinese telecommunications equipment gaining EU market share. Those manufacturers, however, faced opposition from other large European manufacturers such as Ericsson, Alcatel-Lucent SA and Nokia

Siemens Networks, which fear that Chinese retaliation in response to attempts to control the import of Chinese goods will bring a loss of their own lucrative markets in China (Reuters 2013).

Opinions on how to deal with China's trade strategy are also divided in the United States, where labour favours sanctions against China's 'unfair' trade practices but business is ambivalent or split. Some US firms facing Chinese import competition welcome trade sanctions against China, but US firms exporting from China benefit from China's trade policies, and there are others who fear Chinese government retaliation (Subramanian 2013: 14).

The state and the disadvantage of bigness

Throughout China's long history, physical size and a large population have enabled subnational (provincial and local) governments to enjoy a large degree of autonomy from the central government.[8] This has posed enormous challenges to national governance. China's central government has generally found it difficult to enforce national policies at the local level without the cooperation of subnational governments. Post Mao, Beijing finds that implementing its liberal market reforms and strategic industry policies requires active cooperation from subnational governments, but local economic interests activated by these market reforms often lead subnational governments to oppose or moderate national policies.

Localities in the People's Republic of China (PRC) enjoyed a fair amount of autonomy even at the height of central planning when there was continuous tension between the centre and subnational governments. Conflicts between the national and subnational levels, especially over public finance, have a long history that predates the PRC. The centre's historical dependence on the tax collection efforts of subnational governments made rich provinces powerful political actors long before the PRC was created and this has continued to empower them in the current political system (Zhong 2003). The political influence of provinces is formalised in the system, with 'province' a rank in the national political administrative hierarchy equal to a national ministry, and—although not stated formally—richer provinces and their representatives rank higher than their poorer counterparts.

---

8   The subnational government hierarchy advances through township, county, prefecture or municipality, and province. Important municipalities such as Beijing and Shanghai have provincial status. Each level is responsible for overseeing the work carried out by lower levels and has two important officials. The one representing the CCP, the party secretary responsible for national policy implementation, is always administratively above the other, who heads the local People's Government.

Especially since reforms were begun post Mao, subnational governments have utilised their considerable autonomy to become major economic players. They are commonly shareholders in local industrialisation, promoting the development of various industries—from those involved in producing consumer durables to those involved in high-technology production such as civil aviation manufacturing. Local industrialisation efforts are not just to establish globally competitive industries. Subnational governments also promote local industrialisation to create local employment and to maximise local tax revenues. In promoting local economic interests, subnational governments even erected their own regional trade barriers against products made in other localities (Shen and Dai 1990). The disposition of China's powerful provinces towards strategic industry policies and the quest by subnational governments to create local employment and raise local tax revenues have led many specialists to argue that subnational governments and local economic interests, not the central government, are the major impediments to China's WTO compliance (Johnston 2003: 15).

China's strategic industry policy has the powerful backing of national and subnational governments, but there is no guarantee that it will be able to duplicate the success of the post–World War II state-led industry policies of Japan, South Korea and Taiwan. The investigation by Haley and Haley (2013) into state subsidies of Chinese industry identified some dysfunctions that cast doubt on the policy's likely success. Haley and Haley found that competition among subnational governments has led to the expansion of some industries, such as paper and paper products, which have little or no chance of ever becoming competitive. Where there is the prospect of success, as in industries such as automobiles and automobile parts, subnational competition has served to fragment industry and prevent the full exploitation of economies of scale (Haley and Haley 2013: 96–150).

In recent years land-related taxes have been an important source of local revenue. According to Liu (2010: 2), 80 to 90 per cent of local government infrastructure financing comes from land leasing and bank loans with collateral that depends on land and property valuations. Local governments therefore have an interest in high land and property prices and are reluctant to control (on the contrary, they encourage) over-investment in real estate. Local governments in principle are not allowed to run budget deficits. The central government has, however, allowed them to set up local government financing vehicles (LGFVs), which require minimum set-up capital, in order to raise funds from banks for local investment. Many of these investments are—against the wishes of the central government—speculative. There are concerns that many local governments will end up with large hidden deficits (Feng 2010).

Local officials have a built-in incentive to maximise the funds available for their personal benefit by maximising local fiscal profit—that is, fiscal revenue minus expenditure on local services. The desire to maximise local fiscal profit encourages local speculative investments that promise quick short-term returns. As a result of the CCP's preference for social management over political reform, the quality of local governance is often weak (Fewsmith 2013). Although China has a huge floating labour population, in the countryside households are still largely tied to their land because of the poor functioning of the rural land market. This severely restricts individuals' choice to vote with their feet to discipline local officials for poor performance (Gordon and Li 2011).

The party/state will always be with us

When the CCP abandoned central planning post Mao, its adoption of a more liberal approach to managing the national economy caused an inherent ideological contradiction with communist orthodoxy. The CCP remains in power as a monopolistic party, but it has had to reinvent itself to do so. This reinvention has meant changing the 'body and soul' of the party. In practice, this involves changing the characteristics of party members ('body'), especially party elites, and redefining party ideology ('soul').

Former CCP general-secretary Jiang Zemin, in his report to the Sixteenth Party Congress in 2002, invoked the notion that whether a person is politically advanced (*xianjin*) or backward (*luohou*) does not depend on whether or how much personal property the person owns. A person's political thinking depends on his or her '*biaoxian*' (compliant and supportive behaviour towards the party), how they have acquired and how they use any property they may have, and their contribution to building socialism with Chinese characteristics (Jiang 2002: 15). Thus, the CCP does not have to be led by the working class, which paves the way for the party to change its 'body'.

The CCP changes its 'body' in two ways. The first is through the reinvention of party elites. Many members of the elite remake themselves into technocrats and entrepreneurs in the service of market reform in order to remain relevant to the party and to maintain their power and influence within it. Second, the party accepts a new category of elite members who are brought into the CCP from 'advanced elements of other social strata' to prevent the creation of power centres external to the party.

The CCP so far appears to be able to reinvent itself successfully by reconfiguring its support base through co-opting the new social strata empowered by market reform. The party is keen to co-opt the growing elite of skilled professionals, managers and private entrepreneurs. Their bargaining power vis-a-vis the party/state has continued to strengthen while marketisation gives them wealth, leverage and space to pursue their interests within a political marketplace. Perhaps nothing better illustrates how far the CCP has reinvented itself than the attendance of seven of China's richest business leaders at the Eighteenth Party Congress in November 2012 to elect China's leaders for the next five years. Those present included Wanda Group boss Wang Jianlin, who has an estimated fortune of US$10 billion, construction equipment maker Liang Wengen (US$7.3 billion) and clothing mogul Zhou Haijiang (US$1.3 billion). A *Wall Street Journal* report claimed that 160 of China's 1,024 richest people with a total family net worth of US$221 billion were members of the Party Congress, parliament and the Chinese People's Political Consultative Council (Areddy and Grimaldi 2012).

Reinvention has not only been crucial for enabling the CCP to remain in power as a monopolistic party; it also ensures that China's market reforms will not lead to completely free markets. A monopolistic party will not allow free-market competition primarily because such competition serves to erode the monopolistic party's continued control of the economy's financial resources, which is essential if the party is to preserve its monopoly on political power. Allowing competitors the use of a level playing field runs counter to the CCP's imperative to secure control over the country's financial resources lest other groups external to the party obtain significant independent sources of finance that can provide them with the capability to pose a serious challenge to the party's monopoly on power. This imperative explains the cautious response among China analysts to Premier Li Keqiang's May 2013 speech in which he announced plans to reduce the state's role in the economy (Barboza and Buckley 2013; Li 2013). Their caution proved to be judicious, as Chinese political leaders at the Third Plenum of the Eighteenth Party Congress in November 2013 reaffirmed 'the leading role of the state-owned economy' (CPC 2013).

The state and resource security

China's demand for resources has been commensurate with the growth of the national economy. China has designated energy-related industries as strategic, so it is not surprising that its political leaders have not entrusted resource security to the market. China is now the world's largest oil importer, and in 2011 alone it invested US$12 billion in oil and gas fields all over the world (Arango and Krauss 2013). China's SOEs have invested heavily in Africa to secure supplies of energy and minerals, including in Gabon (iron ore), Guinea (bauxite, diamonds, iron ore, uranium), Zambia (copper) and Angola, Sudan and Nigeria (oil) (Doriye 2010: 26).

Oil-rich African countries have become strategically important to China. In 2008 Angola displaced Saudi Arabia as the biggest supplier of oil to China, supplying 18 per cent of China's oil consumption (Faucon and Swartz 2009: A4). In Iraq, Chinese SOEs have offered generous terms to secure half of Iraq's oil production—1.5 million barrels a day (Arango and Krauss 2013). Besides generous terms of purchase, China also provides loans to resource-rich developing countries in its quest for resource security. In both 2009 and 2010, the value of loans to developing countries from China exceeded loans from the World Bank (Kurlantzick 2013).

China has also been actively investing in farmland in Africa to improve its own food security. Much farmland in China has been converted to industrial use and policymakers have regarded this and climate change as threatening the nation's food security. Lobell et al. (2011) estimated that climate change alone could potentially increase global food prices by 6.4 to 19 per cent. China is a large food producer and any loss of farmland could impact significantly on world food supply and prices. China's investment in African farmland mirrors its investment strategy in energy and minerals, where China's SOEs, with funding from state banks such as Exim Bank and China Development Bank, negotiated deals with their FDI hosts (Doriye 2010: 29). In February 2009, Chinese state-owned commercial banks had also concluded deals worth more than US\$40 billion with state oil firms in Brazil, Iran, Russia and Venezuela (Drezner 2009: 43).

China's SOEs, encouraged by the nation's Tenth Five-Year Plan's 'going outside' strategy (Zhu 2001), are active in securing China's resource security, but according to Lieberthal and Wang (2012: 36), these SOEs and other, non-resource-related SOEs act largely independently of one another and commercial considerations drive their decisions. They often compete with one another and their operations are not based on a grand strategy formulated by China Inc., although SOEs, especially those that are resource-related, obtain favourable treatment from state banks.

Getting the state out of the way

China's industry policies that follow or defy comparative advantage can sometimes convey an impression that the country is governed by an omnipresent, overbearing Chinese state. In reality, China's state authority is fragmented, as mentioned above, and is often deliberately decentralised. China does not, for example, have a uniform minimum wage standard. Provincial and lower-level governments are free to set minimum wages appropriate for their locality. It was only in 2002 that provincial and municipal governments extended the minimum wage to domestic migrant workers (Lam 2006: 97). The Twelfth Five-Year Plan, released in 2011, set the ambitious goal of increasing minimum wages by at least 13 per cent a year so that by 2015 the average minimum wage across the nation would be 40 per cent of the average wage (NPC 2011). Achieving this goal will depend on the strength of local economies and the quality of local governance, with less spent on local services meaning more personal benefits for local officials.

Real average wages in China increased more than 200 per cent in the 10 years to 2010. At the height of the impact of the global financial crisis on Asia in 2008 and 2009, Asia excluding China recorded two consecutive years of negative real wage growth, of 2 and 0.9 per cent. Asia with China included, however, posted positive real wage growth of 3.9 and 5.9 per cent (ILO 2013: 20). Despite Chinese workers enjoying significant growth in real wages, such growth still lags behind productivity growth (Schellekens 2013: 2).

There is much official discussion on increasing domestic consumption by rebalancing the economy away from investment, but the state has not actively intervened in the labour market to influence wage outcomes. Wages in China are determined in practice by a largely unregulated labour market. The state regulates the labour market on paper, but enforcement is a different matter. China levies a social insurance contribution charge on employed workers equivalent to an average implicit employment tax of 45 per cent of the wage rate, which is high by international standards. As a result of this levy on employers, however, many of those in the competitive private sector avoid formal employment contracts (WB and DRC 2012: 33).

Workers, on the whole, have not been able to extract a larger share of the gains from the increase in the economy's productivity. The relatively high average wages paid to workers employed by 'national champions' in key industries do not compensate for the low average wages paid to workers in the private sector. The establishment of national champions has worsened wage inequality. National champions are largely immune from private sector competition, earn monopolistic profits and are able to pay premium wages to their workers. Between 1995 and 2002, workers in the state sector enjoyed an annual wage premium 44 per cent above the wage paid to non-state workers. The premium increased to 81 per cent in 2007 (Xia et al. 2013: 18).

Government administration was restructured as well as SOEs. China's government, in the name of reform, shifted a large share of the responsibility for funding services such as health and education from the state to the individual. The result is a fall in government administration employment. By 2011, the fall in employment in SOEs and government administration had reduced public sector employment as a share of the nation's total labour force to 10.2 per cent, which was below that of France (26.7 per cent), Germany (15 per cent) and the

United States (16.9 per cent) (Rutkowski 2013). Most of the cuts in government services and employment took place in the countryside. In urban China, the state remains a major provider of services and employment. In 2007, the public sector share of urban employment was still 30 per cent (Xia et al. 2013: 18).

In line with neoliberal thinking, China has reduced the direct provision of public services and seeks to aid the poor with direct cash transfers. In 1999 China introduced the Minimum Livelihood Guarantee Scheme (*Dibao*) under which cash transfers are made to urban poor on a means-tested basis. By 2003 the scheme covered 22 million people, or 6 per cent of the urban population (Ravallion 2009), but it was only introduced nationwide in 2007. To supplement *Dibao*, local and central governments provide additional cash subsidies to the poor for health, education and housing. Many local governments also provide work support programs. Since *Dibao* became national, state aid to the poor, especially those living in rural areas, has increased significantly. The increase has not kept up with inflation, though, and can only provide just less than one-quarter of the average level of consumption (Gao 2011). *Dibao* is a work in progress and it is fair to conclude that after more than three decades post-Mao China has less of a welfare state than most Western democracies.[9]

Conclusion

The role of the state in China's economy is complex and evolving with the post-Mao economic transition under way. In the early years of reform the state focused industry policy on developing the necessary constituency of reformers in the party/state bureaucracy and pushing ahead with a comparative-advantage following industry policy to develop and expand the market. With market roots established through this policy, the state sought to move beyond this, in pursuit of other sources of economic advantage. It adopted strategic industry policy to take advantage of the economies of scale and scope conferred by China's large geophysical and population size, and through this policy to intervene in the economy to create national champions in the strategic and pillar industries it has selected and protected. The CCP also understands that to maintain its monopolistic political hold it must retain dominant financial power or at least maximise party control over it, which is another imperative to the party/state creating national champions, even though this disables fair market competition in those industries.

---

9   In a Pew Research Center (2013: 20) study, the proportion of survey respondents in China who considered inequality to be a very big problem (52 per cent) was not much higher than survey respondents who thought so in Germany (51 per cent) and the United Kingdom (50 per cent).

The state is simultaneously disengaging from non-key sectors and getting out of the way of the lives of ordinary people. This has created a highly flexible labour market, but it has also, by implication, forced people to take more responsibility for their personal economic well-being. The state no longer guarantees essential services such as education and health, which it used to provide but has now partially or largely privatised. Meanwhile, the state is actively staying involved in the important role it plays in improving China's resource security since China is a major resource consumer and highly dependent on resource imports.

Market reform at the hand of the party/state has ended suffocation of the private sector by central planning. The end of central planning, however, has not meant the end of state intervention in the economy. The state has disengaged from some areas of the economy but has engaged forcefully in others, and it cannot disengage from the monopolistic CCP. China's position today as an export powerhouse deeply integrated into the global economy attests to the success of China's market reform and economic policies. The achievements of state intervention in China's market reforms are consistent with the research of Rodrik (2013: 28), who showed that the most successful developing economies in the past decade 'have not been the ones with the least state intervention'. State intervention in China, however, is not without political and social costs. The privileged position granted to SOEs in key industries, the fragmentation of industry and state authority, and the focus on social management ahead of political reform have compromised China's otherwise impressive economic achievements, with growing unease among Chinese citizens over ever greater corruption and inequality.

Nevertheless, the distinctive role of the Chinese state in judiciously deregulating and re-regulating the economy in the past three decades clearly has much to offer those who are rethinking economics in the twenty-first century.[10] With this in mind, the Chinese economy should be studied not just for the lessons it can teach us about China. The Chinese economy should also be studied for the lessons it can teach us about the problematic nature of many of the key assumptions in conventional Western economic thought, particularly regarding the impacts of state activity on the economy.

---

10   In 2013, with uncertainty over the global economy, people in China responded most optimistically in a Pew international survey (Pew Research Center 2013: 4). In the United Kingdom, only 15 per cent rated the economy as good in 2013 while 69 per cent did so in 2007. The equivalent figures for the United States and Germany are 33 and 50 per cent, and 75 and 63 per cent respectively. But the figures for China are 88 and 82 per cent. Among the Chinese respondents, 80 per cent indicated that they believed their economy would improve in the next 12 months. In the United States, Germany and the United Kingdom, respectively, only 44, 27 and 22 per cent of those polled thought so.

References

Amiti, Mary and Freund, Caroline. 2008. *The anatomy of China's export growth*. Policy Research Working Paper No. 468. Washington, DC: The World Bank.

Arango, Tim and Krauss, Clifford. 2013. China is reaping biggest benefits of Iraq oil boom. *The New York Times*, 2 June. URL: www.nytimes.com/2013/06/03/world/middleeast/china-is-reaping-biggest-benefits-of-iraq-oil-boom.html. Consulted 4 June 2013.

Areddy, James T. and Grimaldi, James V. 2012. Defying Mao, rich Chinese crash the communist party. *Wall Street Journal*, 29 December. URL: wsj.com/article/SB10001424127887323723104578187360101389762.html. Consulted 13 June 2013.

Barboza, David and Buckley, Chris. 2013. China plans to reduce the state's role in the economy. *The New York Times*, 24 May. URL: www.nytimes.com/2013/05/25/business/global/beijing-signals-a-shift-on-economic-policy.html?pagewanted=all&_r=0. Consulted 27 May 2013.

Chen, Qingqing, Goh, Chor-Ching, Sun, Bo and Xu, Lixin Colin. 2011. *Market integration in China*. Policy Research Working Paper No. 5630. Washington, DC: The World Bank. URL: elibrary.worldbank.org/content/workingpaper/10.1596/1813-9450-5630. Consulted 4 June 2013.

Chen, Yun. 1987 [1979]. Jihua yu shichang wenti [Issues of plan and market]. In CPC Central Committee Secretariat Research Office and CPC Document Research, eds. *Jianchi gaige, kaifa, gaohuo: Shiyijie sanzhong quanhui yilai youguan zhongyao wenxian zhaibian* [Persist in reform, opening up, and vitalise: Excerpts of key documents from the Third Plenum of the Eleventh Party Congress]. Reprint. Beijing: Renmin chubanshe.

CPC [Communist Party of China Central Committee]. 1984. *China's economic structure reform*. Beijing: Foreign Languages Press.

CPC. 1993. Decision of the CPC Central Committee on some issues concerning the establishment of a socialist market economic structure. *Beijing Review* 22–28 November: 12–31. Original Chinese version in *Renmin ribao* [People's Daily] 17 November.

CPC. 2013. *Zhongguo gongchandang dishibajie zhongyang weiyuanhui disanci quanti huiyi gongbao* [Communique of the Third Plenum of the Eighteenth Party Congress of the Communist Party of China]. Beijing: CPC. URL: finance.sina.com.cn/china/20131112/194917300619.shtml. Consulted 13 November.

Doriye, Elirehema. 2010. The next stage of sovereign wealth investment: China buys Africa. *Journal of Financial Regulation and Compliance* 18(1): 23–31.

DRC [Development Research Centre of the State Council]. 1999. *1998 nian jingji yunxing de tedian yu chuanzai de wenti* [Characteristics and problems of the functioning of the economy in 1998]. Diaocha yanjiu baogao [Investigation and Research Report]. March. Beijing: DRC.

Drezner, Daniel W. 2009. Bad debts: Assessing China's financial influence on great power politics. *International Security* 34(2): 7–45.

Faucon, Benoit and Swartz, Spencer. 2009. Africa pushes back China on oil search. *The Wall Street Journal* 30 September: A4.

Feng, Zhe. 2010. Liu Mingkang: zuida fengxian reng jizhong yu difang rongzi pingtai [Liu Mingkang: The greatest risk remains concentrated in local financial platforms]. 2 December. URL: finance.sina.com.cn/roll/20101220/14359134045.shtml. Consulted 3 June 2011.

Fewsmith, Joseph. 2013. *The logic and limits of political reform in China*. Cambridge: Cambridge University Press.

Gao, Qin. 2011. Anti-poverty family policies in China: A critical evaluation. Assessing family policies: Confronting family poverty and social exclusion and ensuring work family balance. United Nations Department of Economic and Social Affairs Division for Social Policy and Development Expert Group Meeting, 1–3 June, New York.

Gordon, Roger H. and Li, Wei. 2011. *Provincial and local governments in China: Fiscal institutions and government behavior*. Working Paper No. 16694. Cambridge, Mass.: National Bureau of Economic Research.

Haley, Usha C.V. and Haley, George T. 2013. *Subsidies to Chinese industry: State capitalism, business strategy, and trade policy*. Oxford: Oxford University Press.

Heilmann, Sebastian and Shih, Lea. 2013. *The rise of industrial policy in China, 1978–2012*. Harvard–Yenching Institute Working Paper. Cambridge, MA: Harvard University.

Hua, Sheng, Zhang, Xuejun and Luo, Xiaopeng. 1988. Zhongguo gaige shinian: huigu, fansi he qianjing [Ten years of Chinese economic reform: Review, reflection and prospects]. *Jingji yanjiu* [Economic Research] December: 11–30.

ILO [International Labour Organisation]. 2013. *Global wage report 2012/13: Wages and equitable growth*. Geneva: ILO.

Jiang, Zemin. 1995. Zhengque chuli shehui zhuyi xiandaihua jianshe de ruogan da guanxi [The correct handling of several great relationships in the construction of socialist modernisation]. *Renmin riabo haiwaiban* [People's Daily Overseas Edition] 28 September.

Jiang, Zemin. 2002. Quanmian jianshe xiaokang shehui, kaichuang Zhongguo tese shehuizhuyi shiye xin jumian [Comprehensively build a comfortable well-off society, start a new phase in socialism with Chinese characteristics]. In *Zhongguo gongchandang dishiliuci quanguo daibiao dahui wenjian huibian* [Compilation of documents from the 16th Party Congress of the Communist Party of China]. Beijing: Renmin chubanshe.

Johnston, Alastair Ian. 2003. Is China a status quo power? *International Security* 27(4): 5–56.

Krugman, Paul. 1984. Import protection as export protection: International competition in the presence of oligopoly and economies of scale. In Henryk Kierzkowski, ed. *Monopolistic competition in international trade*. Oxford: Oxford University Press.

Kurlantzick, Joshua. 2013. Why the 'China model' isn't going away. *The Atlantic Monthly*, 21 March. URL: www.theatlantic.com/china/archive/2013/03/why-the-china-model-isnt-going-away/274237/. Consulted 19 June 2013.

Lam, Willy Wo-Lap. 2006. *Chinese politics in the Hu Jintao era: New leaders— New challenges*. New York: M.E. Sharpe.

Li, Keqiang. 2013. Zai guowuyuan jigou zhineng zhuanbian dongyuan dianshi dianhua huiyi shang de jianghua [Speech delivered at the teleconference on mobilising to transform the functions of organs of the State Council]. *Renmin ribao* [People's Daily] 13 May: 2. URL: paper.people.com.cn/rmrb/html/2013-05/15/nw.D110000renmrb_20130515_1-02.htm. Consulted 16 May 2013.

Lieberthal, Kenneth and Wang, Jisi. 2012. *Addressing US–China strategic distrust*. Washington, DC: John L. Thornton China Center, Brookings Institution.

Liew, Leong H. 1995. Gradualism in China's economic reform and the role for a strong central state. *Journal of Economic Issues* 29(3): 883–95.

Liew, Leong H. 2005. China's engagement with neo-liberalism: Path dependency, geography and party self-reinvention. *Journal of Development Studies* 41(2): 331–52.

Lin, Justin Yifu. 2012. *New structural economics: A framework for rethinking development and policy*. Washington, DC: The World Bank.

Liu, Lili. 2010. Strengthening subnational debt financing and managing risks. *Review of Economic Research* 46(16 August): F-9. Beijing: Ministry of Finance.

Lobell, David B., Schlenker, Wolfram and Costa-Roberts, Justin. 2011. Climate trends and global crop production since 1980. *Science* May. URL: iis-db. stanford.edu/pubs/23212/Science_5_11.pdf. Consulted 6 May 2011.

Mattoo, Aaditya and Subramanian, Arvind. 2011. *China and the world trading system*. Policy Research Working Paper No. 5897. Washington, DC: The World Bank.

Naughton, Barry. 1995. *Growing out of the plan: Chinese economic reform 1978–1993*. Cambridge: Cambridge University Press.

NPC [National People's Congress]. 2011. Zhonghua Renmin Gongheguo guomin jingji he shehui fazhan dishierge wunian guihua gangyao [People's Republic of China Twelfth Economic and Social Development Five-Year Plan]. *Renmin ribao* [People's Daily]. URL: politics.people.com.cn/GB/14163461.html. Consulted 12 May 2011.

Pew Research Center. 2013. *Economies of emerging markets better rated during difficult times*. 23 May. Washington, DC: Pew Research Center. URL: www. pewresearch.org. Consulted 18 June 2013.

Rabinovitch, Simon and Anderlini, Jamil. 2013. China blocks renminbi MasterCard dealings. *Australian Financial Review* 4 June: 20.

Ramo, Joshua Cooper. 2004. *The Beijing consensus*. London: The Foreign Policy Centre. URL: www.fpc.org.uk/publications/theBeijingConsensus. Consulted 15 April 2009.

Ravallion, Martin. 2009. How relevant is targeting to the success of the antipoverty program? *World Bank Research Observer* 24: 205–31.

Razeen, Sally. 2011. *Chinese trade policy after (almost) ten years in the WTO: A post-crisis stocktake*. Occasional Paper No. 2/2011. Brussels: European Centre for International Political Economy.

Reuters. 2013. EU chief tells China he won't yield on solar panels. *Business Spectator*, 29 May. URL: www.businessspectator.com.au/news/2013/5/29/solar-energy/eu-trade-chief-tells-china-he-wont-yield-solar-panels. Consulted 3 June 2013.

Rodrik, Dani. 2013. *The past, present, and future of economic growth*. Working Paper No. 1 (June). London: Global Citizen Foundation.

Rutkowski, Ryan. 2013. A shrinking leviathan: State employment in China looms smaller than expected. *China Economic Watch* 24 January. Washington, DC: Petersen Institute for International Economics.

Schellekens, Philip. 2013. *A changing China: Implications for developing countries*. Economic Premise No. 118. Washington, DC: The World Bank. URL: documents.worldbank.org/curated/en/2013/05/17747448/changing-china-implications-developing-countries. Consulted 30 May 2013.

Shen, Liren and Dai, Yuanchen. 1990. Wo guo duhou jingji de xingcheng jiqi biduan he genyuan [The duchy economies: Form, origin and negative features]. *Jingji yanjiu* [Economic Research] March: 12–19.

Subramanian, Arvind. 2011. *Eclipse: Living in the shadow of China's economic dominance*. Washington, DC: Peterson Institute of International Economics.

Subramanian, Arvind. 2013. *Preserving the open global economic system: A strategic blueprint for China and the United States*. Policy Brief No. PB13-16. Washington, DC: Petersen Institute for International Economics.

WB and DRC [The World Bank and Development Research Center of the State Council, the People's Republic of China]. 2012. *China 2030: Building a modern, harmonious, and creative high-income society*. Washington, DC: The World Bank.

Xia, Qingjie, Song, Lina, Li, Shi and Appleton, Simon. 2013. *The effects of the state sector on wage inequality in urban China: 1988–2007*. CGC Discussion Paper No. 19, February. Oxford: China Growth Centre, Oxford University.

Zhong, Yang. 2003. *Local government and politics in China: Challenges from below*. Armonk, NY: M.E. Sharpe.

Zhou, Jing and Latorre, Maria C. 2013. *How FDI influences the triangular trade pattern among China, East Asia and the US. A CGE analysis of the sector of electronics in China*. April. West Lafayette, Ind.: GTAP Resource Centre. URL: www.gtap.agecon.purdue.edu/resources/download/6245.pdf. Consulted 4 June 2013.

Zhu, Rongji. 2001. Report on the outline of the Tenth Five-Year Plan for National Economic and Social Development. Delivered at the Fourth Session of the Ninth National People's Congress. 5 March, Beijing. URL: english.gov.cn/official/2005-07/29/content_18334.htm. Consulted 29 May 2014.

PART III: AUSTRALIAN SOCIAL SCIENCES IN THE ASIAN CENTURY AND BEYOND

9

Australia's future in
the Asian Century[1]

Ken Henry

Australia is a continent, an island nation, a distinct geographic, cultural and political entity—with unique flora and fauna, and unique people, too. Our people are Australian. They inhabit a land rich in natural resources whose neighbourhood is Asia. Australia's geographic location and abundance of natural resources have been key determinants of its economic structure for as long as it has had an economy. Since European settlement, Australia has been a significant exporter of agricultural products and bulk commodities—first wool and more recently iron ore and coal. In the twenty-first century, this feature distinguishes Australia from most other countries at a similar stage of economic development.

Trends in the international terms of trade—measuring the physical quantity of imports that can be purchased with a given quantity of exports—have not always been favourable to us. In the last quarter of the twentieth century, the popular view was that Australia's particular natural endowments had consigned it to ever-falling terms of trade. This prospect helped motivate much of the policy reforms of the 1980s and 1990s. Those reforms paid substantial dividends in economic performance—most notably, through a boost to productivity.

1   This chapter was originally presented as the Cunningham Lecture, Academy of the Social Sciences in Australia, 20 November 2012, Canberra.

Even so, by the turn of the twenty-first century, with the world in awe of impressive developments in information and communications technologies and the advent of electronic commerce, Australia's natural resource endowments and its geographic location were considered by many to be a curse. Australia was being described, in disparaging terms, as an 'old economy', producing things that the rest of the world was finding ways of doing without. Commentators were lamenting Australia's distance from the major European and North American centres of global economic activity.

Today, in the Asian Century, Australia is often described as being 'in the right place at the right time', its geographic location and abundance of natural resources seen as valuable assets. Australia's terms of trade are some 80 per cent above their level at the turn of the century. In contrast, the real prices of information and communications technologies have fallen appreciably. Both of these things can be explained by the internationalisation of China—its reopening to the world—and its extraordinary growth as a manufacturing powerhouse, with a thirst for raw materials that Australia has in abundance.

Yet, abundant as they are, Australia's natural resources will not last forever. At present rates of extraction, Australia's known reserves of iron ore will be exhausted within a human lifetime, and known reserves of black coal will be exhausted within a century. Today, these two products make up more than one-third of Australia's total exports. As a whole, mining contributes about 60 per cent of Australia's total exports, and at present rates of extraction those exports will last, on average, about 75 years.

Of course, there will be further discoveries of mineral deposits in Australia. Rates of extraction could fall, too, as other producers expand capacity and importing countries transform their economies in ways that reduce reliance on raw materials. It is also possible, though, that rates of extraction will increase, given that more than half the world's population has not yet experienced industrialisation. Even if rates of extraction slow somewhat, it is not fanciful to imagine that before the end of this century, Australia will be importing many of the raw materials it is presently exporting in volume. If that is not the case—that is, if it turns out that extraction slows at an appreciably faster rate—there is a high probability that world commodity prices will also fall appreciably, even reverting to a long-term declining trend.

In either event, Australians of the future will identify this generation as the one which extracted unparalleled monetary reward from the continent's natural resources—a monetisation of non-renewable resources unmatched in any previous generation, and unlikely to be matched in any that follows. Those future generations—our children's children—will have reason to examine whether we made the most of a mining boom that we knew could not last forever. In this way, they set a test for this generation. During the year that I led the development of the then government's White Paper on *Australia in the Asian Century*, I found myself wondering, often, who would want to sit that test.

Developing a White Paper on Australia in the Asian Century

In the past three decades, I have been involved in more policy development exercises than I can remember. I do remember, though, some things about some of them. I remember that most were shielded against external involvement. I remember, too, that stakeholder consultation, which typically came after the announcement of a policy position, was not generally a positive process—not for me, and not for those on the other side of the table.

The exercise that produced the White Paper on *Australia in the Asian Century* was very different (Commonwealth of Australia 2012). It was an open process. Members of a small group of officials who had been put together to manage the development of the White Paper met, face-to-face, with hundreds of people in Australia, and dozens overseas. We received numerous written submissions—more than the number received for the defence White Paper in 2009, despite that exercise running for a longer period, and more than the late 1990s financial system inquiry, too. We engaged with people from business, state and territory governments, scientific and educational institutions, sporting organisations, cultural organisations and community groups. All were positive. All had constructive things to say. We listened, assimilated, synthesised, and only then drafted the White Paper text. Most of what appears in the last five chapters of the White Paper is a synthesis of what we were told in these consultations.

Most of those with whom we engaged wanted to see us adopt a strategic approach to the issues identified in our terms of reference. They counselled us against developing a set of initiatives for immediate implementation, emphasising instead the need for a compelling narrative that starts with a vision for Australia's future in the Asian Century. Many were highly critical of a lot of policy announcements of recent times, most of which they saw as ad hoc and reactive, lacking coherence. They were also—most of them—very critical of the intensely partisan nature of contemporary political discourse and media behaviour, something they considered to be undermining the development of rational approaches to many important policy issues. They considered that it would be a tragedy if this piece of work were to be affected in the same way.

Present angst

In the meantime, we are preoccupied with debates about the many consequences of an unusual mining boom—consequences of an intense competition for scarce domestic factors of production. Some of the concerns might be exaggerated, but there is no doubting their power to capture the attention of the Australian media, to dominate political discourse and to distort policy debate. All of these matters should be discussed; but if this generation cannot lift itself above them then we definitely will fail the test of future generations of Australians. What this generation needs is a compelling vision.

Future vision: Australia in the Asian Century

Supported by the three 'external' members of the advisory panel established to guide the development of the White Paper, the small group of officials developed a vision of a future Australia in the Asian Century. It is a vision of a prosperous and secure nation, with sustainably rising living standards and quality of life, which is integrated into our diverse region and open to the world; a nation whose people understand and, together with partners in the region, have the capabilities to deal confidently with the challenges of this Asian Century and to make the most of its extraordinary opportunities.

In our vision, Australian businesses are deeply integrated into the economies of Asia, through trade and investment linkages and in partnership with regional businesses, employing people in Australia and from across the region to supply global markets. We see a highly skilled and educated, dynamic and optimistic Australian community that understands the region's diversity and builds enduring relationships with its people through tourism, education, science and research collaboration, and cultural exchange. We see Australian governments, at all levels and in all parts of Australia, strengthening productive relationships in the region, based on consultation, collaboration and mutual respect.

Core propositions

Our vision emerged from a set of core propositions that provide the architecture for Australia's future in the Asian Century. First, the rise of Asia is reshaping the world, and this reshaping has some way to run. Second, the regional developments that have been our focus are occurring against the backdrop of truly profound global challenges. Third, Australia is well placed and is adapting to the rise of Asia, though the gap between our potential and our present reality is expanding rapidly. Fourth, regional economies are moving up the value chain, and this has implications for Australia. Fifth, our future is in our hands.

The rise of Asia is reshaping the world

Global growth has shifted strongly to our region in the past decade.[2] Global power is now also shifting, with implications for international relations that are not yet settled.

The speed and reach of these changes are unprecedented. They have already changed the shape of the global economy. Yet they have a long way to run. Very likely, they will continue right through this century. No doubt, there will be economic cycles, but these will be around an upward-sloping trend.[3]

Asian growth has been ignited by a new wave of internally generated economic liberalisation. That growth, and the development of new technologies to facilitate communications and trade, has transformed domestic economies and global markets. As Asian economies have grown, hundreds of millions of people have been lifted out of poverty, new businesses have emerged and others have been transformed, and governments and societies have modernised and become more outward looking.

In just the past 20 years, China and India have almost trebled their share of the global economy, and increased their absolute economic size six times over. Indonesia's economy has been growing at about 5 per cent a year for the past decade, and its economy is now larger than Australia's in purchasing power parity terms. Forty per cent of global economic activity now occurs in Asia. The White Paper reports projections that, by 2025, that will rise to almost one-half. One-quarter of the globe's economic activity will occur in China. Asia will have four of the top-10 biggest economies in the world: China first, India third, Japan fourth and Indonesia tenth.

Today there are about 500 million people in Asia who would be regarded as being middle class (Kharas and Gertz 2010). By 2020 that is expected to rise to 1.7 billion people, and by 2030 to more than three billion, with Asia then accounting for about 60 per cent of global middle-class consumption.

---

2   See 'Figure 2.1: Asia to become the centre of global economic activity' (Commonwealth of Australia 2012: 59).
3   See 'Chart 2.2: Share of world output growth' (Commonwealth of Australia 2012: 51).

Regional development is occurring against the backdrop of profound global challenges

The global financial crisis has left a difficult legacy, with governments in the United States and Europe confronting weak public-sector balance sheets and fragile macroeconomic and financial systems. Asian countries have a significant role to play in restoring the health of the global economy, contributing to global infrastructure efforts, strengthening global and regional financial architecture, reforming international financial institutions, and building a global financial safety net.

There are other challenges, of longer duration, with both regional and global dimensions. Many countries, on all continents, are confronting challenges of water security, food security, energy security, climate security, broad-scale ecosystem destruction, national and transnational terrorism, and population ageing. It is legitimate to describe these challenges to the sustainability of human activity in security terms. How these interrelated challenges are managed could have implications for political stability in a number of countries, military strategy in several, and profound implications for the relationship between humans, other animals and broader ecosystems in all. The issues are complex, but not impossibly so.

Water security

Between 1960 and 2000, Asia's consumption of meat increased by 700 per cent. While one kilogram of rice takes a truly staggering 10,000 litres of water to produce, one kilogram of meat takes somewhere between 30,000 and 70,000 litres. It is not surprising that 80 per cent of Asia's fresh water is devoted to irrigated agriculture. That is notwithstanding some formidable constraints: 50 of the 412 rivers in the Philippines are dead; more than 50 per cent of the water in China's Hai River Basin is unusable; all seven of the main rivers in West Java, supplying water to Jakarta, are heavily polluted; and the Ganges and Yellow rivers are so badly polluted that they cannot be used for agriculture along more than half their lengths.

Food security

During a so-called 'green revolution' between 1961 and 2004, agricultural yields in Asia increased at an average annual rate of 2.8 per cent. This revolution was no miracle. It relied on the adoption of higher-yielding crop varieties, the intensive use of fertilisers and a massive expansion of irrigation activity.

In its reliance on water depletion, including of groundwater aquifers, and in the considerable soil degradation it has caused, food security in the present has stolen something from the future. In China, for example, 25 per cent of the landmass is desert, and new desert is being created at the rate of 2,500 square kilometres a year. At that rate, between now and the end of the century, China will create a new desert the size of the State of Victoria.

Between 1961 and 2007, the consumption of fish more than doubled in Southeast Asia and trebled in North Asia. The world's oceans have been exploited to their maximum potential. About one-third of global fish stocks have been overexploited; a further half are fully exploited.

Yet, on conservative estimates, global food demand is projected to increase by 70 per cent over the next four decades.[4] Most of the increase in demand will be in Asia. Satisfying that demand will be no easy matter. It will raise confronting issues for traditional farming methods, of course. And it will raise very significant animal welfare issues as well.

Energy security

A typical 90 square metre apartment in China requires six tonnes of steel. That steel, in turn, requires three tonnes of coking coal and more than 10 tonnes of iron ore. Steel production requires a lot of energy. Between 1990 and 2009, energy consumption in Asia more than doubled, with the region's share of global energy consumption increasing from 25 to 40 per cent. Fossil fuels account for 82 per cent of Asia's energy use, coal making up 47 per cent. By 2035, China and India alone will consume 30 per cent of global energy production. China's consumption will be 70 per cent larger than that of the United States. Its coal use alone will be 2.5 times that of the entire Organisation for Economic Cooperation and Development (OECD).

Climate security

China currently accounts for 25 per cent of global greenhouse gas emissions. Asia as a whole produces 40 per cent. The region as a whole is acutely vulnerable to climate change. More than 10 million people in Asia—inhabiting the lower-lying parts of Bangladesh, China, India and Vietnam—are presently at risk of events causing life-threatening flooding. By the end of this century, that number will grow to something close to 100 million. Without adequate adaptation, there will be significant economic, social and environmental costs throughout the region. Adaptation is also costly.

---

4   See 'Chart C.1: Demand for food will grow' (Commonwealth of Australia 2012: 214).

Human security

It is not uncommon for security analysts to 'nest' conventional, or 'hard', security issues among broader human security considerations. These human dimensions are not simply an 'add-on'. There are important causal links, not only among the various human dimensions, but also between these and conventional security concerns.

Much has been written about the regional security implications of China's re-emergence. Some analysts have been concerned by the growth in China's military spending—a trebling in the past decade.[5] Of course, it should be remembered that the United States, with less than one-quarter of China's population, doubled its defence spending in the same period, currently spending about eight times what China is spending.

There is a broader perspective here, though. The key regional security question raised by China's re-emergence is this: will China be able to achieve water security, food security and energy security for its 1.3 billion people without threatening the peace and stability of the region? China's security ambitions in these several dimensions are legitimate. Denying its 1.3 billion people an opportunity for development that we in the West have enjoyed is indefensible. Yet the world will not find it easy to satisfy China's legitimate ambition.

There is no case in human history of one country's industrialisation, on its own, threatening global sustainability, but China's industrialisation could do so, if not managed well.[6] Today, China has an average income per capita that is about one-fifth that of the United States. Its per capita energy consumption is about one-quarter. Because of its population size, though, its total energy consumption is already slightly larger than that of the United States. Thus, if China's income per capita were to catch up to where the United States is today, and if China's energy intensity were to mirror that of the United States, China would be consuming more than four times what the United States is presently consuming. That would have global consequences, and not only for climate change.

There is consensus, though not unanimity, that any attempt to 'contain' China militarily would be stupid. Neither would it prove feasible if tested. In thinking about regional security requirements, there is a need to go beyond these rather obvious points. Regional peace and stability have to be the responsibility of all countries in the region. All countries should be asking themselves how they can engage with China in ways that enhance China's prospects of achieving water, food and energy security without threatening regional peace and stability.

---

5   See 'Chart 8.1: Regional defence expenditure' (Commonwealth of Australia 2012: 226).
6   See 'Chart 1.6: Energy and metals consumption per person, selected countries' (Commonwealth of Australia 2012: 44).

Such engagement is unlikely to be a burden. On the contrary, there are significant commercial opportunities for Australian businesses, and research opportunities for our scientific and academic institutions, in partnering with others in China and elsewhere in the region in projects to enhance the sustainability of economic activity. Opportunities exist in efforts to enhance energy efficiency and to develop new energy technologies, in projects to improve water efficiency, in soil restoration, in biodiversity conservation, and in environmentally sensitive urban design and construction methods. In all these areas, and many others, China is open to external expertise, indicating a strong interest in collaboration.

Regional security will be advanced through effective collaboration in efforts to ensure that China's legitimate development aspirations are not compromised by a lack of security in water, food and energy. On their own, these collaborative efforts might not prove sufficient; but nothing else, including no set of military alliances of any quality, provides a guarantee of regional peace and stability either.

Other challenges

Three other trends are challenging policymakers in many countries in the region: increasing inequality in the distribution of income and wealth; congestion externalities associated with rapid urbanisation; and population ageing.

While the lot of Asia's poor has been improving on average, the well-being of its rich has been improving more rapidly—their incomes have been increasing at a much faster rate and they enjoy better access to education, water, sanitation and health services. Gaps are widening along rural–urban, gender and ethnic lines.

The tempo and scale with which urbanisation is occurring are testing governments across the region, including in Australia, of course. Some are coping better than others. Cities such as Shanghai, Mumbai, Jakarta and Manila are grappling with the consequences of infrastructure and service shortfalls, choking pollution and highly congested traffic. These problems are also pronounced in Asia's intermediate and smaller-sized cities, where population growth is booming.

As with much of the advanced world—again including Australia—many Asian economies are grappling with the implications of rapidly ageing populations. Over the course of the next decade, the proportion of Asia's total population that is of prime working age will plateau and by 2025 will begin to decline, with serious implications for workforce participation, health care and aged care. This hides much diversity across the region, though, with some economies, including the second most populous, India, continuing to have opportunities to reap a 'demographic dividend' with the right investments in human capability.

There is reason for optimism

Challenging as these several developments are, there is cause for optimism. The challenges are well understood; one has only to read China's impressive Twelfth Five-Year plan to appreciate that point. Citizens throughout the region are indicating a willingness to work together to find collaborative solutions to problems. Active involvement in collaborative solutions will unlock unprecedented opportunity for billions of people in the Asian Century, in developed and developing nations alike.

Australia is well placed and is adapting to the rise of Asia

Against that backdrop, Australia appears to be in good shape. Unlike most of the rest of the developed world, in Australia, government balance sheets are strong. Our financial system is sound. Our economic policy frameworks and governance institutions, developed over several decades, insulated the Australian economy from the external shocks associated with the Asian financial crisis of the late 1990s; the 'tech wreck', global stock market correction and widespread developed-world recession a few years later; and the recent global financial crisis. These frameworks and institutions represent 'created endowments'—a legacy of an earlier generation of Australians.

Our foreign policy and strategic frameworks have built strong bilateral relationships across the region that enable us to influence and shape regional and, at times, global outcomes.

Our natural endowments have a strong measure of complementarity with the world's fastest-growing economies. We have a large endowment of environmental assets, though we need to do a better job of protecting them. We have abundant mineral and energy reserves, though they will not last forever. We have the capacity to produce greater volumes of high-protein foods, though we need to find more sustainable farming practices, and, as a series of recent deplorable events have illustrated graphically, we need a much sharper focus on animal welfare concerns. In this Asian Century, we also have locational advantage.

Our human capital endowments are also significant. We have a highly skilled, diverse and creative population that has deepening connections with the region and demonstrated capability in innovation, design and complex problem solving.

Our people-to-people ties with the region are growing deeper. The face of Australia is changing as migrants, students and visitors from Asia bring new perspectives, energy and skills. One in 10 Australians was born in Asia.

Today, China and India are the principal source countries of Australian immigration. Increasingly, Australians also live, study and work in the region, strengthening the exchange of ideas and cultures.

Our governments at all levels are increasingly outward looking, and we are collaborating with regional counterparts across a broad sweep of interests in ways unimaginable a decade ago.

It would be a grave mistake, however, to think that we have done all we need to do in order to guard against the risks, and make the most of the opportunities, associated with the Asian Century—a point I will enlarge on below.

Regional economies are moving up the value chain

As Asian economies modernise and grow, they are also moving up the value chain, investing in skills and technology, infrastructure and social safety nets. Their costs of production are already increasing (especially in the industrialised east of China), but so too is their capacity to produce high-value, high-innovation goods and services. Asia recently overtook Europe in the share of the world's research and development undertaken. China and Indonesia, in particular, are investing heavily in human capital development, including through the construction of world-class universities. In 2010, China had 22 universities in the top 500 in the world—up from 12 in 2003.

As the Asian middle class grows, so does domestic consumption.[7] Asia is set to become the world's largest consumer market. The rapid rise and creative use of communication technology and social media in Asia are also transforming markets in the region. In 2005 less than one-quarter of the population in Asia and the Pacific had a mobile phone. By 2011, that had grown to three-quarters. In the same period, the number of internet users in Asia and the Pacific trebled, from 344 million to more than one billion.

Australia's future is in our hands

While the opportunities confronting Australia are unarguably promising, success cannot be taken for granted. Indeed, the challenge for government, business and the community is immense. It is no exaggeration to say that a new mindset is required. Success in this century means a willingness to adapt continually. Several factors provide necessary foundations for this integration, including free trade in goods and services, capital mobility, the globalisation of ideas, and people movements—but much more is required.

---

7 'Figure 2.2: Growing consumer markets of Asia, Australia in the Asian Century' (Commonwealth of Australia 2012: 63).

In consulting with people on the White Paper, we came to the view that Australia needs to act in five key dimensions. These provide the structure for the second part of the White Paper.

First, Australia's prosperity will come from *building on our strengths*, reinforcing the domestic foundations of our society and our productive, open and resilient economy. That means building on past reforms and investing across the five pillars of productivity: skills and education, innovation, infrastructure, tax reform, and regulatory reform.

Second, we must do even more to build the *capabilities* that will help Australia succeed. This generation's greatest responsibility is to invest in our people through education and skills to drive Australia's productivity performance and ensure that all Australians can participate in, and contribute to, the Asian Century.

Third, Australia's commercial engagement in the region will be most successful if highly innovative, competitive Australian firms and institutions develop *collaborative relationships* with others in the region. Australian firms need new business models and new mindsets to operate in and connect with Asian markets. The Australian government needs to involve itself in initiatives that make the region more open and integrated, encouraging trade, investment and partnerships.

Fourth, Australia's future is irrevocably tied to the ongoing prosperity and *sustainable security* of our diverse region. Australia has much to offer through cooperation with other nations to support sustainable security in the region. The Australian government has a role to play in contributing to trust and cooperation, bilaterally and through existing regional mechanisms; and the Australian government should continue to support a greater role for Asian countries in a rules-based regional and global order.

Fifth, Australia needs to strengthen its deep and broad *relationships* across the region at every level. These links are social and cultural as much as they are political and economic, developing out of shared experience in commerce, institutions, travel, arts, sport, education and the exchange of ideas and knowledge. Our engagement to date would best be described as episodic, constructed around significant events, with insubstantial, fragile linkages between these. Many of the people with whom we consulted argued persuasively that we need a more strategic approach to our bilateral relationships. We were told that Australia's governments, businesses, unions, community groups and educational and cultural institutions all have an important role to play.

A need for new mindsets

Time and time again, in our consultations, we found ourselves being persuaded that new mindsets were required. We were told that our traditional approach to openness is not sufficiently ambitious. We have to pursue regional harmonisation (or mutual recognition) across a broad sweep of areas: educational qualifications, occupational skills recognition, financial regulation, corporate governance, and so on.

Australian businesses need products and know-how that are valued in the region. That means understanding our comparative advantage and adding value through innovation and the development of long-term relationships.

We came to the view that the twenty-first-century business model is likely to be very different from the successful business models of the last quarter of the twentieth century. The best recipe for long-term success comes from making the most of complementary interests and working collaboratively with partners in Asia, not just competing against them. In some cases, Australian businesses will be able to access large Asian markets through export, including as part of regional supply chains. In other cases, the business opportunities will be secured through the establishment of enterprises, including business partnerships, in Asian countries. Australian businesses will need the capabilities to do both.

'Collaboration', 'cooperation', 'partnership', 'matching capabilities' and 'engagement' are part of the language of this century, just as 'international competitiveness' was the language of the last quarter of the past century. This is not to downplay productivity and competition. Productivity and domestic competition are among the conditions that will allow Australians to secure opportunities for collaboration and cooperation in the region. The central point is one that has been understood by economists since the time of Adam Smith: the gains from trade arise not from mimicry, but from differences that define complementarity. In this Asian Century, Australia's complementary differences include exceptional standards of corporate governance and workplace safety, an insistence on quality and an intolerance of corruption.

Our conclusion was that, for Australian businesses and individuals who develop the capability to engage in this way, there is a vast landscape of new opportunity, especially in supplying goods and services to an increasingly prosperous Asia, and in ventures to help address the challenges confronting several large regional neighbours in respect of water security, energy security, food security, green growth, urban design, health care and aged care. However, only a small proportion of Australia's population has these capabilities at present. They need to be built in all Australians. We need Australians with the knowledge and skills to develop strong relationships in the region. To build partnerships we need the capacities to understand and operate in cultures, languages and mindsets other than our own. Within Australia we need to ensure we have the advisory, decision-making and representational structures in place to make informed decisions in an increasingly complex environment.

Our major bilateral relationships need to be transformed into comprehensive partnerships involving government, business, community organisations and citizens generally. Common experience through commerce, institutions, travel, arts, culture and sport, as well as education, ideas and knowledge exchange, should increase.

The then government indicated in the White Paper that Australia should place an initial priority on deepening relations with five of our Asian neighbours: China, India, Indonesia, Japan and South Korea. In making these a focus, the government also said that we should not neglect other countries in the region. Indeed, there is a case for stepping up efforts to engage and deepen relations with Vietnam and the other countries of the Association of Southeast Asian Nations (ASEAN).

The government has a major role to play in planning and building for the Asian Century. The White Paper sets out core policy principles to guide government action over the coming years, and it articulates policy pathways to deliver real change. The White Paper, however, does more than that. It identifies national objectives out to 2025, to guide decision-making and planning right across the Australian economy and society. It is a call to action—not just for our elected parliamentary representatives but also for all Australians.

Assessing the White Paper

Some Australians are cynical about the 'vision thing'. Absurdly, they draw a distinction between 'vision' and 'substance'. Of course, some of these people do not want political leaders who have a clear sense of direction and purpose, able to build a coherent policy narrative around a powerful vision. They would prefer to have leaders who are easier to manipulate. This, however, is a small, if noisy, minority.

The reaction to the White Paper from people of goodwill and reason has been positive. As I read it, reasonable people are accepting of the direction articulated in the document. They are persuaded of the vision. They welcome it, but many want more detail—and they want things done soon. What this says to me is that the White Paper's narrative has been found compelling. In that important sense, the document has served a purpose.

The White Paper was designed not only to persuade people of the need for action, but also to chart the course for future action—by this generation. It was designed to sketch the pathways all of us will have to pursue if we are to meet the expectations of future generations of Australians. The pathways are many. Most demand a whole-of-community effort.

Some of the people who participated in the consultations on the White Paper had a clear sense of the things this generation of Australians will have to do if it is to have any hope of its descendants awarding it a passing grade in the test I outlined earlier. We heard that we will have to demonstrate that we converted mineral and energy wealth into enduring national capability through sustainably higher rates of national saving; path-breaking advances in science and technology; more effective protection of vulnerable species and ecosystems; high-yielding investments in human capability and physical capital, including both economic and social infrastructure; and the development of effective relationships in the region to support the pursuit of commercial and cultural exchange. We heard also that we will have to demonstrate that we shared the benefits widely so that all Australians had the opportunity to provide their descendants with a better life; notably, we will have to deal a mortal blow to Indigenous disadvantage.

Given the enormity of the challenges we confront, and the generally poor quality of public policy discussion in Australia at present, it is natural to ask who would want to take responsibility for Australia's future. Who would want to sit the test that is being set by future generations of Australians?

Conventionally, governments are expected to look after the interests of those cohorts not yet born. What happens to this country of ours after we are gone is not something for the rest of us to worry about. This, however, makes no sense, especially in a democracy. Whenever there is a trade-off to be made between the instant gratification of the present generation and the well-being of future generations, is the government to stand in opposition to its own electors? Imagine that.

In contrast with this fantasy, the truth is at once more challenging and more motivating. If this generation is going to satisfy the legitimate expectations of future generations of Australians, if it is going to pass the test they set for us, all of us are going to have to assume responsibility for this nation's future in the Asian Century.

References

Commonwealth of Australia. 2012. *Australia in the Asian Century*. White Paper. Canberra: Commonwealth of Australia. URL: pandora.nla.gov. au/pan/133850/20130914-0122/asiancentury.dpmc.gov.au/index.html. Consulted 27 October 2014.

Kharas, Homi and Gertz, Geoffrey. 2010. The new global middle class: A crossover from West to East. In Cheng Li, ed. *China's emerging middle class: Beyond economic transformation*. Washington, DC: Brookings Institution.

Asia literacy: A deeply problematic metaphor

Ariel Heryanto

In separate ways, two issues have concerned scholars in Australia and beyond. The first challenge concerns a desire to respond adequately to the widely accepted critique of Euro-American centricism, which is deeply embedded in much of the social sciences and humanities. The second issue hovers around ways to respond to the unsettling impacts of digital technology, which has radically altered our everyday social relations, along with knowledge production, dissemination and preservation. Neither challenge is new. Far from resolving these old issues, however, we have instead been confronted with an even sharper awareness of their complexity. Most of the time, analysts address these issues as two separate areas of inquiry.

Here, I wish to discuss one case, with much broader relevance, where the two issues intersect. I refer to the study of twenty-first-century Indonesia, a former European colony in Asia and Australia's giant neighbour. I look at the problematic notion of 'Asia literacy' as widely used in Australia, across many professions and circles, including the government, the business community and the education sector. I argue that this key phrase is strongly biased, inadvertently recuperating the old Euro-American centricism already disavowed in much of the Western world. The phrase is also unashamedly obsolete in the early twenty-first century, which is marked by the rapid expansion of digital media technology around the globe, not least in Asia.

Notwithstanding the general admission of its multiple meanings—metaphorically or otherwise—'Asia literacy' unequivocally articulates the notion of Asia as a fixed text for reading.[1] Despite the international acknowledgment of Asia's vigorous and dynamic character, including in the White Paper *Australia in the Asian Century* (Commonwealth of Australia 2012), the phrase assumes that underneath, or superseding, the superanimated Asia exists a more or less coherent, text-like 'Asian' thing (as essence, system or structure), which is assumed to exist 'out there', just waiting to be read, interpreted and commented on by active people who are equipped with the required competency or 'literacy'. In fact, 'reading texts', as a mode of learning shaped by a print-dominated era, is neither the sole nor the best method of learning. This is especially problematic in any discussion of developing knowledge about Asia, and increasingly so in a digitised century. Furthermore, Asia—whatever that might mean—is not, and has never been, simply the muted and helpless object of a reading class of outsiders.

Orality-oriented social life

Life in Indonesia, as in many other societies around the world, is strongly orality oriented. While most Indonesians are nominally literate, there is a low level of functional literacy. The country has a high official literacy rate: more than 90 per cent. This statistic means that most Indonesians have the ability to recognise the alphabet and mathematical figures. It does not mean, however, that literacy plays a major function in their daily life. Even among the nation's literati and graduates of higher education, many prefer to share important information and messages through face-to-face communication or through new media devices that bear many of the features of orality and conversational communication.

At the turn of the twenty-first century, Sen and Hill reported on publishing in Indonesia:

> The book publishing industry in Indonesia is small by regional standards. Through the 1980s Indonesia published 4,000–5,000 titles per year. In 1992, this figure went up to over 6,000, but Indonesia still produced fewer books per head of population than most of its neighbours and even in absolute terms remained lower than South Korea and Thailand, which have much smaller populations. Indonesia's Central Bureau of Statistics … does not even include book-reading

---

1   'Literally', all words are metaphors, as there is no one-to-one relationship between a word (signifier), its meaning (signified) and the reality to which it refers. There cannot be a truly literal meaning of any word, in the common sense of the words 'literal' or 'literally'. Some words appear to have acquired some literal meanings because their metaphoric qualities have been forgotten, taken for granted or a more recent figurative use of the same word has been introduced successfully.

in its 'socio-cultural' data, which measures the usage of all other media (radio, television, newspapers and magazines) as well as sports and community participation. (Sen and Hill 2000: 24)

Statistics are an inadequate measure of the real situation. In Indonesia, major bookshops keep most newly published titles for no more than three months. Some of the best collections of books are privately owned, and many of these books cannot be found in public or university libraries. No matter where they are kept, books in this tropical country suffer incessantly from extremely high levels of humidity and year-round abundant sunlight, which support the rapid growth of mould, plus various insects and termites. At a more fundamental level, Sen and Hill add a note about the status of books in the country:

> Even what constitutes a 'book' is not always obvious. Many published manuscripts in Indonesia, some by respected intellectuals and sold in bookshops, contain no ISBN (International Standard Book Number), which in the context of the international publishing industry is a formal requirement for all books. Some name no Indonesian publisher or printer. (Sen and Hill 2000: 22)

One widely shared post on Facebook is a quote from Albert Einstein (1879–1955): 'Everybody is a genius. But if you judge a fish by its ability to climb a tree it will live its whole life believing that it is stupid.' If civilisation, intelligence, wisdom or education were measured exclusively in terms of functional literacy and book publishing, Indonesia would be a permanently sad story. One need only think of two of the world's most well-known teachers, who did not put their teachings in written form: Socrates and Jesus. Many scholars have noted that Indonesia is among the slowest and least-developed of its Southeast Asian neighbours in modern schooling, and in university training in the social sciences and the humanities (Booth 1999; Nordholt and Visser 1995). According to some reports, research output (presumably only in English!) on Indonesia authored by non-Indonesians has consistently been several times greater than that by Indonesians (Gerke and Evers 2006).[2]

Indonesia has many talented musicians, with some making headlines in the media beyond the territory of the nation-state, but many of these artists do not read musical notes, including the prominent composer Melly Goeslaw. One of the best poets in contemporary Indonesia is soft-spoken Sapardi Djoko Damono, but his poetry is barely read in the nation, and his published anthology is hard to find in bookshops. More people have heard his name than have read his work. In contrast, the poet Rendra (1935–2009) is one of the best-known

---

2   Gerke and Evers (2006: 3) make a disclaimer about their data being less than entirely 'true', and their analysis as 'objective'. They base their assessment on data 'from data banks that are maintained in the United States [which] control which scholarly output is regarded as valuable enough to be enshrined in the Social Sciences Citation Index, the Sociological Abstracts, or similar data banks'.

Indonesian public figures for his performances of poetry reading. Whenever he read his poetry in public, several thousand people listened attentively as if at a rock concert. In 1978 and 1990, the militarist regime of the New Order banned Rendra's performances, but none of his books (Murray 1991: 8–9). Indonesia had a blind president, Abdurrahman Wahid (1940–2009), who ruled by hearing and speaking, instead of reading and writing. Except for Sukarno (1901–70), the first president, Wahid was Indonesia's most revered president, both during his life and after his death.

While Indonesia performs poorly in functional literacy, it is outstanding when it comes to engaging with old and new electronic media, whose characteristics (being instant, highly interactive and fluid) resemble the orality mode of communication rather than the literacy mode. The nation is one of the world's largest markets for radio sets (Sen 2003: 586). Today, more than '90% of Indonesians (over 10 years old) account watching television as one of their main social and cultural activities' (Lim 2011: 1). That amounts to more than 220 million people, and 15 per cent of them enjoy the satellite television network (Lim 2011: 2). In 2010 Indonesia was home to the fourth-largest number of Facebook users in the world, rising from rank seven in the previous year. Two years earlier, Indonesia had not been in the ranking. In 2011, however, it jumped to second position (Burcher 2012). According to Sun Jung, 'Indonesian is the third most used language' in the average worldwide traffic of 'K-pop' (Korean popular music) on Google Trends. This can be attributed to the large number of young Indonesian K-pop fans who are 'technology-savvy digital natives who have never known a world without the Internet' (Jung 2011).

In its most basic or primary model, oral communication requires the physical co-presence of two or more interlocutors, expressing themselves not only through spoken words but, more importantly, also through intonation, through what is not said and by body language, in specific spatial and temporal conditions of real-time interactions that can never be repeated. Understandably, in such circumstances, life tends to be highly communal, with little or no space for privacy. In today's contexts, such fundamentals have been widely extended and there can be found modified expressions in old and new media that operate in ways reminiscent of oral conversations. Unsurprisingly, emotional icons (emoticons) are essential in short message texting and social media postings among young people, expressing nostalgia for conversations in person.

In the more literacy-dependent societies, the ideas of 'author', 'text' and 'audience' are all clearly separated as autonomous entities. Texts are broken up and clearly marked as separate chapters, sections, paragraphs, sentences, words and characters—as in social life. Marshall McLuhan (1911–80) argued that the 'breaking up of every kind of experience into uniform units in order to produce faster action and change of form (applied knowledge) has been the secret of

Western power over man and nature alike' (McLuhan 1964: 87). A sacred oath is commonly used to formalise an agreement in an orality-oriented society, just as a written contract is privileged in literacy-dependent nations. Attempting to read quietly in a busy public space is normal in literacy-oriented societies, while it would be taken as strange or antisocial in many other societies, including Indonesia. A literacy-saturated society must verbalise pleasantries such as 'please' or 'thank you', because they can be easily transcribed in writing. In many places across Asia, many of the standard pleasantries are found in constant smiles, giggles and body language, which cannot be coded in the alphabet or punctuation. I will return to the issue of Indonesia's omnipresent smiling in the concluding section.

A common cultural shock confronting first-time foreign visitors to Indonesia is the series of intrusive-sounding questions issued from complete strangers or recent acquaintances: Where are you going? Are you married? Why not? Have you taken a bath? These expressions, like most, are not readily translated into English, but can be crudely understood to mean 'how are you doing?'. Something is fatally lost and something else is unavoidably added in any act of translation.

Obviously, no modern society today is purely orality oriented, literacy dependent or digitally based. Different modes of communication coexist and compete with one another. Many millions of Indonesians travel frequently, do business or spend extended time in literacy-oriented societies, and vice versa. Such experiences can have a far-reaching impact. Therefore, the distinction I suggest here should be taken more as an analytical framework, rather than a set of descriptive empirical categories.

As hinted at above, and contrary to the assumptions made by many children of the Enlightenment, the revolutionary power of new technologies has been more confronting to those in the highly literate societies (Fernback 2003) than to those in the more orality-oriented ones. New media easily finds a warm reception in societies like Indonesia, as it fits well with existing norms and social practices, characterised by fluid, instantaneous and highly collective participatory modes of communication (Heryanto 2010). For all these reasons, 'Asia literacy' is not the best approach to understanding Indonesia, or many other parts of Asia, nor for that matter anything or anyone throughout the world in this century.

Ways of hearing and seeing

Marshall McLuhan, in the 1960s and 1970s, was the first to radically challenge some of the most familiar paradigms of understanding the nature of social relations and historical change, in his focus on media technology. In contrast with the past, and currently common, inquiry of what technology has done or can do *for* social beings, McLuhan and those who followed in his steps were ingeniously concerned with what technology has done or can do *to* us, and to our ways of understanding the world, others and ourselves. Following McLuhan, I mean by 'technology' the broadest sense of the term, encompassing speech, maps, trains, money or prisons.

Put in the simplest terms, McLuhan identified three major epochs in our history, each marked by one dominant mode of communication in a given society: orality, print and electronic media technology. These are neither three clearly cut nor entirely separable periods or social orders. As mentioned above, and as will be further elaborated and illustrated below, McLuhan was not suggesting a straightforward, linear or uniform view of history, with one phase ending where another one begins. Whether his view represents a technological determinism, as some critics have accused, remains open to debate. Those who built on his early work elaborated his perspective, particularly in the areas concerning the interface between two or more modes of communication.

When a newer technology arrives, the older one never entirely disappears. In order to be accepted by an existing social order, the new technology must be presented in an attractive and non-threatening fashion, even if it later develops in fully fledged ways that undermine and ultimately overthrow older regimes of communication. There is always a complex and dynamic process of interfacing between several modes of communication (orality, print literacy and electronic 'prosumption'/consumption) in most contemporary societies.[3] The variations of social life based on different interfaced modes of communication form an important but underdeveloped area of study. McLuhan's work provides the foundation for such a study. Being a product of his time, however, his work does not adequately address many of the questions raised after his death at the end of 1980, when the digital world developed far beyond what could be imagined in his time, although still in line with many of his basic premises.

As has been widely documented by many in anthropology, linguistics and literary studies, in the early days of literacy in many societies, people wrote what they had been saying orally since time immemorial. Punctuation was

---

3   'Prosumption' involves both production and consumption rather than focusing only on production or only on consumption.

new, awkward, rare and simple. Rhymes, proverbs and a conversational style of speech characterised their writing style, rather than high abstraction and analytical statements. People read texts, including newspapers, aloud. Dialogue in the performing arts was sung. As print was rapidly disseminated, orality continued to function, but had to gradually change its function. People did not cease talking as they learned to read and write. Likewise, pencils and pens have remained part of everyday life in the age of tablets and smart phones. Movies did not vanish, but nor could they survive unchanged, with the invention and rapid diffusion of television, DVDs and YouTube. According to a recent report, although sales of cassette tapes 'have declined, 200,000 albums [were] sold on tape in the U.S. in 2012—a fraction of a per cent of the 316 million total albums sold but a 645% increase over 2011 cassette sales' (Rothman 2013: 42).

Orality persisted after the introduction of print. Orality's earlier logic resisted pressure from the print regime, before it underwent transformation and adjusted to a new social environment dictated by the regime of print, in order to survive and remain relevant. As the regime of print consolidated its power, it put more pressure on orality. Ultimately, modern and increasingly literate members of such societies learned how to construct and organise their speech in the way they would eventually compose their words in writing. Rhymes, parables and proverbs faded from speech, or found themselves on the margin of daily intercourse.

The 'ideal type' of change, as outlined above, from one dominant mode of communication to another takes many decades or, more commonly, centuries. The change represents not only or primarily the speed or capacity of communicative technology, 'but alterations in the apparatus through which the world could be "thought" and retrieved in "memory"'. Furthermore, 'technologies of communication were principally things to think with, moulders of mind, shapers of thought: the medium was the message' (Carey 1998). An overemphasis on the mind and on thought, however, risks overlooking or underestimating the greater impersonal changes in social structures. Such a process of change raises hopes and causes confusion and tension. Apprehension, disorientation and panic were common in North America when television became widely accessible in the middle of the past century (the moment McLuhan's unprecedented thoughts were first published). Recently, another round of overwhelming anxiety occurred when the earlier television generation of the 1960s became older and found themselves confronted by a new, younger generation of this early twenty-first century, who could not keep their hands and eyes off their handheld mobile gadgets twenty-four hours a day, seven days a week.

James Carey observes that, with the widespread distribution of new electronic recording devices,

> the monopoly enjoyed by print was to be exploded and that no one means of experiencing the world would dominate as printing had among educated classes for centuries. The new means of reproducing reality also meant that the historic barriers between the arts and between the arts and other departments of life— art and science, work and leisure—would be driven down.
>
> … This erosion of barriers between the arts meant as well the erosion of barriers between the audiences. The division of culture into high and low; folk and popular; mass and elite; highbrow, lowbrow, and middlebrow—barriers and distinctions that were themselves the product of printing—would have to be discarded under the impact of new forms of communication which simply did not recognize these distinctions. (Carey 1998)

For some, such change was strongly unwelcome. Few articulated the elitist sentiment of North America at that time more eloquently than Dwight MacDonald in the mid-1950s:

> The separation of Folk Art and High Culture in fairly watertight compartments corresponded to the sharp line once drawn between the common people and the aristocracy. The eruption of the masses on to the political stage has broken down this compartmentation, with disastrous cultural results. (MacDonald 1998: 24)
>
> Like nineteenth-century capitalism, Mass Culture is a dynamic, revolutionary force, breaking down the old barriers of class, tradition, taste, and dissolving all cultural distinctions. It mixes and scrambles everything together, producing what might be called homogenized culture, after another American achievement, the homogenization process that distributes the globules of cream evenly throughout the milk instead of allowing them to float separately on top. It thus destroys all values, since value judgments imply discrimination. Mass Culture is very, very democratic: it absolutely refuses to discriminate against, or between, anything or anybody. All is grist to its mill, and all comes out finely ground indeed. (MacDonald 1998: 25)

One major historical product of industrial capitalism and literacy in the West is the notion of 'privacy', along with 'authorship' and the work of authors as 'private property' (McLuhan and Fiore 1967: 122). These notions have been highly valued for at least two centuries. Now it has been made glaringly obvious that privacy has become one of the most vulnerable casualties of the rapid development of digital media. Photocopying machines and digital recorders have undermined copyright as 'private property', and invented the author-cum-publisher. In the wake of whistleblower Edward Snowden's disclosures to the mass media in 2013 about the secret interception operation by the US National Security Agency, surveys suggest that the majority of Americans support the [government operation], even if they don't entirely trust the government's explanations. According to a recent *Washington Post/ABC News* poll, after digesting Snowden's news, a solid majority feel that it's more important to fully investigate terrorist threats than to protect personal privacy. (Wolf 2013: 39)

Many Americans tolerated their privacy being compromised, not only because of the real or perceived threats of terrorism or because the state apparatuses are considered too powerful to resist, but also because, as Wolf puts it aptly, '[p]rivacy is not the only illusion in the new age of data; government secrecy is too. Big Brother might be watching, but he is also being watched' (Wolf 2013: 39)—as the cases of Bradley Manning, Wikileaks and Snowden illustrate. We live in a village-like world: a global village.

Of course, years before Snowden made the headlines, privacy had already been rendered obsolete for millions of Facebook users around the world. Regularly, I have witnessed couples who have been married happily for decades post messages or photographs about each other's appearance or daily activities, and post such comments for the whole world to see. Someone told me how her friend took a picture of a meal in a restaurant with her mobile device and posted it on Facebook for the general public. Instantaneously, her companion sitting across the table commented on the posted image on the same social media platform. While preparing this chapter, a well-respected public figure in Indonesia posted on Facebook a series of his own medical reports just issued from a hospital where he had undergone serious clinical examination!

Changes to the notion, status and value of privacy are not taking place everywhere at the same time and in the same way for all people. These variations do not adhere to simple political, economic, national lines or exist exclusively among specific age groups. This is well illustrated by how Facebook operates, and explains why it is so overwhelmingly popular, transcending so many of those familiar categories. Lev Grossman (2010) recalls that '[p]eople hated Facebook's News Feed when it was introduced in 2006. They thought it was creepy and intrusive … and now Facebook is unimaginable without it.' Chris Cox, Facebook's vice-president, elaborated further in an interview with Grossman:

> When caller ID came out, people went psycho. You know, because, Oh my God, now people are going to know I'm calling them! This is terrible! I'm going to end up being tracked, and Big Brother and Orwell and all that! The reality is now you won't pick up a call unless you know who's calling you. (Grossman 2010)

The introduction of electronic media technology and its impact have generated tensions and social change comparable with earlier societies hit by the spread of literacy and print. They are not, however, and never can be, a full repeat. The process varies across different societies, and thus its impact varies as well.

The impact of digital media has been harsher and more painful for highly literacy-dependent societies than for strongly orality-oriented societies. We are not, therefore, witnessing a kind of technological determinism. There is no suggestion of a deterministic, uniform or linear history that all societies undergo—from orality to literacy to the new media participation often dubbed 'prosumerism' (the amalgamation of producer and consumer).

New ways of learning about the new world

Australian universities are committed to upholding the privacy protections of participants in their respective sponsored research projects. A national body regulates and oversees a mandatory and meticulous formal review of ethical issues in all research plans. All of this is commendable, but its operation often requires more flexibility than many university human research ethics committees are willing or able to accommodate. This is especially true for social research conducted in many parts of Asia, where the notion of privacy is non-existent, irrelevant or significantly different from that generally understood in Australia and most Western societies.

I am aware that to suggest some variation between daily life in Australia (notionally conceptualised as a Western society) and Asia (the 'East') can be easily misconstrued as recuperating the old-fashioned and false dichotomy of East versus West. To suggest, however, that all of these societies are flatly and universally homogeneous would be ridiculous. One alternative approach to identifying and analysing social variations beyond the East/West divide is to take into account the configuration or interfaced modes of communication across social collectives. This technologically based category is to complement, and not substitute, the already familiar practice of categorising social life along 'economic organization (mercantilism, industrialism, capitalism, socialism) or politics (the divine right of kings, the social contract, the dictatorship of the proletariat)' (Carey 1998), or nation-state categories.

Like nations, prisons and factories, our schools and universities are very much products of the logic of the old print technology in Europe and North America. These institutions are currently struggling to survive the overwhelming impact of digital media technology on learning environments, which has made it not only imaginable and possible, but also desirable, to teach and learn in a classroom without walls, without a fixed class timetable and, not least of all, without the hassles of finding a car parking space. This new environment changes not only where, when or how we learn things, but more importantly, what we learn and why. In ways comparable with the struggle of the church in Europe when confronted by the spread of print and the translation of sacred words into vernacular languages several centuries ago, universities today have tried hard to manage their situation in order to salvage the old, established notions of certified knowledge, authority and ethical integrity by incorporating digital media technology into knowledge production and dissemination. Sooner or later we will regard such efforts as similar to insisting that a computer mouse is a new kind of pen or a mobile tablet device is a new kind of book.

Those who run schools and universities have gradually acknowledged that this new media technology does not simply offer options for learning, but rather asserts its logic and forces educational institutions to change the way things are done in the administration office, in classrooms and on campus grounds. Few, however, perceive the power of the technology to undermine some of the key fundamentals of the establishment and operation of these modern institutions and, for better or worse, to transform them into something radically different. In the view of McLuhan and Fiore:

> Today's television child is attuned to up-to-the-minute 'adult' news—inflation, rioting, war, taxes, crime, bathing beauties—and is bewildered when he enters the nineteenth-century environment that still characterizes the educational establishment where information is scarce but ordered and structured by fragmented, classified patterns, subjects, and schedules. (McLuhan and Fiore 1967: 18)

Regardless of the tactics employed by old regimes against change, one need only look at the mass media industry to envisage what transformation our universities might experience in the future. When the form and function of print media initially intersected with online space, print products were simply reproduced in digital form on websites. Similarly, many university lecturers simply uploaded their text in pdf (portable document format) on the course website—just as early writers composed in rhymes and proverbs. Before long, universities realised that the new media did not simply extend their old operations and products into a new online space. Now, the new media not only alters the content—as journalists increasingly gather information initially or exclusively from the Internet—but also the websites feature a set of completely new materials such as interactive graphics, audio and video materials, and real-time coverage, which were all non-existent in earlier forms of the industry.

The fact that McLuhan's work has not been taken more seriously and applied more broadly across the social sciences and humanities, beyond media studies in his home base of Canada, suggests that his insights were far ahead of his time. To gauge how slow and conservative our intellectual capacity has been to grapple with the full potential and impact of digital media, it is useful to look back at our efforts in coming to terms with the significance and consequences of print. Six centuries after Johannes Gutenberg invented movable-type printing, we are still struggling to critically comprehend and fully grasp the impact of print technology on human history. Only in the late twentieth century did we seriously engage in the debate on how literacy and print capitalism might be foundational in the creation of nations, following the publication of Benedict Anderson's *Imagined communities*. To be fair, it must be remembered that Anderson's arguments are far more complex and nuanced than can be summed up here. For our immediate concerns, let us focus on one of his central arguments concerning the 'genesis of nationalism' (Anderson 1983: 30).

Anderson attributes the birth of nations to a series of historical conditions related to the decline of sacred communities. In his view, '[b]eneath the decline of sacred communities, languages and lineages, a fundamental change was taking place in modes of apprehending the world, which, more than anything else, made it possible to "think" the nation' (Anderson 1983: 28). He was referring to the 'idea of *simultaneity*' (emphasis in the original), and argues that

> [w]hat has come to take the place of the mediaeval conception of simultaneity-along-time is, to borrow again from Benjamin, an idea of 'homogeneous, empty time,' in which simultaneity is, as it were, transverse, cross-time, marked not by prefiguring and fulfilment, but by temporal coincidence, and measured by clock and calendar … The idea of a sociological organism moving calendrically through homogeneous, empty time is a precise analogue of the idea of the nation, which also is conceived as a solid community moving steadily down (or up) history. (Anderson 1983: 30–31)

It is significant that Anderson published his innovative work only in the early 1980s, to widespread interest. In other words, it was only after computers had become a daily necessity to many professionals in major industrial centres around the globe. Only then could scholars find themselves in a better position to analyse the conditions under which a new conception of homogeneous time prevailed and nations were born. It is only after word processing, the Internet and mobile media communications began to impact significantly on the sense and sensibilities of a centuries-long print regime that people have been properly equipped to undertake a critical examination of what print has done *to* human beings across the globe, rather than *for* them.

In line with most anti-humanist theorists of the twentieth century, Anderson's portrayal of the nation is conceived as a product not primarily of human efforts. Rather, certain historical conditions and media technologies have required and enabled the articulation of new forms of solidarity, new aspirations and social orders that have found their expression in 'nations'. Referring to 'the novel and the newspaper', he asserts that they 'provided the technical means for "re-presenting" the *kind* of imagined community that is the nation' (Anderson 1983: 30; emphasis in original).

We should not, however, stop there. A couple of decades after this new awareness of what print might have done to human history, we still cannot say with full confidence that the print regime is fully under our gaze and an object of our analysis, detached from our analytical framework. Anderson's subsequent thesis about 'long-distance nationalism' is an intriguing case in point, because it betrays some of his earlier thesis. If he is correct about the potency of specific media technology for transforming human history—in this case, the critical contribution made by print media, such as the novel and the newspaper, to the birth of nations—in the wake of the spread of electronic media, one would expect Anderson to anticipate the decline of nations and nationalism, and imagine the rise of a new consciousness in human history, new conceptions of time and space, with radically new communities and forms of solidarity ('post-nation' is an inadequate metaphor, but suggestive). Instead, he argues that the new media has generated only a new version of nationalism called 'long-distance nationalism':

> It would be very difficult to say that today Indian nationalism is less serious than Chinese, East Timorese [less] than Thai, Indonesian [less] than Japanese, or Taiwanese [less] than Korean. If one asks why this should be so, especially today, an explanation is impossible without thinking about the role of the electronic media, which for most people now exercise[s] an even more powerful influence than print, the original mother of nationalism.

> … One could even argue, as I have done in another context, that electronic communications, combined with the huge migrations created by the present world-economic system, are creating a virulent new form of nationalism, which I call long-distance nationalism: a nationalism that no longer depends as it once did on territorial location in a home country. (Anderson 2001: 42)

If the electronic media fundamentally enhances nationalism, there should be another and more critical re-examination of the thesis about the fundamental service of print literacy in the birth of nations.

For McLuhan and Fiore (1967: 45), '[t]he rational man in our Western culture is a visual man. The fact that most conscious experience has little "visuality" in it is lost on him.' Consequently:

> They suspect the ear; they don't trust it. In general we feel more secure when things are visible, when we can 'see for ourselves'. We admonish children, for instance, to 'believe only half of what they see, and nothing of what they hear'. All kinds of 'shorthand' systems of notation have been developed to help us see what we hear.

> We insist on employing visual metaphors even when we refer to purely psychological states, such as tendency and duration. For instance, we say thereafter when we really mean thenafter … We are so visually biased that we call our wisest men visionaries, or seers! (McLuhan and Fiore 1967: 117)

This is not to say that people in less literacy-oriented societies are not biased or are less biased. Rather, we are differently biased, and more often than not we are all unaware of our own biases. For these reasons, cross-cultural experience is both potentially risky and enriching. Australia's commitment to understanding Asia and deeply engaging with Asians in various forms is highly commendable, not least for allowing Australians to better understand themselves in the process of learning about 'others'. This can be done successfully if Australians let go of the Asia literacy paradigm, and seek new and better approaches to 'reading' Asia and Asians as other than text-like characters (in the double sense). One step in that direction is to acknowledge some of the fundamental differences in daily life between many parts of Asia with strong orality-oriented features and those in other parts of the world such as Australia. I wish to conclude with a couple of cases to illustrate these differences.

Politically incorrect habits

It is normal for first-time foreign visitors, unless they come from similar social environments, to misunderstand how and why certain things are done in Indonesia. One well-documented example is the strong reaction by many Indonesians and many other Asians to the widely published image dated 15 January 1998 of Michel Camdessus, then International Monetary Fund (IMF) managing director, with his arms folded, standing and watching then president Suharto of Indonesia bowing to the table as he signed the country's bailout package. In another case, Australians were outraged at the published image of Amrozi, one of the Bali bombers, smiling along with the Indonesian police in 2002. I wish to argue that in both cases a misunderstanding took place, in part due to the work of different modes of communication and the materiality of language—being one of the oldest media technologies in our history—and its impact on our often taken-for-granted banal sensibilities, norms and social values.

By the late 1990s, a great number of Indonesians (including the military elite and not just the student political activists who took to the streets) felt that they had had more than enough of Suharto's rule. Whether the 1998 IMF bailout package was wise has been a topic of debate, which is not our immediate concern here. What is of concern is Camdessus's posture in the image. Remarkably, despite the widespread repugnance to the aged dictator and impatience to be rid of Suharto, many Indonesians and their neighbouring nationals took offence at Camdessus's posture. Significantly, most angry Indonesians did not express their feelings in writing.

Ten years after the infamous picture was published, Chris Giles (2007) commented on the photo as he looked back and offered further analysis of the merits of the bailout package: 'For Asia, Mr Suharto's humiliation and subsequent downfall after more than 30 years in power symbolised the domineering attitude of the west.' In response to Giles, Dennis de Tray of the Center for Global Development (in Washington, DC) wrote a letter to the magazine and concluded his note with these words:

> I have always found it profoundly unfair that someone [Camdessus] who went out of his way to support what we all saw as a last ditch effort to save Indonesia has been pilloried simply because he stood where he was told to stand, and has the same habit I have: he folds his arms when he is standing. (de Tracy 2007)

While many Asians found Camdessus's posture offensive, only those who spoke Indonesian could have had an additional insight into what makes the posture offensive. Indonesian has a popular idiomatic expression '*berpangku tangan*' (fold one's arms), referring to the state of being selfish, lazy or uncaring about the plight of others in their immediate environment. To fold one's arms is usually seen as a display of power and arrogance in Indonesia, an orality-oriented society, where communal solidarity is supposed to be highly valued. By no means is this to suggest that Indonesians are generally any more sociable and charitable than anyone in Australia or elsewhere. In fact, people with disabilities, the elderly and pregnant women are generally treated more kindly in public spaces in Australia than in Indonesia. Pedestrians are better respected on zebra crossings on Australian streets than in Indonesia. In Indonesia, however, one is expected to not fold one's arms in front of someone else in a difficult situation, even if one has no interest in assisting those in difficulty.

To some extent, de Tracy is correct that it is hard to blame common habits, especially when such habits are not considered bad or offensive in their home environment. It is only fair that such respect and understanding are shown reciprocally. Smiles and a few giggles are a common habit across many societies including in Indonesia, Malaysia, Thailand, Burma and Vietnam, where oral culture is commonly strong. In these cultures, smiling does not necessarily signify being happy, amused or friendly. Smiles and giggles are considered to go well with any topic of conversation, including about a vacation, having just escaped a traffic accident, a recent illness or the death of a loved one. I have met some Indonesians who cannot utter a complete sentence without a burst of giggles, regardless of the topic of conversation. Many foreigners in Indonesia are often offended when they have minor accidents, such as stumbling or falling to the ground, because Indonesians will laugh heartily when witnessing the accident. Smiles and giggles are so deeply ingrained in daily interactions in Indonesia—just as bowing is in Japan—that most Indonesians are not even aware of their own or others' smiles. In everyday conversations with fellow Indonesians, what would strike them is a lack or total absence of such smiles, suggesting the other party may be experiencing pain, serious sadness or anger.

My first overseas trip was to the United States as an exchange student for a year. It struck me that it was not usual for American people to smile, unless there was something that made them happy or amused. In public places, I noticed some grumpy-looking people wore a pin with an icon and text that says 'smile'! You needed to be literate to read and appreciate it. As an exchange student in a public high school, I took a speech class, where students had to make short speeches in front of the class every week. Our teacher assessed, analysed and commented on each presentation. One unexpected criticism that I received from the teacher—and the only one that I will remember for the rest of my life—was that I smiled 'too much' when speaking, and smiled when there was nothing funny. Since then, I consciously worked very hard to learn not to smile 'too much'. I was not aware of the consequences until a long-distance call from a relative, who giggled when I told him that I was suffering from a bad cold. I was puzzled, but not offended. For the first time, I had the ability to hear the typical and 'strange' Indonesian giggles that shock and puzzle many foreigners.

All of the above came back to mind in November 2002, when I followed the uproar in Australia in response to the published image of the Bali bomber Amrozi smiling during an interview in Denpasar (Bali) with Indonesia's police chief. Amrozi was eventually executed in 2008, but this smiling incident hit the media headlines in Australia, and became the source of a major public outcry. Significantly, no Indonesian media showed interest in the incident. After all, this is a country that had recently emerged from more than three decades of military dictatorship under Suharto, who was known as the 'smiling general', and who came to power in the wake of the massacre of nearly one million people in 1965–66. The Indonesian public and media, including the *Bali Post*, were neither impressed nor disturbed by Amrozi's smile. Indonesia's largest daily, *Kompas*, took some interest—not in the controversial smiles, but in Australia's response to them. It ran a piece of news with the headline '*Gambar Amrozi tersenyum timbulkan kemarahan Australia*' (The image of Amrozi smiling provoked Australia's outrage) (Kompas 2002).

Several sympathetic Australian journalists and Indonesian commentators have offered explanations about the disturbing scene to the Australian public. Most attribute it to 'cultural differences' between the two countries, exacerbated by the difficult circumstances in which the Indonesian police operate. Those giving cultural explanations stressed that Australians might well have failed to understand that smiling in the Indonesian context does not necessarily imply delight, amusement, friendliness or malice. I have no objections to such cultural explanations, but I have discord with those who attempted to infer a rationalist reason in the smiles; such explanations were provided in effect to demonstrate the 'objective rationality' behind the smiles. The smiles were interpreted as if they were some kind of calculated strategy on the part of the suspect and his captors to achieve political gains or to hide embarrassment.

In light of what I have discussed above, I am sure Amrozi smiled unconsciously. No calculation, clever or otherwise, was involved. More precisely, the bomber and the police smiled because they could not help it, because that was the way they had been brought up since childhood—similar to Camdessus folding his arms. The Indonesian public took no issue with the smiles, either because these smiles appeared insignificant or because the public simply failed to notice them. As Pierre Bourdieu remarked, culture is what goes without saying, just as it comes without questioning (1977: 166–7).

In many orality-oriented languages in Indonesia, smiles are built-in, just as tenses or gender are in European languages. Neither gender nor tense exists in Indonesian grammar. One common pitfall for most native English speakers (including Australians) who learn Indonesian is in pronouncing words that start with /c/, /j/, /p/ or /t/. In English these phonemes are aspirated consonants, while in Indonesian not a single consonant is aspirated. To pronounce words such as 'Jakarta' in Indonesian properly, native speakers of English must make an extra effort to spread one's lips widely enough. In other words, like it or not, one has to smile as one speaks, without expressing a sense of delight or amusement.

One wonders whether Amrozi's smile would have provoked such a strong reaction from the Australian public if more Australians had fluency in instead of 'knowledge about' Indonesian language and culture. Australia's commitment to Asia literacy includes a greater commitment to learning four priority Asian languages, including Indonesian. However, the foregoing suggests that Australians will enhance their knowledge capacity and learn a lot more about Indonesia, and consequently themselves, by learning to listen and speak the language, instead of trying to 'master' the language and become highly 'literate' by focusing on written texts.

References

Anderson, Benedict. 1983. *Imagined communities: Reflections on the origin and spread of nationalism*. London: Verso.

Anderson, Benedict. 2001. Western nationalism and Eastern nationalism: Is there a difference that matters? *New Left Review* 9(May–June): 31–42.

Booth, Anne. 1999. Education and economic development in Southeast Asia: Myths and realities. Paper delivered at the Second International Malaysian Studies Conference. 2–4 August, University of Malaya, Kuala Lumpur. URL: phuakl.tripod.com/pssm/conference/Anne_Booth.htm. Consulted 7 December 2014.

Bourdieu, Pierre. 1977. *Outline of a theory of practice*. Trans. Richard Nice. Cambridge: Cambridge University Press.

Burcher, Nick. 2012. Facebook usage statistics by country December 2008– December 2011. 4 January. URL: www.nickburcher.com/2012/01/facebook-usage-statistics-by-country.html. Consulted 4 April 2012.

Carey, James. 1998. Marshall McLuhan: Genealogy and legacy. *Canadian Journal of Communication* 23(March). URL: www.cjc-online.ca/index.php/journal/article/view/1045/951. Consulted 10 August 2013.

Commonwealth of Australia. 2012. *Australia in the Asian Century*. White Paper. Canberra: Commonwealth of Australia. URL: asiancentury.dpmc.gov.au/white-paper. Consulted 7 October 2013.

de Tray, Dennis. 2007. A clearer picture of the day Suharto signed. *Financial Times* 5 July.

Fernback, Jan. 2003. Legends on the net: An examination of computer-mediated communication as a locus of oral culture. *New Media and Society* 5(1): 29–45.

Gerke, Solvay and Evers, Hans-Dieter. 2006. Globalizing local knowledge: Social science research on Southeast Asia, 1970–2000. *Sojourn* 21(1): 1–21.

Giles, Chris. 2007. Wrong lessons from Asia's crisis. *Financial Times* 2 July.

Grossman, Lev. 2010. Mark Zuckerberg. *Time* 15 December. URL: www.time.com/time/specials/packages/article/0,28804,2036683_2037183_2037185,00.html. Consulted 4 April 2012.

Heryanto, Ariel. 2010. Entertainment, domestication, and dispersal: Street politics as popular culture. In Edward Aspinall and Marcus Mietzner, eds. *Problems of democratisation in Indonesia: Elections, institutions and society*. Singapore: ISEAS.

Jung, Sun. 2011. Race and ethnicity in fandom: Praxis K-pop, Indonesian fandom, and social media. *Transformative Works and Cultures* (8). doi:10.3983/twc.2011.0289. Consulted 7 January 2012.

Kompas. 2002. Gambar Amrozi tersenyum timbulkan kemarahan Australia. *Kompas* 15 November. URL: www.kompas.co.id/kompas-cetak/0211/15/ln/ gamb02.htm. Consulted 15 November 2002.

Lim, Merlyna. 2011. @crossroads: Democratization and corporatization of media in Indonesia. URL: participatorymedia.lab.asu.edu/files/Lim_Media_ Ford_2011.pdf. Consulted 7 December 2014.

MacDonald, Dwight. 1998 [1957]. A theory of mass culture. In John Storey, ed. *Cultural theory and popular culture: A reader*, 2nd edn. Athens: The University of Georgia Press.

McLuhan, Marshall. 1964. *Understanding media*, 2nd edn. New York: McGraw-Hill.

McLuhan, Marshall and Fiore, Quentin. 1967. *The medium is the massage*. New York: Bantam Books.

Murray, Alison. 1991. Kampung culture and radical chic in Jakarta. *RIMA* 25(Winter): 1–16.

Nordholt, Nico Schulte and Visser, Leontine. eds. 1995. *Social sciences in Southeast Asia: From particularism to universalism*. Amsterdam: VU University Press.

Rothman, Lily. 2013. Rewound. *Time* 19 August: 41–43.

Sen, Krishna. 2003. Radio days: Media-politics in Indonesia. *The Pacific Review* 16(4): 573–89.

Sen, Krishna and Hill, David. 2000. *Media, culture and politics in Indonesia*. Melbourne: Oxford University Press.

Wolf, Michael. 2013. Privacy is mostly an illusion. *Time* 19 August: 36–39.

11

Challenges for Australian higher education in the Asian Century

Simon Marginson

Introduction

Australia is an odd construction: a nation with British/European heritage on the southeastern edge of Asia positioned between its history and its geography. While its demography is becoming more Asian, its flag still carries the imperial ensign. It needs to embrace both, but British antecedents have left it linguistically and culturally singular and it has yet to develop the cultural, political and intellectual resources to manage multiple identities. Thick multisectoral engagement will stimulate the formation of those resources. The former Gillard government's White Paper *Australia in the Asian Century* (the 'Henry Report') names higher education as one of the principal sectors through which Australia's regional engagement will develop. The White Paper states:

> A growing proportion of global scientific research is taking place in Asia. Partnerships with research and technology communities are crucial to supporting Australia's ability to access new ideas and to build our future competitiveness (Commonwealth of Australia 2012: 266).

As noted in the introduction to this book, the Abbott Liberal government has also encouraged engagement with Asian universities. This has a collaborative aspect and, for some, a competitive aspect. In 2014, Commonwealth Education Minister Christopher Pyne mentioned the need for Australian universities to be better resourced so as to compete with universities from China—as one justification for his proposal to introduce deregulated tuition fees (Pyne 2014). This chapter examines the challenges Australian universities face in engaging with universities in the Asian region.

There is some basis for optimism about higher education. After two decades of education exports, ties with the region have thickened and the gathering weight of universities in China and elsewhere enhances the pull factor. Australian universities still, however, connect better with North America, the United Kingdom and Western Europe than with Asia; and, apart from The Australian National University, they are building regional activity off a low base. While they are becoming more regionally involved, they are not yet regionally identified. The great transformation has yet to occur. Some in Australian universities, as in business and government, still see themselves operating as the British in Asia. That stance has no legs at all in the region. Australian universities can be part of the problem. All the same, the Henry Report is right: they are also part of the solution. Australian universities are enterprising institutions, the legacy of the Dawkins reforms of 1987–90 (Croucher et al. 2013); and many university leaders are alive to the modernisation dynamics in East Asia and parts of Southeast Asia, the emerging Asian universities and the potential thus created. Of course, Australian universities will need to move. Higher education and research science are highly globalised, and if the universities do not go with East Asia they will become undermined and marginalised even at home.

In this chapter, I analyse the changing geopolitics of knowledge, the rise of regional universities and the strategic implications for Australian higher education institutions.

Global and regional patterns

Though Australian universities and science are the products of post-1945 nation-building programs, it is impossible to fully understand them through the lens of 'methodological nationalism'—the idea that the nation-state is 'the natural and necessary form of society in modernity' (Cherlino 2007: 9–10). Increasingly, nations and institutions are conditioned by global and regional flows and patterns. At the same time, these flows and patterns are filtered through national and local systems, institutions and behaviours. Universities are all globalised, state-regulated and partly state-dependent. The past 25 years have seen a great worldwide expansion in the social and economic reach of higher education and research science, moving beyond the advanced industrial economies to include middle-income and developing nations. The spread of the research university is associated with communicative globalisation and networking (Marginson 2011b), the growing economic role of knowledge-intensive work and technological innovations, urbanisation and the expansion of the middle class. The capitalist economy is absorbing pre-capitalist rural sectors in Asia, Africa and Latin America. Cities now house more than 50 per cent of the world's population. The European Union Institute for Strategic Economic Studies estimates the global middle class—people earning US$10–100 a day—will increase from 1.8 billion in 2009 to 4.9 billion in 2030, including three billion in Asia (de Vasconcelos 2012: 28–30). Middle-class families want higher education.

From 2000 to 2010, the gross tertiary enrolment ratio (GTER) in East Asia and the Pacific rose from 16 to 29 per cent (UNESCO 2013). Research science has grown likewise. All nations now need capability in education, science and technology—though not all can pay for it—just as they need clean water, stable governance and globally viable finance.

Nations need universities that participate in the global knowledge network on an equal basis. Nations and cities without the capacity to interpret and understand research—a capacity that must rest on trained personnel capable of creating research—are locked into continued dependence. The growth of research is sustained by collaborations and the globalisation of knowledge within one-world English-language science. It also takes the competitive form of an economic arms race in research and development (R&D) and innovation in which global research rankings signify the competitive position. Between 1995 and 2009, Asian output of journal papers in science grew from 77,000 to almost 190,000 (NSF 2013). Capacity in higher education and science has been pluralised. In 2009, 48 countries published more than 1,000 science papers (Table 11.1)—a proxy for a science system that partly reproduces itself—compared with 38 in 1995 (NSF 2013). China, Hong Kong Special Administrative Region (SAR), Taiwan, South Korea in East Asia and Singapore in Southeast Asia have joined Japan as high-participation, high-science education and research systems. These 'post-Confucian' systems (Marginson 2011a)[1] share a dynamic growth trajectory.

---

1   In an earlier essay on East Asian higher education, I used the term 'Confucian model' (Marginson 2011a). Respondents, especially those from East Asia, endorsed the description of East Asian-specific cultural elements but it was apparent that the term 'Confucian' carried unintended meanings reflecting prior usage in historical-cultural analysis and business studies as a form of cultural essentialism. It was never the intention to define all East Asian or educational phenomena as 'Confucian'. Cultural practices are not singular or fixed. Higher education and research in East Asia and Singapore are a complex, open and moving hybrid, shaped by indigenous elements, Western imperial intervention and the contemporary American research university. The term Confucian was not intended as a universal explanation but to emphasise two distinctive features of all higher education in the region: Confucian family practices of education as self-cultivation and social advancement, and the Sinic state. 'Post-Confucian' carries less unwanted baggage than 'Confucian'. It creates more space for hybridity with Western universities and global science. It should also be noted, however, that these post-Confucian states include liberal-capitalist democracies, socialist states and the Special Administrative Regions of Hong Kong and Macau.

Table 11.1 Nations publishing more than 1,000 science papers in 2009

Anglo-sphere		European Union		Non-EU Europe		Asia		Latin America		Middle East and Africa	
United States	206,601	Germany	45,003	Russia	14,016	China	74,019	Brazil	12,306	Iran	6,313*
United Kingdom	45,649	France	31,748	Switzerland	9,469	Japan	49,627	Mexico	4,123	Israel	6,304
Canada	29,017	Italy	26,755	Turkey	8,301	South Korea	22,271	Argentina	3,655	South Africa	2,864
Australia	18,923	Spain	21,543	Norway	4,440	India	19,917	Chile	1,868*	Egypt	2,247
New Zealand	3,188	Netherlands	14,866	Ukraine	1,639	Taiwan	14,000			Tunisia	1,022*
		Sweden	9,478	Serbia	1,173*	Singapore	4,169				
		Poland	7,355	Croatia	1,164*	Thailand	2,033*				
		Belgium	7,218			Malaysia	1,351*				
		Denmark	5,306			Pakistan	1,043*				
		Finland	4,949								
		Greece	4,881								
		Austria	4,832								
		Portugal	4,157*								
		Czech Republic	3,946								
		Ireland	2,799								
		Hungary	2,397								
		Romania	1,367*								
		Slovenia	1,234*								
		Slovakia	1,000								

* Countries that have entered the 1,000 papers group since 1995

Source: Adapted from NSF (2013).

Table 11.2 Top-10 school systems in learning achievement of 15-year-olds in the three Program of International Student Assessment (PISA) disciplines, mean student scores, 2009

	Reading		Mathematics		Science	
1	Shanghai China	570	Shanghai China	613	Shanghai China	580
2	Hong Kong SAR	545	Singapore	573	Hong Kong SAR	555
3	Singapore	542	Hong Kong SAR	561	Singapore	531
4	Japan	538	Taiwan	560	Japan	547
5	South Korea	536	South Korea	554	Finland	545
6	Finland	524	Macau SAR	538	Estonia	541
7	Taiwan	523	Japan	536	South Korea	538
8	Canada	523	Liechtenstein	535	Vietnam	528
9	Ireland	523	Switzerland	531	Poland	526
10	Poland	518	Netherlands	523	Liechtenstein/Canada	525
	Australia (19th)	*504*	*Australia (eq. 13th)*	*512*	*Australia (eq. 19th)*	*521*
	United Kingdom	*499*	*United Kingdom*	*494*	*United Kingdom*	*514*
	United States	*498*	*United States*	*481*	*United States*	*497*

Source: Adapted from OECD (2013b).

Unlike Europe, in East Asia higher education is not moving on the basis of regulated regional cooperation, but it is moving in parallel. The post-Confucian countries differ from each other in many ways including language and political systems. There are tensions. Nevertheless, they have four common features that have facilitated their take-off: the comprehensive and active Sinic state, Confucian educational practices at home, internationalisation strategies that enable them to rapidly absorb Western modernisation in higher education and science, and economic growth sufficient to pay for educational infrastructure and research.

Higher education and research in East Asia and Singapore

Participation in tertiary education

Despite diversity in political and economic systems, the countries I have characterised as the post-Confucian systems are moving towards universal participation. The GTER exceeds 85 per cent in South Korea and Taiwan; Macau SAR is at 65 per cent and Japan and Hong Kong SAR at 60 per cent. Hong Kong and Singapore are moving away from the non-universal systems inherited from Britain by building subdegree numbers. In China the GTER moved from 5 per cent to 26 per cent between 1990 and 2010 (UNESCO 2013). The 2020 target is 40 per cent, which is near the present Organisation for Economic Cooperation and Development (OECD) average. Institutional quality varies. The top-200 universities have been lifted. The challenge is to improve other institutions and lift participation in the poorer provinces. Nevertheless, the post-Confucian systems largely avoid the Anglo-American trade-off between advances in quality and in quantity.

Government and households share the cost of participation, enabling the state to focus part of its funding on elite national research universities, their students and (in some systems) social equity. A feature of post-Confucian systems—in marked contrast with Europe—is that poor families often invest heavily in schooling, extra tutoring and classes. Post-Confucian families can spend as much on education as Australians spend on housing. In Korea in 2010, 72.7 per cent of the cost of tertiary institutions was paid privately, including 47.1 per cent by households, with 27.3 per cent financed by government. In Japan, the private sector share was 65.6 per cent (OECD 2013a: 207); in China about 40 per cent. Levin (2011) finds Koreans spend *3 per cent of gross domestic product (GDP)* on non-formal schooling.

Public and private investment in schooling, combined with parental focus on student achievement, state reform programs and the pressure of examinations, prepare post-Confucian students for tertiary education at an advanced level (Table 11.2). The 2012 OECD Program of International Student Assessment (PISA) found that in mean student scores in mathematics, the top-seven systems in the world were Shanghai (613), Singapore (573), Hong Kong SAR (561), Taiwan (560), South Korea (554), Macau SAR (538) and Japan (536). Post-Confucian systems performed almost as well in PISA science, with the top-four systems, and in PISA reading, with the top-five systems (OECD 2013b).

Research science

Except in China, post-Confucian investment in R&D as a proportion of GDP is on par with Western Europe. South Korea invested 3.74 per cent of GDP in 2010, and Taiwan 2.9 per cent, compared with 3.96 per cent in Finland, 2.88 per cent in the United States and 2.21 per cent in Australia (NSF 2013). China's investment was 1.7 per cent of GDP. It is increasing investment by 0.1 per cent a year. The national target is 2.5 per cent by 2020.

Figure 11.1 Total spending on R&D, top 11 countries, 2000 and 2010, US$ billion

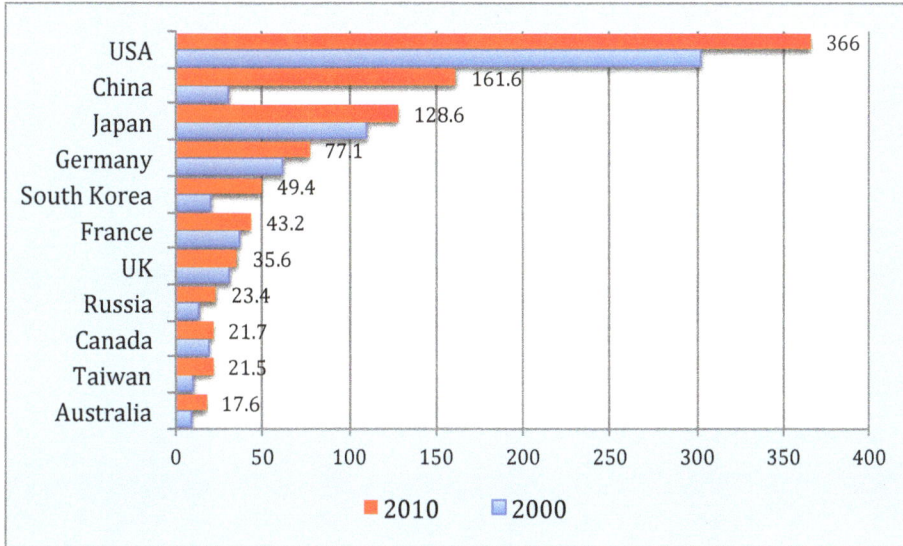

Data for 2010 or nearest year, expressed in constant 2005 USD
Source: Adapted from OECD (2013c).

If spending continues to grow at this rate, China's R&D will pass that of the United States in the next five years. As in South Korea, in China, a relatively low proportion of spending goes to universities—one yuan in 10—but the universities access other government monies by partnering with the state enterprises that conduct most R&D in China. East Asia now invests more than Europe and the United Kingdom combined. In 2009 North America invested $433 billion in R&D, Europe $319 billion and East, Southeast and South Asia $402 billion—31.5 per cent of the global total (NSF 2013).

Figure 11.1 shows that three of the world's five largest R&D investor nations are post-Confucian—China, Japan and South Korea—while Taiwan is in the top 10 (OECD 2013c). In constant 2005 prices, China's R&D rose from $30.4 billion in 2000 to $161.6 billion in 2010—*multiplying by five times in a decade*. Post-Confucian research systems are strongly biased towards applied research and commercialisation. Basic university research is less well supported proportionately than in the United States or Western Europe. Nevertheless, with all research budgets rising, except in Japan, both university research funding and scholarly papers are growing vigorously (again, except in Japan).

Figure 11.2 Number of journal papers produced in 2009, 14 leading countries

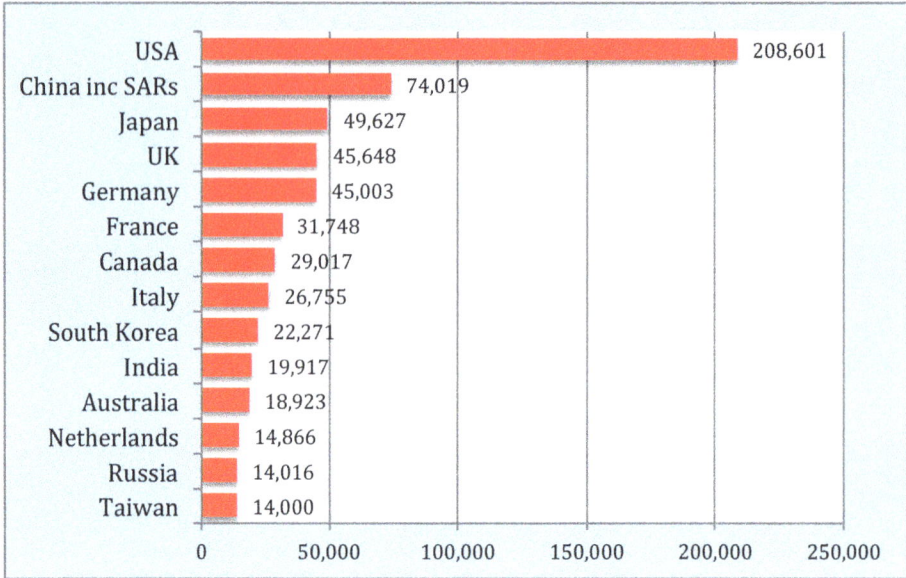

Source: Adapted from NSF (2013).

Figure 11.2 is based on ISI/Thomson Web of Knowledge data, which include economics, demography, psychology, sociology and some education as well as physical and life sciences and applied sciences. Legitimate questions have been raised about how effective ISI/Thomson's global reach really is (Connell in this volume; Cruz 2008). Nonetheless, it serves as one indicator of the forward march of the post-Confucian science systems: the coverage of English-language publishing in the orthodox sciences, at least, is comprehensive. In 2009 two of the three largest science producers were post-Confucian and South Korea was in ninth place, ahead of Australia, while Taiwan was in fourteenth place (NSF 2013).

Of the non–post-Confucian systems in Asia, Singapore produced 4,187 papers in 2009, Thailand 2,033, Malaysia 1,351 and Pakistan 1,043. The world's fourth most populous nation, Indonesia, had 262 papers. There were 260 in Bangladesh, 223 in the Philippines and 326 in post-Confucian Vietnam (where the nation is too poor for the take-off)—all with large populations but lacking indigenous science systems. Journal papers are largely the work of doctoral students abroad. On graduation, such students typically either migrate to the nation of education or return home to career positions but leave the field of research.

Figure 11.3 Output of journal papers in science, 1995 to 2009, seven countries

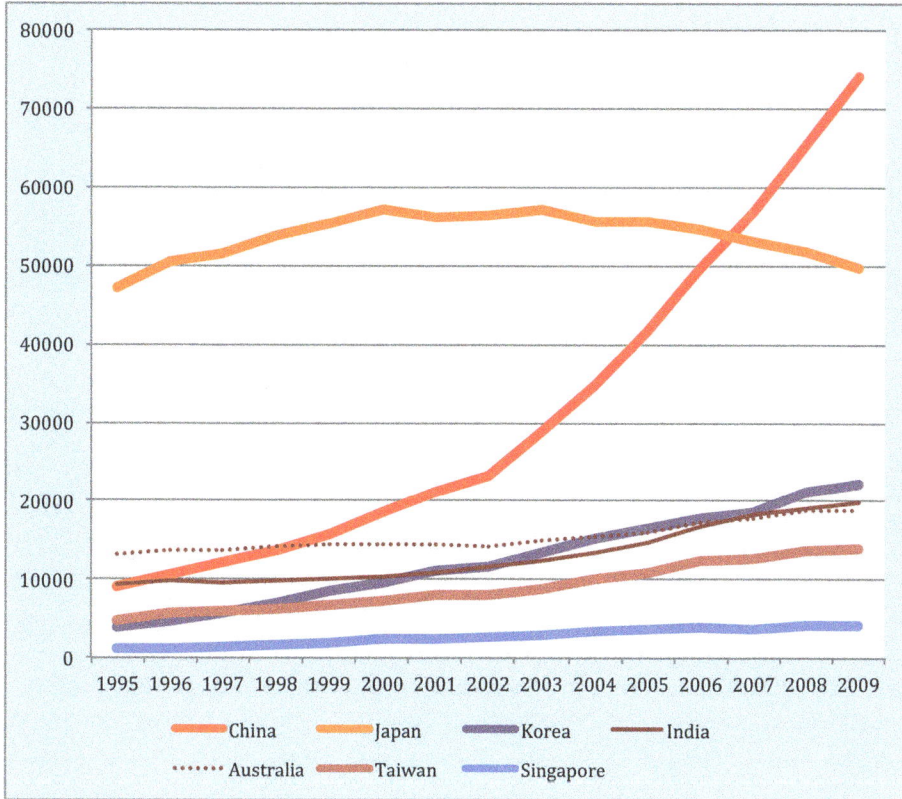

Source: Adapted from NSF (2013).

The advance of Chinese science is extraordinary (Figure 11.3). China was the world's twelfth-largest producer in 1995; it was second in 2009. *Since 2000, annual output has grown by 17 per cent per year*. When the world's largest nation expands research at unprecedented rates over a prolonged period, global knowledge flows are decisively changed. In future, much of human knowledge will come from China. The growth of science has been almost as rapid in South Korea, where annual output has now passed that of India, even though India has 30 times the population of South Korea. Journal paper output has also ballooned in Singapore and Taiwan. In 1995 India produced more research papers than China but growth has begun to quicken only in the past half-decade, stimulated by central government funding of R&D. Japan's science system matured in the 1970s and 1980s and the annual number of papers is now falling (NSF 2013).

Research quantity has moved ahead of research quality. In 2010 China, Japan, Korea, Taiwan, Singapore, India, Thailand, Malaysia, Indonesia and the Philippines produced 21.9 per cent of all science papers, but only 10.6 per cent of papers in the top 1 per cent by citation rate. The United States produced 27.8 per cent of papers and 48.9 per cent of the top 1 per cent of papers. China published 7.5 per cent of papers and 3.6 per cent of the top papers. The patterns are uneven by discipline. The strengths of post-Confucian research systems are in the physical science-based disciplines, which underpin transport, communications, energy, urban construction and infrastructure. In engineering, chemistry, computer science, physics and mathematics, China's share of published research is relatively high—in engineering, China had 12.5 per cent of all papers and 12.3 per cent of the top 1 per cent—and quality is improving rapidly. In 2000 China had 0.6 per cent of the top 1 per cent most cited chemistry papers; in 2010 it had 10.6 per cent. In medicine and biological sciences, however, China generated less than 1 per cent of the top papers in 2010 (NSF 2013).

Note that in Figure 11.3 Australia began in 1995 as the largest research producer after Japan. In 2009 it was fifth, behind China, Japan, South Korea and India.

World-class universities

Governments in East Asia and Singapore place a high priority on developing 'world-class universities' (WCUs), concentrations of status and research comparable with North America and the United Kingdom/Western Europe. WCU policy builds on pre-given national hierarchies, like the pre–World War II imperial universities in Japan, Peking University (1898) in China and Seoul National University (1946) in Korea. There are also successful more recent foundations, such as the Hong Kong University of Science and Technology, which opened in 1991 (Postiglione 2011). WCUs are supported by special investment funding such as the 211 and 985 programs in China and Brain 21 in Korea (Shin 2009).

It takes time for WCU investment to show in global rankings. There are lags between investment and published science, between publication and citation, and between citation and change in the rankings. China's investment is now beginning to secure results. In the Shanghai Academic Ranking of World Universities (ARWU 2013), the number of top-500 universities in mainland China increased from 8 to 28 between 2005 and 2013. There were five more in Hong Kong SAR. In 2011 Tsinghua was the only top-200 university; in 2013 there were five: Tsinghua, Peking, Zhejiang, Fudan and Shanghai Jiao Tong. Investments in R&D now taking place will show in the rankings in 10 to 15 years, though the full effects will take a generation or more. By 2025–30, leading universities in China, South Korea, Taiwan and Singapore will be highly placed and there will be many more in the top 200.

The Shanghai ranking also lists the top-100 institutions in five broad research fields. There are 24 post-Confucian universities in the world top 100 in engineering; China and Taiwan between them have 16. The City University of Hong Kong is twenty-fifth in the world, Hong Kong University of Science and Technology thirty-fourth, alongside Tsinghua. National Taiwan University, a major player in computing research, is twenty-sixth. Australia has five engineering schools in the world top 100 but none in the top 50 (ARWU 2013).

A more precise picture is provided by the Leiden University Centre for Science and Technology Studies (Leiden 2013). It ranks universities using separated single indicators, including volume of science papers, citations, cites per paper and papers in the top 10 per cent of their field by citation rate.[2] Table 11.3 lists the 30 leading Asia-Pacific universities, including Australian universities, by their number of top 10 per cent papers (second-last column). The table also includes total papers and proportion of papers in the top 10 per cent. Despite the limits of citation counts as a measure of quality, including the omission of much of social science and all humanities, the second-last column in Table 11.3 is a useful summary of the scientific firepower of a university—its 'quantity of quality' in research.

Eight regional universities produce more than the University of Sydney. The two Singapore institutions are large research producers with a high percentage of top 10 per cent papers. In terms of total output and highly cited papers, the National University of Singapore is as strong as European universities other than Oxford and Cambridge. There are 12 mainland Chinese universities in the top 30, plus three from Hong Kong. Tsinghua and Peking universities have citation rates comparable with leading Australian universities of equivalent size. There is an interesting group of small to medium-sized science and technology specialists. Nankai and the University of Science and Technology in China have excellent citation rates, as do the three Hong Kong universities and Hong Kong University of Science and Technology and Postech in Korea, which are both too small to figure in the table (Leiden 2013).

Of the world's top-100 universities by proportion of papers in the top 10 per cent of their field, 17 are in the Asia-Pacific region, including five in Australia. One regional university is in the world top 30: the National University of Singapore (twenty-ninth). On this measure, Australia's strongest university is Melbourne, at forty-first in the world and third in the region. Melbourne has moved ahead of The Australian National University in all the citation quality indicators in the Leiden ranking.

---

2   The citation data are provided in both raw form and on a field-normalised basis, whereby the Leiden group adjusts the raw data to account for different rates of publication and citation in research fields.

Table 11.3 Thirty leading research universities in the Asia-Pacific, on the basis of number of science papers in 2008–11 in the top 10 per cent of the research field on citation rate (per cent)

University	Total journal papers 2008–11	Proportion of papers in top 10% by citation	Number of papers in top 10% by citation	World rank on number of papers in top 10%
Harvard University (USA)	29,812	21.8	6,492	1
University of Cambridge (UK)	11,742	17.1	2,009	11
National University of Singapore (Singapore)	9,890	13.7	1,353	29
University of Tokyo (Japan)	14,175	9.0	1,274	31
University of Melbourne (Australia)	8,516	13.0	1,111	41
Zhejiang University (China)	11,427	9.2	1,054	45
Tsinghua University (China)	8,891	11.7	1,037	47
Kyoto University (Japan)	11,343	8.6	980	49
University of Queensland (Australia)	7,858	12.3	970	51
Nanyang University of Technology (Singapore)	6,673	13.7	912	59
Peking University (China)	8,419	10.8	905	60
University of Sydney (Australia)	8,655	10.3	894	61
Seoul National University (South Korea)	10,799	8.1	871	64
Shanghai Jiao Tong University (China)	9,899	7.8	770	81
Fudan University (China)	7,076	10.7	756	83
Monash University (Australia)	6,345	11.2	711	94
Osaka University (Japan)	8,714	7.8	681	96
University of New South Wales (Australia)	6,322	10.8	680	97
University of Science and Technology (China)	4,914	13.3	653	100
University of Hong Kong (Hong Kong SAR)	5,820	11.2	651	101
Tohoku University (Japan)	8,654	6.7	579	117
Nanjing University (China)	5,724	10.1	578	118
Chinese University of Hong Kong (Hong Kong SAR)	4,998	10.7	533	133
Nankai University (China)	3,673	14.4	531	136
Sun Yat-Sen University (China)	5,624	9.4	527	139
The Australian National University (Australia)	4,209	12.1	511	144

University	Total journal papers 2008–11	Proportion of papers in top 10% by citation	Number of papers in top 10% by citation	World rank on number of papers in top 10%
Korea Advanced Institute of S&T (South Korea)	4,483	11.2	500	149
Jilin University (China)	4,986	9.8	490	152
Harbin Institute of Technology (China)	5,202	9.3	486	155
Shandong University (China)	5,592	8.4	468	169
Yonsei University (South Korea)	6,592	7.1	466	170
Hong Kong Polytechnic University (Hong Kong SAR)	4,054	10.9	440	183

Source: Adapted from Leiden (2013).

Dynamics of the post-Confucian model

Beginning with Japan in the 1960s to 1980s, followed by Taiwan, Korea and Singapore in the 1990s, and China in the past decade, the post-Confucian systems have achieved three objectives simultaneously: the generalisation of participation, the rapid growth of research science, and world-class universities. No other system of higher education and university research has moved forward at this pace in all three areas—and the post-Confucian systems have done it within low-tax polities. In 2007, public spending as a share of GDP was less than 15 per cent in Hong Kong SAR, Japan and Taiwan, 19.3 per cent in China and 20.8 per cent in Korea (ADB 2010), compared with more than 50 per cent in parts of Europe.

How was it done? What are the conditions and drivers? As noted above, the key elements have been economic growth—all post-Confucian countries except China and Vietnam now enjoy per capita incomes at Western European levels—the distinctive Sinic state, Confucian educational practices in the home, and state-driven internationalisation strategies.

The comprehensive and centralising Sinic state originated in China's Qin and Han dynasties in the third century BCE and has followed a different path to the limited liberal state of John Locke and Adam Smith. Perhaps it is better equipped than Western states for the accelerated upgrading of universities and R&D. In the limited liberal state, the state's right to tax and intervene is habitually questioned, whereas East Asians mostly accept the state as supervisor of society and social conduct. Dissidents, as in Tiananmen Square in 1989, rarely rail against the legitimacy of state action as such. Rather they call on the state to discharge its responsibilities in a proper manner, to behave as a state should behave:

> In the East Asian cultural context, government leadership is deemed indispensable for a smooth functioning of the domestic market economy and vital for enhancing national comparative advantage in international competition. The central government is expected to have a holistic vision of the well-being of the nation and a long-term plan to help people maintain an adequate livelihood ... Strong government with moral authority, a sort of ritualized symbolic power fully accepted by the overwhelming majority, is acclaimed as a blessing. (Tu 1996: 7)

The post-Confucian states see higher education and research as essential to economic growth and global effectiveness. They take the long view of their role. Government as a vocation has higher standing than in English-speaking countries. Many of the best graduates from top universities head for state office, not the professions or business.

In the home, the Confucian commitment to self-cultivation via learning was first established on a mass basis in the Song Dynasty 1,000 years ago. Post-Confucian respect for education is more deeply rooted than in Europe and North America, where mass education dates from the nineteenth century. For example, prior to the mid-nineteenth-century Western intervention in Japan, school participation, especially among females, was equal to or greater than in Europe. The 11,000 village schools were a strong basis for Meiji modernisation (Henshall 2007: 43). Education is seen as part of the duty of child to parent and the duty of parent to child, the source of personal virtue, social standing and meritocratic advance. The family and individual schooling are joined to social ordering by the 'one-off' examination systems that select students into the leading universities.

East Asian higher education is also shaped by norms and models from Europe and the American research university, entrenched through relentless internationalisation programs (Wang et al. 2011): sponsored mobility of students and scholars and measures to attract back the diaspora; recruitment of foreign scholar-researchers; English language learning, incentives for global publishing in English, and English medium graduate studies and international education; benchmarking of universities and disciplines against counterparts in North America and Europe, and rankings to drive WCU ambitions; and new public management reform of organisation. Since Meiji Japan, catch-up with the West has been *the* policy driver, though competition with other Asian nations is increasingly important. The post-Confucian systems of higher education and research are East–West hybrids. They are also something new: a distinctive post-Confucian form of modernisation. Western influence has not displaced educational or political tradition. The relation between tradition and modernity is one of exchange, not displacement. Much of the potency of the post-Confucian model of education derives from its indigenous elements: Confucian tradition at home and the constructive state policy.

Partnerships with rising Asia

Australia has five universities in the ARWU top 100—the University of Melbourne, The Australian National University, the University of Queensland, the University of Western Australia and the University of Sydney—though none in the top 50. The Leiden data position the top Australian research universities as equivalent to the top regional universities rather than ahead of them, and behind Singapore and some science and technology universities in citation quality. Australia is above world average citation rates in 17 of 20 disciplines, but only five disciplines are above the European average: veterinary science, energy, engineering, earth and planetary science, and medicine. The United Kingdom is above the European average in all disciplines (Chubb 2013). While the leading Australian institutions perhaps have the firepower to partner in Asia, what do they bring to potential partnerships that is superior to the United Kingdom, the United States and Canada? Are they making use of their priceless geographical proximity to deepen the cultural interface?

This raises the question of regional identity, which is both geographical and cultural. In the global setting, regional formation in higher education (and other spheres) depends on four elements. First, systems must be sufficiently resourced to enable partnership and not dependency. Second, geographical proximity is important. Third, common cultural elements, as in Iberian Latin America, are significant. Fourth, political will is necessary. National education systems must *want* to regionalise, as with the Bologna Accord in Europe and the European Research Area. At this stage, the post-Confucian countries fulfil the first three conditions but the will is weak. The Association for Southeast Asian Nations (ASEAN) has the political will to develop regionally but, with the exception of Singapore, its higher education systems are underdeveloped, and there is less cultural commonality than in post-Confucian Asia or Western Europe. Both Northeast Asia and Southeast Asia have limited themselves to small-scale mobility schemes such as staff and student exchanges between leading universities.

Given that regional consciousness is embryonic, collective inclusion of Australian higher education in Asian higher education is not a prospect. Australia is on the geographical edge; there is no will to bring Australia in, and there is a cultural gulf between Australia and most regional systems with the partial exception of Hong Kong and Singapore. The only potential for Australian–Asian regional structures is in research (to be discussed below). Australian integration into Asian higher education is a matter for bilateral negotiations and one-to-one dealings between institutions. Here, to work more effectively, Australian universities will need to deepen their cultural understanding of East Asia and its nations. Australia, with its relative strength in Asian studies and Asian languages, is well placed to do so.

The cross-cultural dimension

There is more than one kind of state and more than one kind of university. Political and educational cultures condition the potentials of government and where universities collaborate. Most systems are partly regional, reflecting historical overlaps and clustered cultures. Informal regional groupings include post-Confucian, Westminster and US systems, Nordic (Valimaa 2011), Germanic, Francophone, Russian (Smolentseva 2003), Latin American (Marginson 2012), South Asian, and Saudi Arabian and the Gulf states.

Table 11.4 compares post-Confucian, US and Westminster systems.

Table 11.4 Comparison of post-Confucian and English-language country systems

	Post-Confucian systems (East Asia & Singapore)	US system	Westminster systems (UK, Australia, New Zealand)
Character of nation-state	Comprehensive, central, delegates to provinces. Politics in command of economy and civil society. State draws best graduates	Limited, division of powers, separate from civil society and economy. Anti-statism common. Federal	Limited, division of powers, separate from civil society and economy. Some anti-statism. Unitary
Educational culture	Confucian commitment to self-cultivation via learning. Education as filial duty and producer of status via exam competition (and producer of global competitiveness)	Twentieth-century meritocratic and competitive ideology. Education common road to wealth/status, within advancing prosperity	Post-1945 ideology of state-guaranteed equal opportunity through education as path to wealth and status, open to all in society
State role in higher education	Big. State supervises, shapes, drives and selectively funds institutions. Over time increased delegation to part-controlled presidents	Smaller, from distance. Fosters market ranking via research, student loans. Then steps back. Autonomous presidents	From distance. Policy, regulation, funding supervise market, shape activity. Autonomous vice-chancellors
Financing of higher education	State-financed infrastructure, part of tuition (especially early in model), scholarships, merit aid. Household funds much tuition and private tutoring, even in poor families	State funds some infrastructure, tuition subsidies, student loans. Households vary from high tuition to low, poor families state dependent	Less state-financed infrastructure now. Tuition loans, some aid. Growing household investment but less than East Asia. Austerity

	Post-Confucian systems (East Asia & Singapore)	US system	Westminster systems (UK, Australia, New Zealand)
Dynamics of research	Part household funding of tuition, ideology of WCU, university hierarchy— together enable rapid state investment in research at scale. Applied is dominant. State intervention	Research heavily funded by federal government unburdened by tuition. Industry and philanthropic money. Basic science plus commercial IP	Research funded (more in UK) by government, also finances tuition. Less philanthropy than US. Basic science, applied growth, dreams of IP
Hierarchy and social selection	Steep university hierarchy. 'One-chance' universal competition with selection into prestigious institutions. WCUs are fast track for life	Steep institutional hierarchy mediated by SAAT scores. Some part second chances, mainly public sector. Top WCUs are fast track for life	Competition for place in university hierarchy mediated by school results with some part second chances. WCUs provide strong start
Fostering of world-class universities	Part of tradition, universal target of family aspirations. Support for building of WCUs by funding and regulation. Emerging global agenda	Entrenched hierarchy of Ivy League and flagship state universities, via research grants, tuition hikes, philanthropy. Source of global pride	Ambivalence in national temperament and government policy on status of top institutions. Private and public funding hit ceilings

Source: Author.

University organisation in Australia has much in common with its regional counterparts, especially in science. Yet concepts like state responsibility, civil society, public interest and academic freedom are practised differently in much of East Asia (see also the introduction to this volume). For example, whereas US universities are often understood as part of civil society, or the market, in East Asia it is inconceivable that even private universities could be located outside the state. Japan and South Korea have prestigious private universities, including Yonsei, Korea University and Ewha in South Korea, and Waseda and Keio in Japan. Government regulation, however, plays a larger role in the running of these universities than it does in the case of their counterparts in the United States.

What about academic freedom? Resources affect the capacity to exercise freedoms. The economic instrumentalism common to all post-Confucian systems (and many others) weakens the humanities and humanistic social sciences vis-à-vis the applied sciences and technologies. Political repression also affects freedoms. There is no blanket repression of criticism in post-Confucian universities. Dissent is expressed in distinctive ways. Issues openly debated or subject to ritualistic angst in Australia are often discussed inside the party/ state in China; the universities are part of the state, broadly defined. In leading universities, the atmosphere is often liberal with more potent academic presence in policy issues than in Australia. Yet open public criticism is rare, because it must confront state legitimacy. In the Chinese tradition, scholars have a responsibility to serve the state. This means that they must criticise the state when it departs from the path of legitimate conduct. They openly challenge the regime not whenever they disagree but when they believe it has lost the mandate to govern. This generates acts of individual courage that can trigger state repression—a recurring pattern in China that affects some social scientists and humanists today. Their criticism is not in the form of 'Western-style' assertions of freedom against the state. It is consistent with Sinic tradition and post-Confucian order. Debate is more open in South Korea, Taiwan and Japan, but it takes courage to defy the state and conservative peers.

The meanings of 'university autonomy' and 'academic freedom' vary. There is a universal component—in all systems, faculty like making decisions on their own behalf—and there are culturally variant elements. In the post-Confucian world, the autonomous personality of the university is mostly expressed on behalf of government, not against it. Likewise, academic freedom is understood in terms of authority and responsibility:

> Once one can excel in terms of productivity and meet the State's criteria for producing valuable and useful knowledge, one may enjoy a high level of intellectual authority. This type of intellectual authority is not identical with academic freedom in the Western context, but in some ways it provides even more flexibility and greater power than does academic freedom. There is certainly some overlap between these two concepts, yet clearly a different emphasis. Westerners focus on restrictions to freedom of choice, whereas Chinese scholars looking at the same situation focus on the responsibility of the person in authority to use their power wisely in the collective interest. (Zha 2011: 464)

Freedom is understood more in terms of positive freedom than negative freedom. Does this cultural difference limit research outputs? It is unlikely to reduce the quantity of science. In relation to quality and creativity, time will tell. What about the imagination in the humanities? Here, modern economism may be a larger problem than state tradition. It is likely that the post-Confucian systems will develop new humanistic scholarship that embodies both indigenous and global influences, as is already the case in the arts. This may be key to the evolution of the post-Confucian model. To join this conversation, Australian universities will need a larger capacity in East Asian languages and traditions. East Asians know English, but English-speaking universities know little of East Asia.

Moving forward

Is there scope for non-Confucian higher education to adapt features of the post-Confucian model? Neither the Sinic state nor the Confucian family is readily transplanted. Nevertheless, Australian policymakers could adopt a longer-term view and focus public investment on reforms that would increase participation and the quality and quantity of research. The government did this in 1957–75 in Australia when modern mass higher education and university research were built. The political conditions for such a transformation do not yet exist. The obstacles include small-tax politics and resistance to building selected global research universities. Even The Australian National University's special research funding is being folded back into the one-size-fits-all approach that is the negative legacy of the Dawkins reforms (Marginson and Marshman 2013). Australian institutions are enterprising but of one middling type. In future, regional expectations will be set more by East Asian systems than by Australia. Local universities will need to add more value at the top end to be regionally effective.

Table 11.5 Joint publication of Australian-authored science, by selected partner countries: 1.00 = expected rate of collaboration based on overall collaboration patterns of the two countries

	1995	2010		1995	2010
South Africa	1.86	1.50	New Zealand	4.49	3.92
United Kingdom	1.05	1.16	Singapore	2.01	1.66
Ireland	0.42	0.97	China	1.11	1.06
Canada	0.76	0.89	India	0.61	0.77
United States	0.80	0.75	Taiwan	0.30	0.68
Germany	0.52	0.60	Japan	0.60	0.64
France	0.37	0.58	South Korea	0.33	0.47
Brazil	0.27	0.56	Russia	0.31	0.42

Source: Adapted from NSF (2013).

It is noticeable that even the White Paper agenda in higher education would have rested on universities lacking post-Confucian state support. Here, as elsewhere, everything will depend on the willingness of Australian universities to tool themselves within the current resource envelope and apply that new capacity to collaborations in Asia. As Table 11.5 shows, Australian research collaboration with Singapore is strong, it is above the expected level in China but relatively low with South Korea, Japan and Taiwan. Australian science had a slightly greater international edge in collaboration with China in 1995 (1.11) than 2010 (1.06). The latter figure was similar to the US–Chinese rate (1.05).

The Chief Scientist's Office has suggested one structural initiative that could advance the scope for research collaboration: the formation of an 'Asian-area research zone':

> To gain maximum benefit from our [science, technology, engineering and mathematics (STEM)] investments in knowledge generation, we must link to the work of the international community ... Many of the challenges that confront Australia are similar to those of our regional neighbours. There is now an opportunity to share talents, skills, expertise and infrastructure that arises rarely. Accordingly, it is proposed that Australia seek to enter into a partnership with neighbours to establish an Asian-Area Research Zone. (Chubb 2013: 18)

An Asian-area research zone could be developed as a partnership-based research program similar to the European Research Area. Each participating country could provide a share of the total funding based on size and capacity to pay. Grants would be peer-reviewed and awarded only to cross-country partners and teams. As noted above, there are currently some barriers, including linguistic ones, to increasing Australian humanities and social science academics' formal inclusion in regional arrangements. In scientific research, however, the benefits of cooperation are apparent and there is likely to be more support for the inclusion of Australian researchers. More than education exports, research provides Australians with the opportunity to transcend neo-colonial relations through partnerships of genuine equality. This must be central to Australian strategy in the region.

References

ADB [Asian Development Bank]. 2010. *Key indicators for Asia and the Pacific 2009*. Manila: ADB.

ARWU [Academic Ranking of World Universities]. 2013. *Shanghai Jiao Tong University Graduate School of Education*. Shanghai: Shanghai Ranking Consultancy. URL: www.shanghairanking.com/index.html. Consulted 10 November 2014.

Cherlino, Daniel. 2007. *A social theory of the nation-state*. Oxon: Routledge.

Chubb, Ian. 2013. *Science, technology, engineering and mathematics in the national interest*. Canberra: Chief Scientist's Office. URL: www.chiefscientist. gov.au/wp-content/uploads/STEMstrategy290713FINALweb.pdf. Consulted 10 November 2014.

Commonwealth of Australia. 2012. *Australia in the Asian Century*. White Paper. Canberra: Commonwealth of Australia. URL: www.asiaeducation.edu.au/verve/_resources/australia-in-the-asian-century-white-paper.pdf. Consulted 10 November 2014.

Croucher, Gwilym, Marginson, Simon, Norton, Andrew and Wells, Julie. eds. 2013. *The Dawkins revolution 25 years on*. Melbourne: Melbourne University Publishing.

Cruz, Isagani R. 2008. Challenging ISI Thomson Scientific's journal citation reports: Deconstructing 'objective,', 'impact' and 'global'. *Libraries and the Academy* 8(1): 7–13.

de Vasconcelos, Alvaro. ed. 2012. *Global trends 2030: Citizens in an interconnected and polycentric world*. Paris: European Union Institute for Security Studies. URL: www.iss.europa.eu/publications/detail/article/espas-report-global-trends-2030-citizens-in-an-interconnected-and-polycentric-world/. Consulted 10 November 2014.

Henshall, Ken. 2007. History. In Chris Rowthorn (coordinating author), *Japan*. Melbourne: Lonely Planet.

Leiden University. 2013. *The Leiden ranking 2013*. Leiden: Centre for Science and Technology Studies. URL: www.leidenranking.com/default.aspx. Consulted 10 November 2014.

Levin, Henry. 2011. Teachers college, Columbia University. Conversation with the author. 26 September, Melbourne.

Marginson, Simon. 2011a. Higher education in East Asia and Singapore: Rise of the Confucian model. *Higher Education* 61(5): 587–611.

Marginson, Simon. 2011b. Imagining the global. In Roger King, Simon Marginson and Rajani Naidoo, eds. *Handbook of higher education and globalization*. Cheltenham: Edward Elgar.

Marginson, Simon. 2012. Global university rankings: The strategic issues. Keynote address to conference at National University of Mexico. 17–18 May, Mexico City. URL: www.cshe.unimelb.edu.au/people/marginson_docs/Latin_American_conference_rankings_17-18May2012.pdf. Consulted 10 November 2014.

Marginson, Simon and Marshman, Ian 2013. System and structure. In Gwilym Croucher, Simon Marginson, Andrew Norton and Julie Wells, eds. *The Dawkins revolution 25 years on*. Melbourne: Melbourne University Publishing.

NSF [National Science Foundation]. 2013. *Science and technology indicators 2012*. Arlington, VA: National Science Board. URL: www.nsf.gov/statistics/seind12/. Consulted 10 November 2014.

OECD [Organisation for Economic Cooperation and Development]. 2013a. *Education at a glance 2011: OECD indicators*. Paris: OECD.

OECD. 2013b. *PISA 2012 results in focus. What 15 year olds know and what they can do with what they know*. Paris: OECD.

OECD. 2013c. *Science and technology indicators*. Paris: OECD.

Postiglione, Gerard. 2011. The rise of research universities: The Hong Kong University of Science and Technology. In Phillip Altbach and Jamil Salmi, eds. *The road to academic excellence: The making of world-class research universities*. Washington, DC: The World Bank.

Pyne, Christopher. 2014. Commonwealth Minister for Education. House of Representatives *Hansard* 26 August: 32.

Shin, Jung Cheol. 2009. Building world-class research university: The Brain Korea 21 project. *Higher Education* 58(5): 669–88.

Smolentseva, Anna 2003. Challenges to the Russian academic profession. *Higher Education* 45: 391–424.

Tu, Wei-Ming. 1996. Introduction. In Wei-Ming Tu, ed. *Confucian traditions in East Asian modernity: Moral education and economic culture in Japan and the four mini-dragons*. Cambridge, MA: Harvard University Press.

UNESCO [United Nations Educational, Scientific and Cultural Organisation]. 2013. *Tertiary indicators*. Paris: UNESCO Institute for Statistics. URL: stats. uis.unesco.org/unesco/TableViewer/tableView.aspx?ReportId=167&IF_Language=eng. Consulted 10 November 2014.

Valimaa, Jussi. 2011. The corporatisation of national universities in Finland. In Brian Pusser, Ken Kempner, Simon Marginson and Imanol Ordorika, eds. *Universities and the public sphere: Knowledge creation and state building in the era of globalisation*. New York: Routledge.

Wang, Qing Hui, Wang, Q. and Liu, Nian Cai. 2011. Building world-class universities in China: Shanghai Jiao Tong University. In Phillip Altbach and Jamil Salmi, eds. *The road to academic excellence: The making of world-class research universities*. Washington, DC: The World Bank.

Zha, Qiang. 2011. Is there an emerging Chinese model of the university? In Ruth Hayhoe, Jun Li, Jing Lin and Qiang Zha, eds. 2011. *Portraits of 21st century Chinese universities*. Hong Kong: Springer/Comparative Education Research Centre, University of Hong Kong.